Organizational Culture and Leadership

A Dynamic View

Edgar H. Schein

Organizational Culture and Leadership

Jossey-Bass Publishers

San Francisco • Washington • London • 1985

ORGANIZATIONAL CULTURE AND LEADERSHIP
A Dynamic View
by Edgar H. Schein

Copyright © 1985 by: Jossey-Bass Inc., Publishers
433 California Street
San Francisco, California 94104
&
Jossey-Bass Limited
28 Banner Street
London EC1Y 8QE

Library of Congress Cataloging in Publication Data

Schein, Edgar E.
    Organizational culture and leadership.

    (A joint publication in the Jossey-Bass management
series and the Jossey-Bass social and behavioral science
series)
    Bibliography: p. 329
    Includes index.
    1. Corporate culture. 2. Culture. 3. Leadership.
I. Title. II. Series: Jossey-Bass management series.
III. Series: Jossey-Bass social and behavioral science
series.
HD58.7.S33   1985   302.3'5   84-43034
ISBN 0-87589-639-1 (alk. paper)

Manufactured in the United States of America

The paper in this book meets the guidelines for
permanence and durability of the Committee on
Production Guidelines for Book Longevity of the
Council on Library Resources.

JACKET DESIGN BY WILLI BAUM

FIRST EDITION

Code 8519

A joint publication in
The Jossey-Bass Management Series
and
The Jossey-Bass
Social and Behavioral Science Series

Consulting Editors
Organizations and Management

Warren Bennis
University of Southern California

Richard O. Mason
University of Arizona

Ian I. Mitroff
University of Southern California

Preface

The purpose of this book is, first of all, to clarify the concept of "organizational culture" and, second, to show how the problems of organizational leadership and organizational culture are basically intertwined. I hope to demonstrate that organizational culture helps to explain many organizational phenomena, that culture can aid or hinder organizational effectiveness, and that leadership is the fundamental process by which organizational cultures are formed and changed.

I first became interested in culture because my teaching and consulting experiences in Europe and Mexico *felt* very different from comparable experiences in the United States. A trip to Australia and Singapore in 1980 reinforced this sense of difference across countries, but, at the same time, I noticed another phenomenon: that companies operating in the multinational context sometimes did things in dramatically similar ways, even in widely differing cultures. Companies thus seemed to have cultures of their own that were sometimes strong enough to override or at least modify local cultures.

I had always been sensitive to company cultures, since my process consulting style was based on the notion that only members of the client system could determine what kind of intervention would work for them in their culture, but I had never taken the trouble to analyze in detail what was meant by "their culture" (Schein, 1969). In my studies of organizational socialization and careers, I analyzed the *process* of socialization but gave little attention to the *content* of what people were being taught and were learning (Schein, 1978). In my earlier research on "coercive persuasion," I had attempted to understand how someone's basic ideological beliefs could undergo dramatic change, but there again the focus was on the process rather than the cultural content (Schein, 1961).

Why, then, a book specifically on organizational culture at this time? There are basically five reasons:

1. *The topic has heated up.* The discovery that some Japanese companies could compete successfully with their United States counterparts suddenly focused our attention on both national culture and organizational culture. There has been a rash of books and papers focusing on the concept of culture, and many of these works claim that culture makes a major difference to organizational effectiveness (Ouchi, 1981; Pascale and Athos, 1981; Deal and Kennedy, 1982; Peters and Waterman, 1982; Tichy, 1983; Sathe, 1985; Kilmann, 1984; Wilkins and Ouchi, 1983).

2. *The topic is confusing.* Unfortunately, most of the writers on organizational culture use different definitions, different methods of determining what they mean by culture, and different standards for evaluating how culture affects organizations. These conceptual and methodological differences make it almost impossible to assess the various claims made. One of my main purposes in writing this book now is to clarify what culture is, what it does, and how it relates to organizational effectiveness, so that these various claims can be put into a useful perspective for the manager and the student of organizations.

3. *The analysis of culture can illuminate the study of leadership.* Why link the concept of culture to leadership at all? This link had not really been my original intent, but the further

I got into the topic of organizational culture, the more I realized that culture was the result of entrepreneurial activities by company founders, leaders of movements, institution builders, and social architects. As I began to think through the issues of how culture changes, I again realized the centrality of leadership—the ability to see a need for change and the ability to make it happen. Much of what is mysterious about leadership becomes clearer if we separate leadership from management and link leadership specifically to creating and changing culture.

4. *The field of organization studies is maturing into more interdisciplinary modes of thinking and conducting research.* Ethnographic methods, participant observation, qualitative research, and clinical research are becoming more legitimate. Organizations are increasingly being studied with explicitly interdisciplinary models in mind (Van Maanen, 1979a; Jelinek, Smircich, and Hirsch, 1983; Pondy and others, 1983; Mitroff, 1983). My reading of much of what is being said about culture suggests some confusion about what the concept should mean and what research methods most appropriately bear on it. By looking across the fields, one sees connections that need to be made explicit.

5. *My own perspective has shifted toward a more interdisciplinary view.* This shift takes me back full circle to my graduate work in Harvard's Department of Social Relations in the late 1940s and early 1950s, a time when anthropology, sociology, social psychology, and clinical psychology were making a concerted effort to enhance each other through the joint educational efforts of superstars such as Clyde and Florence Kluckhohn, Talcott Parsons, Samuel Stouffer, George Homans, Henry Murray, Robert White, Gordon Allport, Jerome Bruner, Richard Solomon, and David McClelland. I mention them here because some of their theories and insights have proved crucial in my current effort to understand what culture is all about; and it is only now that I can repay my intellectual debt to them.

In many respects this book is a journey of "integration" for me, in that it attempts to bring together many intellectual strands that have occupied me for many years. The organizing thread has always been the effort to "understand" in the clinical, phenomenological sense. For me a theory is no good if I cannot find illustrations in everyday life of the phenomenon with which the theory deals and if I cannot observe and feel the impact of what the theory or model purports to explain. Since culture is very abstract and we can only build intellectual models of it, it becomes especially important to see whether such models illuminate and can be illuminated by our concrete experience.

I hope in this book to provide a "clarifying" perspective for the scholar/researcher, for the manager who increasingly needs to have broader concepts than those traditionally found in administrative science or "organizational behavior," and for the consultant who must help organizations in times of difficulty. And, most of all, I hope to have a prescription for leaders, because it is leaders who will ultimately face all the difficult questions about organizational culture.

Who Should Read This Book

I have aimed this book at the person who wants to understand organizational culture from either a theoretical or a practical point of view. I hope that many managers, particularly those at senior levels in organizations, will find that this book helps them understand what is going on in their organizations and, to some degree, manage the consequences of what they have come to understand. Notice that I have not said "manage the culture," because it is not clear whether that is possible or even desirable. But the consequences of culture are real, and these must be managed.

This book should be of interest to students and colleagues who want to get acquainted with the concept of culture in the contemporary setting. Culture, as it turns out, is not limited to countries but exists wherever groups exist, so it should be of interest to anyone interested in organizations and groups. What has traditionally been limited to anthropology is expanded here into sociology and, especially, group psychology.

Consultants and helpers to human systems—whether families, teams, or larger organizational units—should find useful theoretical ideas and practical suggestions in the dynamic approach taken here. My clinical perspective orients me to action and help, so the concepts and illustrations are designed to illuminate how culture works, how to figure culture out, and how to intervene appropriately.

I hope that my academic colleagues and researchers will find useful the concepts that are brought to bear on organizational culture in this book. I have been excited by the insights I have been able to obtain by bringing together some of the psychology of groups, leadership theory, anthropological theory, and psychodynamic theory, and hope that they might be similarly excited and intrigued.

Finally, those who aspire to leadership may find food for thought here. What is leadership ultimately about? I hope to provide some provocative answers.

Organization and Contents

The book is organized to reflect the dynamic perspective that I take toward the analysis of organizational culture. Chapter One defines the term, gives two brief case illustrations of what culture is all about, and sets the stage for the remaining chapters. Part One deals with what culture is and what it does, its functions in group and organizational life. Chapter Two first makes a case for why one should study culture. Chapter Three then lays out the major external adaptation and internal integration problems that every group must deal with and attempts to show that culture can best be thought of as the stable solutions to those problems. In Chapter Four I show how culture becomes abstracted into a set of basic underlying assumptions, which deal with certain universal issues that all groups face. The interlocking pattern of these assumptions is the essence of a given culture. In Chapter Five I show how to locate such assumptions in an organization by means of observation, interview, and a joint working out of the answers between an outsider and willing insiders. Chapter Six explores the pros and cons of doing such an analysis and the ethical problems inherent in studying, giving feedback on, and publishing the results of culture studies.

In Part Two the focus shifts to the origins and evolution of culture. The key issue is how to understand the process of coming to share common assumptions, a theme that all culture analyses rely on. Chapter Seven reviews the relevant theories for such an analysis and attempts to weave together concepts from sociodynamic, psychoanalytical, leadership, and learning theory. Chapter Eight shows how the process of culture formation actually works in the setting of a training group, where such a process can be examined. Chapter Nine then extrapolates these processes into organizations by examining several case descriptions of company startups, focusing especially on how entrepreneurs and founders externalize their own assumptions and make them part of their organizations. In Chapter Ten we look at explicit and implicit mechanisms used by founders and leaders to embed and reinforce their assumptions, and in that process to stabilize the evolving culture.

Part Three deals with the problem of culture evolution and change. To set the framework for the argument that culture change is hard to diagnose and even harder to analyze, Chapter Eleven reviews in detail a major change program that I was involved with in one of the companies that is used illustratively throughout the book. Chapter Twelve then provides a framework for examining culture change mechanisms by relating them to the stage of organizational evolution. The proposition that culture serves different functions at different stages leads to the hypothesis that different change mechanisms apply at different stages. Chapter Thirteen shows how hard it is to conceptualize and measure culture change by noting that one's perspective, goals, and implicit theories of change all affect one's definitions and measures.

Chapter Fourteen pulls the various messages of the chapters together and makes explicit the implications of the dynamic perspective for leadership. It turns out that the role of leadership is different at different stages of group evolution and that the real problem of *changing* culture occurs only in mature organizations under certain conditions. But when it is necessary, it tests leadership in an ultimate manner.

Acknowledgments

It is always difficult to repay intellectual debts. Yet I must mention particularly Gordon Allport, Richard Solomon, and Florence Kluckhohn, who gave me insights that I am only now beginning to take advantage of. For the clinical perspective that governs much of my current approach, I am indebted to David Rioch, my mentor at the Walter Reed Army Institute of Research in the mid-1950s. My interest in groups stems from Alex Bavelas and the work done over several years with Leland Bradford, Richard Beckhard, and many others at the National Training Laboratories in Bethel, Maine. Conducting training groups for managers over a fifteen-year period reinforced my understanding of how action and research together lead to understanding. From Richard Beckhard, my colleague of over twenty years, I learned most of what I know about organizational change and consulting.

My thinking about organizational culture, specifically, was most influenced by my colleagues Lotte Bailyn and John Van Maanen. Our spirited debates on concepts and methods have enriched my understanding immeasurably. Many of the ideas were tested on and worked out with students in a doctoral seminar, especially Steve Barley, Jon Chillingarian, Deborah Dougherty, Gibb Dyer, Karen Epstein, Anna Maria Garden, Gideon Kunda, Barbara Lawrence, and Jeanne Lindholm. Barley, Dougherty, Dyer, and Kunda have worked intensively on culture projects of their own and have provided necessary and invaluable critical analysis. Deborah Dougherty in particular has been helpful in searching the recent anthropological literature for theories of culture change. Several of the chapters on change were directly influenced by her insights and her organization of anthropological materials.

Many other colleagues have helped by making suggestions, criticisms, and elaborations. I would like to thank especially Joanne Martin for her incisive feedback and support. Others who have provided feedback and help are Chris Argyris, Paul Evans, Robert and Jaqueline Goodnow, Arnoldo Hax, David

Kolb, Meryl Louis, Fred Neubauer, Eleanor Westney, and the consulting editors of Jossey-Bass—Warren Bennis, Richard Mason, Ian Mitroff, and William Henry. Nancy Dallaire helped by thoroughly editing the first draft. My colleague Bill Johnson provided valuable feedback on the final draft. Dorothy Conway, my copy editor, not only improved the writing but added many original thoughts of her own through her careful reading and probing questions.

Finally, I once again want to acknowledge the important contribution of my wife, Mary, for discussing at length with me the implications of some of what we experience when we travel, for attending some of my lectures and providing incisive critiques, and for generally supporting the work at every stage. I also benefited greatly from the help of my children, Louisa, Elizabeth, and Peter, who have developed an active interest in anthropology and organizations and, because of this, have supplied ideas and insights that helped my thinking at every stage of this writing.

Cambridge, Massachusetts   Edgar H. Schein
November 1984

Contents

xvii

The Author

Edgar H. Schein is the Sloan Fellows Professor of Management at the Sloan School of Management, Massachusetts Institute of Technology. He received his B.A. degree (1947) from the University of Chicago, his M.A. degree (1949) from Stanford University, and his Ph.D. degree (1952) from Harvard University in social psychology.

Schein's main research activities have been in the field of managerial career development and the process of socialization leading to the study of organizational culture. His applied work in organizational development led to the concept of process consultation as a way of dealing with organizational client systems around major change issues. Schein's book, *Organizational Psychology* (1965; 3rd ed., 1980) helped to define that field, and his collaboration with Richard Beckhard and Warren Bennis led to the seminal Addison-Wesley series on organization development. In addition, his publications include the following books: *Coercive Persuasion* (1961), *Interpersonal Dynamics* (1964, with others), *Professional Education: Some New Directions* (1972), and *Career Dynamics* (1978).

Schein was chairman of the Organization Studies Group of the Sloan School of Management from 1972 to 1981, and he has been a consultant to many major corporations in the United States and in Europe.

Organizational Culture and Leadership

A Dynamic View

1

Defining Organizational Culture

Most of us—whether students, employees, managers, researchers, or consultants—live in organizations and have to deal with
them. Yet we continue to find it amazingly difficult to understand and justify much of what we observe and experience in
our organizational life. Too much seems to be "bureaucratic,"
or "political," or just plain "irrational." People in positions of
authority, especially our immediate bosses, often frustrate us or
act incomprehensibly, and those we consider the "leaders" of
our organizations often disappoint us and fail to meet our aspirations. The fields of organizational psychology and sociology
have developed a variety of useful concepts for understanding
individual behavior in organizations and the ways in which organizations structure themselves. But the dynamic of why and
how they grow, change, sometimes fail, and—perhaps most important of all—do things that don't seem to make any sense continues to elude us.

The concept of organizational culture holds promise for

1

illuminating this difficult area. I will try to show that a deeper understanding of cultural issues in organizations is necessary not only to decipher what goes on in them but, even more important, to identify what may be the priority issues for leaders and leadership. Organizational cultures are created by leaders, and one of the most decisive functions of leadership may well be the creation, the management, and—if and when that may become necessary—the destruction of culture. Culture and leadership, when one examines them closely, are two sides of the same coin, and neither can really be understood by itself. In fact, there is a possibility—underemphasized in leadership research— that the *only thing of real importance that leaders do is to create and manage culture* and that the unique talent of leaders is their ability to work with culture. If the concept of leadership as distinguished from management and administration is to have any value, we must recognize the centrality of this culture management function in the leadership concept.

But before we examine closely the tie to leadership, we must fully understand the concept of organizational culture. I would like to begin with two examples from my own consulting experience. In the first case (Company A), I was called in to help a management group improve its communication, interpersonal relationships, and decision making. After sitting in on a number of meetings, I observed, among other things, high levels of interrupting, confrontation, and debate; excessive emotionality about proposed courses of action; great frustration over the difficulty of getting a point of view across; and a sense that every member of the group wanted to win all the time. Over a period of several months, I made many suggestions about better listening, less interrupting, more orderly processing of the agenda, the potential negative effects of high emotionality and conflict, and the need to reduce the frustration level. The group members said that the suggestions were helpful, and they modified certain aspects of their procedure, such as lengthening some of their meetings. However, the basic pattern did not change, no matter what kind of intervention I attempted. I could not understand why my efforts to improve the group's problem-solving process were not more successful.

In the second case (Company B), I was asked, as part of a broader consultation project, to help create a climate for innovation in an organization that felt a need to become more flexible in order to respond to its increasingly dynamic business environment. The organization consisted of many different business units, functional groups, and geographical groups. As I got to know more about these units and their problems, I observed that some very innovative things were going on in many places in the company. I wrote several memos describing these innovations, added other ideas from my own experience, and gave the memos to my contact person in the company, hoping that he would distribute them to other managers who might benefit from the ideas. I also gave the memos to those managers with whom I had direct contact. After some months I discovered that whoever got my memo thought it was helpful and on target, but rarely, if ever, did the memo get past the person to whom I gave it. I suggested meetings of managers from different units to stimulate lateral communication, but found no support at all for such meetings. No matter what I did, I could not seem to get information flowing, especially laterally across divisional, functional, or geographical boundaries. Yet everyone agreed in principle that innovation would be stimulated by more lateral communication and encouraged me to keep on helping.

I did not really understand what happened in either of these cases until I began to examine my own assumptions about how things should work in these organizations and began to test whether my assumptions fitted those operating in my client systems. This step of examining the shared assumptions in the client system takes one into "cultural" analysis and will be the focus from here on. Such analysis is, of course, common when we think of ethnic or national cultures, but not sufficient attention has been paid to the possibility that groups and organizations within a society also develop cultures that affect in a major way how the members think, feel, and act. Unless we learn to analyze such organizational cultures accurately, we cannot really understand why organizations do some of the things they do and why leaders have some of the difficulties that they have.

The concept of organizational culture is especially relevant to gaining an understanding of the mysterious and seemingly irrational things that go on in human systems. And culture *must* be understood if one is to get along at all, as tourists in foreign lands and new employees in organizations often discover to their dismay.

But a concept is not helpful if we misuse it or fail to understand it. My primary purpose in undertaking this book, therefore, is to explain the concept of organizational culture, show how it can best be applied, and relate it to leadership. To put it more precisely, I hope to accomplish the following things in this book:

1. Provide a clear, workable definition of organizational culture that takes into account the accumulated insights of anthropologists, sociologists, and psychologists. Much attention also will be given to what culture *is not,* because there has been a tendency in the last few years to link culture with virtually everything.

2. Develop a conceptual "model" of how culture works—that is, how it begins, what functions it serves, what problems it solves, why it survives, why and how it changes, and whether it can be managed and, if so, how. We need a dynamic evolutionary model of organizational culture, a model that tells us what culture *does,* not only what it is. In our rush to create more effective organizations in the last few years, we may well have latched on to culture as the new panacea, the cure for all our industrial ailments. How valid is this notion, and, if it is valid, how can we use culture constructively?

3. Show how culture, as a conceptual tool, can illuminate individual psychological behavior; what goes on in small groups and in geographically or occupationally based communities; how large organizations work; and how societal, multinational issues can be better understood through increased cultural insight. A dynamic model of culture will be especially useful in improving our understanding of how human systems evolve over time.

4. Show how culture and leadership are really two sides of the same coin. One cannot understand one without the other.

Underlying these several purposes is a chronic fear I have that both students of culture and those consultants and managers who deal with culture in a more pragmatic way continue to misunderstand its real nature and significance. In both the popular and the academic literature, I continue to see simplistic, cavalier statements about culture, which not only confuse matters but positively mislead the reader and promise things that probably cannot be delivered. For example, all the recent writings about improving organizational effectiveness through creating "strong" and "appropriate" cultures continue to proliferate the possibly quite *incorrect* assumption that culture can be changed to suit our purposes. Suppose we find that culture can only "evolve" and that groups with "inappropriate" or "weak" cultures simply will not survive. The desire to change culture may become tantamount to destroying the group and creating a new one, which will build or evolve a new culture. Leaders do at times have to do this, but under what conditions is it possible or practical? Are we aware that we may be suggesting something very drastic when we say "Let's change the culture"?

So throughout this book I will be hammering away at the idea that culture is a *deep* phenomenon, that culture is *complex* and difficult to understand, but that the effort to understand it is worthwhile because much of the mysterious and the irrational in organizations suddenly becomes clear when we do understand it.

A Formal Definition of Organizational Culture

The word "culture" has many meanings and connotations. When we combine it with another commonly used word, "organization," we are almost certain to have conceptual and semantic confusion. In talking about organizational culture with colleagues and members of organizations, I often find that we agree "it" exists and is important in its effects but that we have completely different ideas of what the "it" is. I have also had colleagues tell me pointedly that they do *not* use the concept of culture in their work, but when I ask them what it is they do *not* use, they cannot define "it" clearly. Therefore, before launching into the reasons for studying "it," I must give a clear definition of what I will mean by "it."

Some common meanings are the following:

1. *Observed behavioral regularities* when people interact, such as the language used and the rituals around deference and demeanor (Goffman, 1959, 1967; Van Maanen, 1979b).
2. The *norms* that evolve in working groups, such as the particular norm of "a fair day's work for a fair day's pay" that evolved in the Bank Wiring Room in the Hawthorne studies (Homans, 1950).
3. The *dominant values espoused* by an organization, such as "product quality" or "price leadership" (Deal and Kennedy, 1982).
4. The *philosophy* that guides an organization's policy toward employees and/or customers (Ouchi, 1981; Pascale and Athos, 1981).
5. The *rules* of the game for getting along in the organization, "the ropes" that a newcomer must learn in order to become an accepted member (Schein, 1968, 1978; Van Maanen, 1976, 1979b; Ritti and Funkhouser, 1982).
6. The *feeling* or *climate* that is conveyed in an organization by the physical layout and the way in which members of the organization interact with customers or other outsiders (Tagiuri and Litwin, 1968).

All these meanings, and many others, do, in my view, *reflect* the organization's culture, but none of them *is* the essence of culture. I will argue that the term "culture" should be reserved for the deeper level of *basic assumptions* and *beliefs* that are shared by members of an organization, that operate unconsciously, and that define in a basic "taken-for-granted" fashion an organization's view of itself and its environment. These assumptions and beliefs are *learned* responses to a group's problems of *survival* in its external environment and its problems of *internal integration.* They come to be taken for granted because they solve those problems repeatedly and reliably. This deeper level of assumptions is to be distinguished from the "artifacts" and "values" that are manifestations or surface levels of the culture but not the essence of the culture (Schein, 1981a, 1983, 1984; Dyer, 1982).

But this definition immediately brings us to a problem. What do we mean by the word "group" or "organization," which, by implication, is the locale of a given culture (Louis, 1983)? Organizations are not easy to define in time and space. They are themselves open systems in constant interaction with their many environments, and they consist of many subgroups, occupational units, hierarchical layers, and geographically dispersed segments. If we are to locate a given organization's culture, where do we look, and how general a concept are we looking for?

Culture should be viewed as a property of an independently defined stable social unit. That is, if one can demonstrate that a given set of people have shared a significant number of important experiences in the process of solving external and internal problems, one can assume that such common experiences have led them, over time, to a shared view of the world around them and their place in it. There has to have been enough shared experience to have led to a shared view, and this shared view has to have worked for long enough to have come to be taken for granted and to have dropped out of awareness. Culture, in this sense, is a *learned product of group experience* and is, therefore, to be found only where there is a definable group with a significant history.

Whether or not a given company has a single culture in addition to various subcultures then becomes an empirical question to be answered by locating stable groups within that company and determining what their shared experience has been, as well as determining the shared experiences of the members of the total organization. One may well find that there are several cultures operating within the larger social unit called the company or the organization: a managerial culture, various occupationally based cultures in functional units, group cultures based on geographical proximity, worker cultures based on shared hierarchical experiences, and so on. The organization as a whole may be found to have an overall culture if that whole organization has a significant shared history, but we cannot assume the existence of such a culture ahead of time.

This concept of culture is rooted more in theories of group dynamics and group growth than in anthropological theories of how large cultures evolve. When we study organizations, we do not have to decipher a completely strange language or set of customs and mores. Rather, our problem is to distinguish—within a broader host culture—the unique features of a particular social unit in which we are interested. This social unit often will have a history that can be deciphered, and the key actors in the formation of that culture can often be studied, so that we are not limited, as the anthropologist is often limited, by the lack of historical data.

Because we are looking at evolving social units within a larger host culture, we also can take advantage of learning theories and develop a dynamic concept of organizational culture. Culture is learned, evolves with new experiences, and can be changed if one understands the dynamics of the learning process. If one is concerned about managing or changing culture, one must look to what we know about the learning and unlearning of complex beliefs and assumptions that underlie social behavior.

The word "culture" can be applied to any size of social unit that has had the opportunity to learn and stabilize its view of itself and the environment around it—its basic assumptions. At the broadest level, we have *civilizations* and refer to Western or Eastern cultures; at the next level down, we have *countries* with sufficient ethnic commonality that we speak of American culture or Mexican culture. But we recognize immediately that within a country we also have various *ethnic groups* to which we attribute different cultures. Even more specific is the level of *occupation, profession,* or *occupational community.* If such groups can be defined as stable units with a shared history of experience, they will have developed their own cultures. Finally, we get to the level of analysis that is the focus of this book—*organizations.* Within organizations we will find subunits that can be referred to as *groups,* and such groups may develop group cultures.

To summarize, at any of these structural levels, I will

mean by "culture": *a pattern of basic assumptions—invented, discovered, or developed by a given group as it learns to cope with its problems of external adaptation and internal integration—that has worked well enough to be considered valid and, therefore, to be taught to new members as the correct way to perceive, think, and feel in relation to those problems.*

Because such assumptions have worked repeatedly, they are likely to be taken for granted and to have dropped out of awareness. Note that the definition does not include overt behavior patterns. I believe that overt behavior is always determined both by the cultural predisposition (the assumptions, perceptions, thoughts, and feelings that are patterned) and by the situational contingencies that arise from the external environment. Behavioral regularities could thus be as much a reflection of the environment as of the culture and should, therefore, not be a prime basis for *defining* the culture. Or, to put it another way, when we observe behavior regularities, we do not know whether we are dealing with a cultural artifact or not. Only after we have discovered the deeper layers that I am defining as the culture can we specify what is and what is not an artifact that reflects the culture.

Two Case Examples

To illustrate the problem of definition, I will briefly review the two company examples mentioned earlier. In Company A, hereafter referred to as Action Company, one encounters at the visible level an organization with open office landscape architecture; extreme informality of dress and manners; an absence of status symbols (so that it is hard to decipher who has what status in the organization); a very dynamic environment in the sense of rapid pace, enthusiasm, intensity, energy, and impatience; and, finally, a high level of interpersonal confrontation, argumentativeness, and conflict. One also discovers that people are constantly busy going to meetings of various sorts and expressing considerable ambivalence about committees and meetings. Committees are considered frustrating but necessary, and the level of debate and argument within meetings is intense.

If one goes beyond these surface phenomena and talks to

people about what they do and why, one discovers some of their *values*: high regard for individual creativity, an absolute belief in individual accountability, but, at the same time, a strong commitment to obtaining consensus on important matters before moving ahead to a decision. Individuals at all levels in the organization are expected to think for themselves and take what they consider to be the correct course of action, even if it means going against a previous decision. Insubordination is positively valued if the action leads to a better outcome. The language one hears in the company reflects these values in that it glorifies "arguing back," "doing the right thing," and so on.

Inquiries about what the "boss" wants are typically considered irrelevant, giving one the impression that authority is not much respected in the organization. In fact, there are frequent complaints that decisions made at higher levels do not get implemented, that people at lower levels feel they can reverse a decision if their insight tells them to do something different, and that insubordination is rarely if ever punished. When people in higher authority positions are asked why they are not more decisive, why they let groups work things out, they state that they are "not smart enough" to make the decision by themselves. Consequently, they stimulate group debate and argument and create the kind of group atmosphere that I described above.

To understand this behavior, one must seek the *underlying assumptions* and premises on which this organization is based. The founding group comes from an engineering background, is intensely practical and pragmatic in its orientation, has built a strong and loyal "family" spirit that makes it possible to confront and have conflict without risk of loss of membership, and clearly believes that "truth" lies not in revealed wisdom or authority but in "what works," both technologically and in the marketplace. The assumption that the individual is the source of ideas but that no one individual is smart enough to evaluate his or her own ideas is at the root of the organization's problem-solving/decision-making model. Thus, creativity is always strongly encouraged, but new ideas have to be sold to all potentially affected parties before they will be blessed by higher authority.

Without understanding these assumptions, one cannot decipher most of the behavior observed, particularly the seeming incongruity between intense individualism and intense commitment to group work and consensus. Similarly, one cannot understand why there is simultaneously intense conflict with authority figures and intense loyalty to the organization without also understanding the assumption "We are one family who will take care of each other." Finally, without these assumptions one cannot decipher why a group would want a consultant to help it become more effective, yet ignore most of the suggestions on how to be more effective.

I now realize that what the group members meant by "effective" was, within their cultural assumptions, to be better at sorting out the truth. The group was merely a means to an end; the real process going on in the group was a basic, deep search for solutions that one could have confidence in because they stood up. Once I shifted my focus to improving the *decision* process instead of the *group* process, my interventions were more quickly acted on. For example, I began to help more with agenda setting, time management, clarifying some of the debate, summarizing, consensus testing once debate was running dry, and in other ways focusing on the "task process" rather than the "interpersonal process." But the basic confrontive, interruptive style continued because the culture of the group legitimized operating that way, based on the assumption that truth is determined through confrontive debate.

Company B, hereafter referred to as the Multi Company, offers a sharp contrast. Multi is headquartered in Europe, and most of its managers are European. At the level of what is visible, it is more formal—the formality symbolized by large buildings and offices with closed doors; a hushed atmosphere in the corridors; obvious deference rituals among people who meet each other in the hall; many status symbols, such as private dining rooms for senior managers (in contrast to Action's open cafeteria); the frequent use of academic and other titles, such as Dr. so-and-so; a slower, more deliberate pace; and much more emphasis on planning, schedules, punctuality, and formal preparation of documents for meetings.

Multi managers come across as much more serious, more

thoughtful, less impulsive, more formal, and more concerned about protocol. Whereas Action ties rank and salary fairly strictly to the actual job being performed by the individual, Multi has a system of managerial ranks based on length of service, overall performance, and the personal background of the individual rather than on the actual job being performed at a given time.

In meetings I observed much less direct confrontation and much more respect for individual opinion. Recommendations made by managers in their specific area of accountability are generally respected and implemented. Insubordination tends *not* to be tolerated. Rank and status thus clearly have a higher value in Multi than in Action, whereas personal negotiating skill and the ability to get things done in an ambiguous social environment have a higher value in Action than in Multi.

I could not understand the culture of Multi, however, until I attempted to circulate memos to the various branches of the Multi organization. Although I was supposed to "stimulate innovation," the ideas never got to certain managers unless I presented them personally. When I asked one of my colleagues in the organization *why* the information did not circulate freely, he indicated that unsolicited ideas might not be well received. Only if information was asked for was it acceptable to offer ideas, unless they came down the hierarchy as an official position. To provide unsolicited information or ideas could be seen as a challenge to the information base the manager was using, and that might be regarded as an insult, implying that the person challenged had not thought deeply enough about his own problem or was not really on top of his job.

To understand this and related behavior, it was necessary to consider the underlying assumptions that this company had evolved. It had grown and achieved much of its success through fundamental discoveries made by a number of basic researchers in the company's central research laboratories. Whereas in Action truth is discovered through conflict and debate, in Multi truth has come more from the wisdom of the scientist/researcher. Both companies believe in the individual, but the differing assumptions about the nature of truth led to completely different attitudes toward authority and the role of conflict.

In Multi authority is much more respected, and conflict tends to be avoided. The individual is given areas of freedom by the boss and then is totally respected in those areas. If the role occupant is not well enough educated or skilled enough to make decisions, he is expected to train himself. If he performs poorly in the meantime, that will be tolerated. In both companies there is a "tenure" assumption that once someone has been accepted he is likely to remain unless he fails in a major way.

In Action conflict is valued, and the individual is expected to take initiative and fight for ideas in every arena. In Multi conflict is suppressed once a decision has been made. In Action it is assumed that, if a job is not challenging or is not a good match between what the organization needs and what the individual can give, the individual should be moved to a new assignment or would quit anyway. In Multi the person would be expected to be a good soldier and do the job. Both companies are successful, yet in certain respects their cultures are almost totally different.

Recognition of these assumptions has led me to change my role as a consultant at Multi. I found that if I gave information directly, even if it was unsolicited, it was accepted because I was an "expert." If I wanted information to circulate, I sent it out to the relevant parties on my own initiative. But I have not yet found reliable mechanisms for stimulating lateral communication as a means of achieving the basic goal of increasing innovativeness. (More will be said about this problem in Chapter Eleven.)

Levels of Culture

Throughout the previous discussion, I have referred to various cultural "elements," such as the physical layout of an organization's offices, rules of interaction that are taught to newcomers, basic values that come to be seen as the organization's ideology or philosophy, and the underlying conceptual categories and assumptions that enable people to communicate and to interpret everyday occurrences. As Figure 1 shows, I distinguish among these elements by treating basic assumptions as

Figure 1. Levels of Culture and Their Interaction.

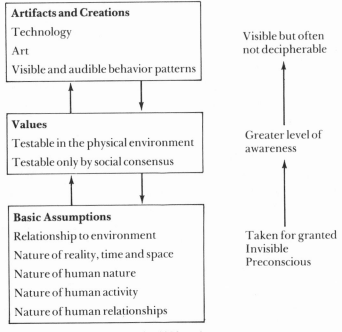

Source: Adapted from Schein, 1980, p. 4.

the essence—what culture really is—and by treating values and behaviors as observed manifestations of the cultural essence. In a sense these are "levels" of the culture, and they need to be carefully distinguished to avoid conceptual confusion.

Level 1: Artifacts. The most visible level of the culture is its artifacts and creations—its constructed physical and social environment. At this level one can look at physical space, the technological output of the group, its written and spoken language, artistic productions, and the overt behavior of its members. Since the insiders of the culture are not necessarily aware of their own artifacts, one cannot always ask about them, but one can always observe them for oneself.

Every facet of a group's life produces artifacts, creating the problem of classification. In reading cultural descriptions, one often notes that different observers choose to report on different sorts of artifacts, leading to noncomparable descriptions. Anthropologists have developed classification systems, but these tend to be so vast and detailed that cultural essence becomes difficult to discern.

Moreover, whereas it is easy to observe artifacts—even subtle ones, such as the way in which status is demonstrated by members—the difficult part is figuring out what the artifacts mean, how they interrelate, what deeper patterns, if any, they reflect. What has been called the "semiotic" approach to cultural analysis (Spradley, 1979; Frake, 1964; Barley, 1983; Manning, 1979; Van Maanen, 1977) deals with this problem by collecting enough data on how people communicate to enable one to understand, from the point of view of the insider, what meanings are to be attached to the visible behavior. If the anthropologist lives in the cultural environment long enough, the meanings gradually become clear.

If one wants to achieve this level of understanding more quickly, one can attempt to analyze the central values that provide the day-to-day operating principles by which the members of the culture guide their behavior.

Level 2: Values. In a sense all cultural learning ultimately reflects someone's original values, their sense of what "ought" to be, as distinct from what is. When a group faces a new task, issue, or problem, the first solution proposed to deal with it can only have the status of a value because there is not as yet a shared basis for determining what is factual and real. Someone in the group, usually the founder, has convictions about the nature of reality and how to deal with it, and will propose a solution based on those convictions. That individual may regard the proposed solution as a belief or principle based on facts, but the group cannot feel that same degree of conviction until it has collectively shared in successful problem solution. For example, in a young business if sales begin to decline, the leader may say "We must increase advertising" because of his* *belief* that "advertising always increases sales." The group, never having experienced this situation before, will hear that assertion as a statement of the leader's *values*: "He thinks that one should always advertise more when one is in trouble." What the leader

---

*The author uses *his* and *he* for reasons of convenience and acknowledges the inequity of the traditional use of masculine pronouns.

initially proposes, therefore, cannot have any status other than a value to be questioned, debated, and challenged.

If the solution works, and the group has a shared perception of that success, the value gradually starts a process of *cognitive transformation* into a belief and, ultimately, an assumption. If this transformation process occurs—and it will occur only if the proposed solution continues to work, thus implying that it is in some larger sense "correct" and must reflect an accurate picture of reality—group members will tend to forget that originally they were not sure and that the values were therefore debated and confronted. As the values begin to be taken for granted, they gradually become beliefs and assumptions and drop out of consciousness, just as habits become unconscious and automatic. Thus, if increased advertising consistently results in increased sales, the group begins to believe that the leader is "right" and has an understanding of how the world really works.

Not all values undergo such transformation. First of all, the solution based on a given value may not work reliably. Only those values that are susceptible of physical or social validation, and that continue to work reliably in solving the group's problems, will become transformed into assumptions. Second, certain value domains, those dealing with the less controllable elements of the environment or with aesthetic matters, may not be testable at all. In such cases consensus through social validation is still possible, but it is not automatic. By social validation I mean that values about how people should relate to each other, exercise power, define what is beautiful, and so on, can be validated by the experience that they reduce uncertainty and anxiety. A group can learn that the holding of certain beliefs and assumptions is necessary as a basis for maintaining the group.

Many values remain conscious and are explicitly articulated because they serve the normative or moral function of guiding members of the group in how to deal with certain key situations. For example, if a company states explicitly in its charter and other public documents that it strongly values people, it may be doing so because it wants everyone to operate by that value, even without any historical experience that such a value actually improves its performance in its environment. A set of values that become embodied in an ideology or organizational philosophy thus can serve as a guide and as a way of dealing with the uncertainty of intrinsically uncontrollable or difficult events. Such values will predict much of the behavior that can be observed at the artifactual level. But if those values are not based on prior cultural learning, they may also come to be seen only as what Argyris and Schön (1978) have called "espoused values," which predict well enough what people will *say* in a variety of situations but which may be out of line with what they will actually *do* in situations where those values should be operating. Thus, the company may *say* that it values people, but its record in that regard may contradict what it says.

If the espoused values are reasonably congruent with the underlying assumptions, then the articulation of those values into a philosophy of operating can be helpful in bringing the group together, serving as a source of identity and core mission (Ouchi, 1981; Pascale and Athos, 1981; Peters and Waterman, 1982). But in analyzing values one must discriminate carefully between those that are congruent with underlying assumptions and those that are, in effect, either rationalizations or aspirations for the future.

If we can spell out the major espoused values of an organization, have we then described and understood its culture? And how do we know whether we have *really* understood it? The answer often lies in our own feelings as observers and analysts. Even after we have listed and articulated the major values of an organization, we still may feel that we are dealing only with a list that does not quite hang together. Often such lists of values are not patterned, sometimes they are even mutually contradictory, sometimes they are incongruent with observed behavior. Large areas of behavior are often left unexplained, leaving us with a feeling that we understand a piece of the culture but still do not have the culture as such in hand. To get at that deeper level of understanding, to decipher the pattern, to predict future behavior correctly, we have to understand more fully the category of "basic assumptions."

Level 3: Basic Underlying Assumptions. When a solution to a problem works repeatedly, it comes to be taken for granted. What was once a hypothesis, supported by only a hunch or a value, comes gradually to be treated as a reality. We come to believe that nature really works this way. Basic assumptions, in this sense, are different from what some anthropologists call "dominant value orientations" (Kluckhohn and Strodtbeck, 1961) in that such dominant orientations reflect the *preferred* solution among several basic alternatives, but all the alternatives are still visible in the culture, and any given member of the culture could, from time to time, behave according to variant as well as dominant orientations. Basic assumptions, in the sense in which I want to define that concept, have become so taken for granted that one finds little variation within a cultural unit. In fact, if a basic assumption is strongly held in a group, members would find behavior based on any other premise inconceivable. For example, in a group whose basic assumption is that the individual's rights supersede those of the group, members would find it inconceivable that they should commit suicide or in some other way sacrifice themselves to the group even if they had dishonored the group. In a company in a capitalist country, it is inconceivable that one might sell products at a financial loss or that it does not matter whether a product works.

What I am calling basic assumptions are congruent with what Argyris has identified as "theories-in-use," the implicit assumptions that actually guide behavior, that tell group members how to perceive, think about, and feel about things (Argyris, 1976; Argyris and Schön, 1974). Basic assumptions, like theories-in-use, tend to be nonconfrontable and nondebatable. To relearn in the area of "theories-in-use," to resurrect, reexamine, and possibly change basic assumptions—a process that Argyris and others have called "double-loop learning"—is intrinsically difficult because assumptions are, by definition, not confrontable or debatable.

Clearly, such unconscious assumptions can distort data. If we assume, on the basis of past experience or education, that other people will take advantage of us whenever they have an opportunity (essentially what McGregor, 1960, meant by his

"Theory X"), we expect to be taken advantage of and then interpret the behavior of others in a way that coincides with those expectations. We observe people sitting idly at their desk and perceive them as loafing rather than thinking out an important problem; we perceive absence from work as shirking rather than doing work at home. In contrast, if we assume—as the previously mentioned Action Company does—that everyone is highly motivated and competent (McGregor's "Theory Y"), we will act in accordance with that assumption. Thus, if someone at Action Company is absent or seems to be idle, the managers ask themselves what has happened to their job assignment process, not what is wrong with the individual. The person is still seen as motivated, but the environment is perceived as somehow turning him or her off. Managerial energy then goes into redesigning the work or the environment to enable the person to become productive once again.

Unconscious assumptions sometimes lead to "Catch 22" situations, as illustrated by a common problem experienced by American supervisors in some other cultures. A manager who comes from an American pragmatic tradition assumes and takes it for granted that solving a problem always has the highest priority. When that manager encounters a subordinate who comes from a different cultural tradition, in which good relationships and protecting the superior's "face" are assumed to have top priority, the following scenario can easily result.

The manager proposes a solution to a given problem. The subordinate knows that the solution will not work, but his unconscious assumption requires that he remain silent because to tell the boss that the proposed solution is wrong is a threat to the boss's face. It would not even occur to the subordinate to do anything other than remain silent or even reassure the boss that they should go ahead and take the action.

The action is taken, the results are negative, and the boss, somewhat surprised and puzzled, asks the subordinate what he would have done. When the subordinate reports that he would have done something different, the boss quite legitimately asks why the subordinate did not speak up sooner. This question puts the subordinate into an impossible bind because the answer itself is a threat to the boss's face. He cannot possibly explain his behavior without committing the very sin he is trying to avoid in the first place—namely, embarrassing the boss. He might even lie at this point and argue that what the boss did was right and only bad luck or uncontrollable circumstances prevented it from succeeding.

From the point of view of the subordinate, the boss's behavior is incomprehensible because it shows lack of self-pride, possibly causing the subordinate to lose respect for that boss. To the boss the subordinate's behavior is equally incomprehensible. He cannot develop any sensible explanation of his subordinate's behavior that is not cynically colored by the assumption that the subordinate at some level just does not care about effective performance and therefore must be gotten rid of. It never occurs to the boss that another assumption—such as "One never embarrasses a superior"—is operating and that, to the subordinate, that assumption is even more powerful than "One gets the job done."

In this instance probably only a third party or some cross-cultural education could help to find common ground whereby both parties could bring their implicit assumptions to the surface. And even after they have surfaced, such assumptions would still operate, forcing the boss and the subordinate to invent a new communication mechanism that would permit each to remain congruent with his culture—for example, agreeing that, before any decision is made and before the boss has stuck his neck out, the subordinate will be asked for suggestions and for factual data that would not be face threatening.

I have dwelled on this long example to illustrate the potency of implicit, unconscious assumptions and to show that such assumptions often deal with fundamental aspects of the culture. But such assumptions are hard to locate. If we examine carefully an organization's artifacts and values, we can try to infer the underlying assumptions that tie things together. Such assumptions can usually be brought to the surface in interviews if both the interviewer and the interviewee are committed to trying to piece together the cultural pattern. But this requires detective work and commitment, not because people are reluctant to surface their assumptions but because they are so taken for granted. Yet when we do surface them, the cultural pattern suddenly clarifies and we begin to feel we really understand what is going on and why.

Ethnographic Versus Clinical Perspective

In reviewing my own "data base," the sources of my own knowledge about organizational culture, I have found it necessary to distinguish the perspective of the *ethnographer* from that of the *clinician.* The ethnographer obtains concrete data in order to understand the culture he is interested in, presumably for intellectual and scientific reasons. Though the ethnographer must be faithful to the observed and experienced data, he brings to the situation a set of concepts or models that motivated the research in the first place. The group members studied are often willing to participate but usually have no particular stake in the intellectual issues that may have motivated the study.

In contrast, a "clinical perspective" is one where the group members are clients who have their own interests as the prime motivator for the involvement of the "outsider," often labeled "consultant" or "therapist" in this context. In the typical ethnographic situation, the researcher must obtain the cooperation of the subjects; in the clinical situation, the client must get the cooperation of the helper/consultant. The psychological contract between client and helper is completely different from that between researcher and subject, leading to a different kind of relationship between them, the revelation of different kinds of data, and the use of different criteria for when enough has been "understood" to terminate the inquiry.

Clients call in helpers when they are frustrated, anxious, unhappy, threatened, or thwarted; when their rational, logical approaches to things do not work. Inevitably, then, the clinical view brings one to the topic of the "irrational" in organizations. I have found and hope to show in this book that one of the simplest ways of understanding the seemingly irrational is to relate such phenomena to culture, because culture often explains things that otherwise seem mysterious, silly, or "irrational."

Consultants also bring with them their models and concepts for obtaining and analyzing information, but the function
of those models is to provide insight into how the client can be
helped. In order to provide help, the consultant must "understand" at some level. Some theories, in fact, argue that only by
attempting to change a system (that is, giving help) does one
demonstrate any real level of understanding (Lewin, 1952;
Schein, 1980). For me this criterion has always been the relevant one for "validating" my understanding, even though that
understanding often is incomplete, since the clinical relationship
does not automatically license the helper to inquire into areas
the client may not wish to pursue or considers irrelevant. On
the other hand, the level of understanding is likely to be deeper
and more dynamic.

The point of spelling all this out now is to let the reader
know that my data base is a clinical one, not an ethnographic
one. I have not been a participant-observer in organizations
other than the ones I had membership in, but in being a consultant I have spent long periods of time in client organizations. I
believe that this clinical perspective provides a useful counter-
point to the pure ethnographic perspective, because the clinician learns things that are different from what an ethnographer
learns. Clients are motivated to reveal certain things when they
are paying for help that may not come out if they are only
"willing" to be studied.

So this kind of inquiry leads, I believe, to a "deeper"
analysis of culture as a phenomenon—deeper in the sense of its
impact on individual members of the organization. This perspective also leads inevitably to a more dynamic view of how things
work, how culture begins, evolves, changes, and sometimes dis-
integrates. And, as we will see, this perspective throws into high
relief what leaders and other change agents can or cannot do to
change culture deliberately.

2

Why Culture
Must Be
Better Understood

At a meeting of training directors and internal consultants in
the Multi organization, the subject of their company culture
came up. There were eight of us in the room, varying in seniority from fifteen years to one year. An organization development consultant, who had been hired a year ago because of his
prior experience in conducting diagnostic projects in companies, was responding to my general outline of how to analyze cultural assumptions. He noted that one of the interesting
features of the Multi culture was the tendency to assume that
only people who had been in the company a long time could
understand how it really operated; as a result, recently arrived
employees found it difficult to make any contribution. The
senior person in the group, who was in charge of an internal
consulting unit that had been functioning for quite a few years
(his own seniority was fifteen years), turned on the young consultant and said angrily: "How can you sit there and make a
statement about the Multi culture when you have been here

barely one year. You are completely wrong. We accept the ideas of new employees." In the shocked silence that followed, we all had occasion to think hard about what the impact of culture really is, and why it is important to understand the concept.

There are three basic reasons why organizational culture must be better understood:

1. Organizational cultures are highly "visible" and "feelable." The phenomenon of culture is real and has impact, whether we are talking about a total society, an occupation, an organization, a group within an organization, or just a meeting. Any phenomenon so real should be better understood.

2. Individual and organizational performance, and the feelings that people in an organization have about that organization, cannot be understood unless one takes into account the organization's culture. There are now many claims that organizational culture can determine the degree of effectiveness of the organization, either through its "strength" or through its "type" (see, for example, Deal and Kennedy, 1982; Brandt, 1981; Peters and Waterman, 1982; Wilkins and Ouchi, 1983; Kets de Vries and Miller, 1984). How valid are these claims and how do we "interpret" them?

3. Organizational culture as a concept has been misunderstood and confused with other concepts, such as "climate," "philosophy," "ideology," "style," "how people are managed," and the like. If we are to get any benefit from the concept, we must first build a common frame of reference for analyzing it and must use it in a theoretically appropriate manner.

Visibility and Feelability of Culture

Cultural impacts are potent and patterned; they have a "demand quality" to them; and they invite us to project our own assumptions if the data are not clear.

Potency. Anyone who has ever traveled knows how potent the impact of different cultures can be. We encounter a new language, strange customs, unfamiliar sights, sounds, and smells, and unpredictable behavioral responses from "locals" that make it hard to relax. Typically, all our senses and sensibilities become involved immediately when we enter a new culture. What we encounter are the culture's "artifacts," its visible and feelable manifestations, and these have powerful impacts.

Though the effect is often less intense, the same range of sensory surprises is likely to occur when we move into an *organization* that has a culture different from the one to which we are accustomed (Louis, 1980). This phenomenon is fairly evident to people who move from one company to another, but is also often felt within a given company when an individual moves from one functional department to another, or from one geographical region to another, suggesting that cultural phenomena even operate at a subgroup level within an organization. We speak of crossing organizational "boundaries" and of the need to be "socialized" into the new group (Schein, 1971; Van Maanen and Schein, 1979).

As "consumers," we often note these sensory differences when we compare stores, banks, airlines, or restaurants. Establishments *look and feel different from one another,* and the service people in different stores or restaurants behave differently toward us, sometimes in puzzling ways that strike us as rude, impersonal, or inconsiderate. The rules by which things get done in different organizations vary, often to our frustration because we cannot decipher how to get what we want. At the Action Company, I learned that if I wanted to make a point I had to fight for air time; at Multi I learned that if I got the floor it was hard to relinquish because people expected me to make some major points.

But what justifies calling such differences, however vivid and visible they may be, "cultural" phenomena? What makes us attribute such differences to anything more than the individual personalities we encounter? Why do we talk about the entire airline, bank, or restaurant as being pleasant or unpleasant, rather than simply attributing such qualities to individual encounters with individual personalities?

Patterning. Psychologically we experience such artifactual phenomena as something more than the effect of individual personalities because (1) we observe that a number of people in the organization seem to behave in the same way, (2) we observe that others in the setting treat the behavior as normal and expected, and (3) we experience the behavior not as random or unmotivated but as *purposive and patterned.* We sense that there is some meaning in what people are doing, that there is a purpose to it that others in the situation seem to understand, even if we ourselves cannot decipher that purpose.

We tend to deal with this kind of situation by making attributions to the organization as a whole: "they" are cutting down on costs, "they" are trying to compete by giving better service, "they" are an organization in which it must be fun to work, or not fun to work, and so on. Furthermore, when we observe that the behavior of a number of people is coordinated into a larger pattern, that there is a consistency among a number of separate elements, we are led to generalizations about how formal or informal a given organization is, how autocratic, bureaucratic, or participative it is, or how open or closed it seems to be.

In any given restaurant or bank, the physical layout, the furniture, the attire and demeanor of the employees, the sound level, and dozens of other cues often reinforce each other, giving the impression of a pattern. Such impressions of "patterning" are based on expectations derived from previous experiences with similar situations.

We can see the operation of this mechanism most clearly when we examine how we react to incongruities. If we go to a restaurant and encounter, on the one hand, wooden plank tables and, on the other hand, waiters dressed in tuxedos, we feel puzzled, possibly uncomfortable. If we notice that others in the setting seem to treat as normal the things that strike us as incongruous, we try to figure it out by looking for a higher-order pattern that would "explain" the incongruity.

Why do we look for such patterns? Why is it not enough simply to register what is out there? First of all, it is inherently anxiety provoking to deal with randomness or meaninglessness, because we cannot predict, and therefore prepare for, what may come next. If there is intrinsically no order in our perceptual world, or too little, or too much stimulation, we invent patterns or meaning even if we have to hallucinate them (Hebb, 1954; Lilly, 1956, 1957; Heider, 1958; Jones and Nisbett, 1971; Pulliam and Dunford, 1980).

Second, we look for patterns in the collective behavior of others because we are acutely aware from observing ourselves how much of our own behavior is patterned, even though the patterns may be invisible to others. We try to present ourselves to others in a consistent and congruent fashion and to convey our own interpretation of the situation (Goffman, 1959; Van Maanen, 1979b). We naturally assume, therefore, even if we cannot decipher the meaning initially, that others "know what they are doing and why they are doing it," or at least are acting out patterns that at one time had conscious meanings and intents, even if now they are just unconsciously motivated habits.

If the behavior of others is ambiguous, we are still capable of attributing to them motives and meanings that make sense to us. Experiments on attribution have shown that when we attempt to explain someone else's behavior we are likely to see it as motivated and patterned, rather than situationally determined or "random" (Jones and Nisbett, 1971). When we explain our own behavior, on the other hand, we can see the situational forces that modify the basic motivational patterns, and thus can see more "randomness" in it. It is probably harder to attribute such situational contingencies to others because we have a need to predict and control. We can do such predicting and controlling of our own situation because we know what is happening. If we try to predict and control others, we need to look for more patterned explanations.

Or, to put it another way, we can tolerate exceptions from predicted patterns in our own behavior because we know what the pattern is from which we are deviating. Knowledge of that pattern is what makes the exception definable and tolerable. When we observe behavior in others and cannot decipher the pattern, we must first put our energy into seeking the pattern before we can even consider the situational exceptions to it. The tendency, then, is to project whatever patterns we have in our own culture as an initial hypothesis about what may be going on in the person from another culture.

To illustrate this point, I recall vividly my own first im-

pressions of the intense debate and conflict in group meetings at
the Action Company. I was puzzled, perplexed, and made anxious by this behavior because it seemed like open warfare
among the individual members of the group; yet they apparently tolerated it, liked each other, and in other ways indicated
that they considered the behavior normal and "OK." I initially
attributed individualistic aggressiveness to their behavior because it was the pattern most similar from my own experience.
Only when I noticed other behavior that was incongruous with
such aggressiveness, such as the degree of affection among group
members, was I alerted to the need to find other explanations
for the pattern.

"*Demand*" *Quality.* When we experience a new cultural
situation, we feel a need to respond, react, "do the right thing,"
fit into the situation, remove the tension of uncertainty, gain
acceptance, establish communication, or the like. We find it difficult just to observe the situation and tolerate the feelings of
alienation and tension that it may arouse. Instead, we need to
determine what is expected of us. Such anxiety can turn into
anger if we sense a pressure to conform without knowing how,
or if we sense that conformity might undermine our own sense
of identity. In other words, experiencing a new cultural situation is rarely a bland or neutral experience. If we understand
and successfully cope, we feel exhilaration; if we do not understand, we feel at least some caution and a subtle sense of danger
because inaccurate deciphering can offend others and lead to
embarrassment for ourselves.

The most poignant examples of misunderstanding and
consequent embarrassment often revolve around basic human
functions, such as eating and elimination, and around the rules
of deference and demeanor in interpersonal situations. A friend
related with humor and pain an incident in which a visitor from
another country, unfamiliar with American family-style service,
was passed the plate of cookies during morning coffee, said
thank you, and proceeded with great effort to eat every single
cookie on the plate. No one knew how to correct the situation
without causing more embarrassment than was already present.

Overprojection. In a new cultural situation, we tend to

attribute meaning and purpose to *all* aspects of the setting, possibly even exaggerating the degree to which the setting actually reflects clear intent on the part of other participants. To take a trivial but common example, American tourists in Paris often regard French waiters as "rude" because of their brusque behavior and their lack of helpfulness. Because waiters in the United States generally seem to be friendly and helpful, these tourists expect all waiters to behave similarly. When they do not, their behavior is interpreted as "rude." Instead, according to French friends of mine, the pattern of doing a minimal amount is merely a reflection of a French cultural norm of "individualism"—take care of yourself and expect others to take care of themselves—a norm particularly likely to operate in the urban environment of Paris. The behavior is, in fact, relatively unmotivated, but the American—attributing more to the behavior pattern than is actually there—interprets it as an *intent to be rude* or to put down the tourist.

At the Action Company, a comparable situation arises when a young manager is hired from an organization where people are more polite to each other than they are at Action. The newcomer may feel personally threatened by the brusque, aggressive, confrontive behavior of senior managers. Projecting aggression onto behavior that is thought of within Action as normal problem solving, the newcomer often reacts in a cautious, passive way. And, of course, the more cautious the newcomer becomes, the more likely he is to fail to conform to the norms of the company. Socialization into the Action Company involves the discovery that one must stand up to confrontation and be able to hold one's own at all times. Even feeling sorry for oneself is unacceptable, and letting others see that one is sorry for oneself is a prescription for failure.

Because such additional projections often reflect our own prior cultural biases rather than the intentions of others, we should be very careful not to attribute too much to stimuli even though they may be very potent. Nor should we assume that, even if we knew the meaning, we would know what to attribute it to. That is, for any given potent stimulus, we have no way of knowing initially whether we are dealing with ethnicity and nationality, the culture of an occupation such as one encounters when one deals with doctors or policemen (Becker and others, 1961; Van Maanen, 1975), the culture of an organization, some subcultural element within the organization reflecting common geography, common tasks, or other common elements that may have led to culture formation, or the idiosyncrasies of a given individual. Often what is perceived to be the characteristic of a particular company, such as a high-technology company, may, in fact, reflect the occupational culture of electrical engineering. Thus, we may feel culture impinging on us but be unable to locate its source.

Effects of Cultural Phenomena on Organizational Effectiveness and Individual Satisfaction

The effects of cultural misunderstanding are painfully obvious in the international arena. Cultural misunderstanding can cause wars and the failure of societies, as when strong subcultures cause the larger culture to lose focus and integration. But do such broad issues have any bearing on *organizational* culture? Do the embarrassments, unwitting insults, offenses, and failures to accomplish things in strange cultures have any counterpart when we are dealing with occupations and organizations in a larger culture, especially our own culture? My own experience and many of the recent writings in the field of organization theory, strategy, and organization development all suggest that an examination of cultural issues at the organizational level is absolutely essential to a basic understanding of what goes on in organizations, how to run them, and how to improve them.

To argue this point more concretely, I want to review several kinds of issues, starting with broad organization/environment issues and proceeding to intraorganizational issues.

Effects of Culture on Strategy. Many companies have found that they can devise new strategies that make sense from a financial, product, or marketing point of view, yet they cannot implement those strategies because they require assumptions, values, and ways of working that are too far out of line with the organization's prior assumptions. For example, the Multi

Company built its business by developing—through an intensive effort in its research labs—"important" products that were "useful to society." When the company began competing in a more diversified market, where product utility was not nearly as important as product marketability, some managers argued for a more pragmatic marketing strategy. Those managers wanted to decrease the research and development budget, increase marketing expenditures, and teach their colleagues how to think like marketers. But they were unable to convince key leaders, and therefore parts of the company were left in a financially vulnerable position. Clearly, the traditions, values, self-concepts, and assumptions about the nature of the business made some aspects of the new strategy "unthinkable" or unacceptable to these key leaders.

Another vivid example from Multi is the previously examined problem with "increasing innovativeness." The senior managers recognized the need to become more innovative, both in the products and in the managerial strategies being utilized. Although tremendous top-management energy went into efforts and programs to increase innovation by increasing the flow of ideas upward and laterally, it proved very difficult to communicate even the concept of free flow of information and ideas to a middle management that had grown up under traditions of "top down" management, where all ideas came from the top and loyalty was the most important value. If young managers or professionals attempted to circulate new ideas laterally or upward, they would be reminded in a most kindly but firm manner that the issue being addressed by the new idea had already been dealt with in prior policy statements and that it was really the obligation and duty of the young manager to follow prior precedents rather than questioning them.

Furthermore, a central assumption in this organization was that a job is a person's "turf," not to be invaded by others. Thus, a strategy of increased lateral communication heightened the probability that people's turf would be invaded by all kinds of new ideas, which would to some degree be viewed as threatening or insulting because they implied that the manager needed help. Possession of organizational turf was a jealously guarded right that only one's boss or someone higher in the hierarchy could tamper with. Thus, ideas could circulate up and down the hierarchy, but it was virtually impossible to stimulate lateral communication.

A third example is provided by Action, a company that grew up and became successful by marketing a very complex product to sophisticated customers. When the company later developed smaller, simpler, less expensive versions of this product, which could be sold to less sophisticated customers, its product designers and its marketing and sales divisions could not deal with the new customer type. The sales and marketing people could not imagine what the concerns of the new, less knowledgeable customer might be, and the product designers continued to be convinced that they could judge product attractiveness themselves. Neither group was motivated to understand the new customer type because, unconsciously, they tended to look down on such customers.

In each of the above examples, one could ask whether the problem was not merely one of communication or inadequate training. Why should these be called "cultural" issues? They are "cultural" because the perceptions and resulting behavior patterns were built on deeply held, long-standing assumptions that were taken for granted because they had led to prior success. Such assumptions were active largely outside of management's awareness and were so deeply held that alternative assumptions or strategies built on different assumptions were virtually undiscussible.

Is culture only a "constraint"? Or can an organization that genuinely understands its overall culture and subcultures use this insight as a source of strategic strength? One example will make this issue clear. A founder of a lawn care company in the Middle West believed strongly that all his employees—including truck drivers, maintenance people, and secretaries—should understand the economics of the business and feel a sense of ownership and responsibility for it. The employees of this company were noticed by customers because they seemed especially intelligent and thoughtful. On a typical visit, while chemicals were being applied to the lawn, the truck driver would engage the homeowner in conversation about the business and build up a personal relationship. The company ran into severe competition and found that its survival depended on its ability to diversify. The *employees* pointed out that, since they knew the homeowners to whom they delivered lawn care, they might be able to expand the range of services and gain a competitive edge in housecleaning, home repair, maintenance, and other activities that hinged on their having credibility and trust. The company launched training programs in these related services and expanded successfully.

More and more management consultants are recognizing these types of problems and are noting explicitly that, because "culture constrains strategy," a company must analyze its culture and learn to manage within its boundaries or, if necessary, change it (Beckhard and Harris, 1977; Schwartz and Davis, 1981; Peters, 1980; Allen and Kraft, 1982; Peters and Waterman, 1982; Stonich, 1982).

Scholars, consultants, and managers who are concerned with improving organizations often get into debates about whether it is enough to change the structure of an organization—by which they mean its patterns of authority, division of labor, method of control (in the sense of who reports to whom and who is responsible for what), and lines of communication—or whether one must change people's attitudes and perceptions as well as structure. And, if both need to change, which should come first? If one views these questions from the perspective of organizational culture, one will recognize that both structure and attitudes are, in a sense, artifacts of the culture; and if one thinks of changing the artifacts without confronting the underlying assumptions, one will not obtain successful change. The organization will simply revert to its prior way of operating. If a group has had enough of a history to develop a culture, that culture will pervade everything.

Failures of Mergers, Acquisitions, and Diversifications. When the management of a company decides to merge with or acquire another company, it usually checks carefully the financial strength, market position, management strength, and various other concrete aspects pertaining to the "health" of the other company. Rarely checked, however, are those aspects that might be considered "cultural": the philosophy or style of the company; its technological origins, which might provide clues as to its basic assumptions; and its beliefs about its mission and its future. Yet, if culture determines and limits strategy, a cultural mismatch in an acquisition or merger is as great a risk as a financial, product, or market mismatch.

Several concrete examples will make this point clear. Some years ago a large packaged-foods company purchased a successful chain of hamburger restaurants but, despite ten years of concerted effort, could not make the acquisition profitable. First of all, the company did not anticipate that many of the best managers of the acquired company would leave because they did not like the philosophy of the new parent company. Instead of hiring new managers with experience in the fast-food business, the parent company assigned some of its own managers to run the new business. This was its second mistake, since these managers did not understand the technology of the fast-food business and hence were unable to utilize many of the marketing techniques that had proved effective in the parent company. Third, the parent company imposed many of the control systems and procedures that had historically proved useful for it—and consequently drove the operating costs of the chain up too high. The parent company's managers found that they could never completely understand franchise operations and hence could not get a "feel" for what it would take to run that kind of business profitably. Eventually the company sold the restaurant chain, having lost many millions of dollars over a decade.

The lack of understanding of the cultural risks of buying a franchised business was brought out even more clearly in another case, where a very stuffy, traditional, moralistic company whose management prided itself on its high ethical standards bought a chain of fast-food restaurants that were locally franchised all around the country. The company's managers discovered, much to their chagrin, that one of the biggest of these restaurants in a nearby state had become the local brothel. The activities of the town were so well integrated around this restaurant that the alternative of closing it down posed the risk of drawing precisely the kind of attention this company wanted at all costs to avoid. The managers asked themselves, *after the fact,* "Should we have known what our acquisition involved on this more subtle level? Should we have understood our own value system better, to ensure compatibility?"

A third example highlights the clash of two sets of assumptions about authority. A first-generation company, run by a founder who injected strong beliefs that one succeeds by stimulating initiative and egalitarianism, was bought by another first-generation company, which was run by a strong autocratic entrepreneur who had trained his employees to be highly disciplined and formal. The purchasing company wanted and needed the new managerial talent it acquired, but within one year of the purchase, most of the best managers from the acquired company had left because they could not adapt to the formal autocratic style of the parent company. The autocratic entrepreneur could not understand why this had happened and had no sensitivity to the cultural differences between the two companies.

What is striking in each of these cases is the lack of insight on the part of the acquiring company into its own organizational culture, its own unconscious assumptions about how a business should be run. As one contemplates some recent major cross-industry mergers, such as Du Pont with Conoco, U.S. Steel with Marathon Oil, or American Express with Shearson, one can only wonder how these corporate giants will mesh not only their businesses but their cultures. The histories of these companies, as well as their differing technologies, suggest that substantial cultural differences almost certainly exist between them.

Similar "cross-cultural" problems arise when organizations diversify into new geographical areas or when they move into new technologies, new product lines, or new markets. In each case they will encounter regional or occupational subcultures, which require different kinds of managerial behavior in order to get things accomplished. The problem is often initially conceptualized as "merely" introducing a new technology or product into a new setting, when, in fact, the real problem is that the new technology or product threatens to change local

cultural assumptions to an unknown degree, and is therefore resisted. Or the diversification, like the merger, may require the
learning of a new culture, which turns out to be incompatible
with the present culture of the organization.

After mergers, acquisitions, or diversifications have run
into trouble, managers frequently say that cultural incompatibilities were at the root of it, but somehow these factors rarely
get taken into account during the initial decision-making process. Recently there has been a growing trend to attempt to
assess these factors, but the tools for assessing cultural differences are still relatively crude. One of the major purposes of this
book is to make such tools more readily available and, thereby,
to increase the possibility of improving the merger/acquisition/
diversification process.

Failure to Integrate New Technologies. The introduction
of any new technology into an occupation, organization, or society can be seen as a culture change problem. Occupations
typically build their practices, values, and basic self-image
around their underlying technology. Similarly, an organization
that is successful because of its mastery of a given technology
develops its self-image around that technology. If the technology changes in a substantial fashion, the organization or occupation not only must learn new practices but must redefine itself
in more substantial ways that involve deep cultural assumptions.
For example, with the introduction of low-cost frozen foods
and efficient home refrigeration, many of the canning companies faced either conversion to frozen foods or extinction.
Only those companies that were able to change their whole
sense of what their business was, essentially a cultural change,
were able to survive. Similar stories are told about railroads failing to survive because they could not redefine themselves as
being in the transportation business and could not adapt to new
transportation technologies.

The clearest current examples are probably to be found
in relation to automation, computers, and data-processing technology. One of the strongest elements of an organizational culture is the status system that arises out of the traditional technology, a system often based on the possession of key items of

information or critical skills. With the introduction of sophisticated computerized information systems and automation, it becomes painfully obvious that in many crucial areas the subordinate knows more than the boss, or that groups who previously had no power now have a great deal. People who are in power often anticipate such changes and realize that the best way to avoid the loss of their own power is to resist the new technology altogether. Even if the organizational logic of power redistribution is so convincing that some employees and managers can go along with the change, a second source of "cultural" resistance would be the uncertainty and anxiety associated with the transition itself. The period of transition very likely would involve some time when the very criteria of power and status would be so ambiguous that all people involved in the transition would be made uncomfortable, even the ones who would in the end benefit.

If the new technology is to succeed, those advocating it must recognize from the outset that the resistance to it is not to the technology per se but to the cultural change implications of its introduction. Data-processing technology is usually brought in with the argument that the organization will become more efficient, and little attention is paid to the implications for power realignments. And even when such power issues are dealt with, too little attention is given to still another cultural factor—namely, that the new technology brings with it its own *occupational* culture. Only when change is under way do managers realize that with the new technology comes a whole new set of assumptions, values, and behavior patterns developed in the data-processing occupation.

The data-processing fraternity has its own vocabulary, its own norms, its own traditions, its own vision of its importance, and its own perspective on how the technology ought to be used, none of which may match the language, perspectives, and norms of the potential users of the system (Brooks, 1975; Keen, 1977). The data-processing professional is often convergent in his thinking process, intolerant of ambiguity, impersonal, concrete and output oriented, compulsive and precise, and, therefore, likely to misunderstand and clash with the general manager, who perceives his world as ambiguous, imperfect, and imprecise.

For example, in a large manufacturing company that wanted help with management development, the data-processing managers had come up through a professional career path that gave them considerable familiarity with the various systems the company was using in its business. This familiarity led them to expect that they would be ideal candidates for general manager positions, and they were frustrated by the fact that they rarely obtained promotions to such positions. The general managers, on the other hand, said that the data-processing managers were inexperienced, did not know how to handle people, and had a poor sense of how to exercise responsibility. They felt that knowledge of the systems was not nearly enough to compensate for the interpersonal weaknesses, and they asserted that the data-processing group would "never" make it into senior management slots.

My own observations of the two groups in several meetings revealed a further aspect of the problem. The data-processing managers used their occupational jargon liberally, which was a direct threat to the "face" of general managers, who did not understand many of the terms and, worse, resented being made to feel ignorant. One could see the conflict developing between the two subcultures; and, of course, the dominant subculture of general management won out, in that data-processing managers were, in fact, never considered for general manager jobs. Unfortunately, in the process of working out the intergroup conflict, the issue of how to improve the company's efficiency through better use of the data-processing technology temporarily got lost.

An interesting example can be followed currently in medicine, where the introduction of computerized diagnostic procedures may make a generation of older doctors obsolete in one critical area of their job. For instance, the introduction of the sophisticated radiological diagnosis that is made possible by ultrasound technology, computerized tomography, and other devices puts relatively more power into the hands of well-trained technicians and makes the older radiologist dependent on those technicians. The realignment of status, power, and working habits is clearly going to be a major cultural change in radiology departments (Barley, 1984a, 1984b). The implication is that the successful introduction of any new technology must be viewed in part as a problem of meshing several occupational subcultures and/or changing the dominant organizational culture (Allen, 1977).

Intergroup Conflicts Within the Organization. Groups can form on the basis of physical proximity, shared fate, common occupation, common work experience, similar ethnic background, or similar rank level (such as labor or management). Once a group acquires a history, it also acquires a culture. If groups get into conflict with each other, that conflict is very difficult to reduce—mainly because a group needs to maintain its identity, and one of the best ways of maintaining that identity is to compare and contrast itself with other groups. In other words, *inter*group comparison, competition, and/or conflict helps to build and maintain *intra*group culture (Sherif and others, 1961; Blake and Mouton, 1961; Alderfer, 1977). This formation of "subcultures" is essentially the same phenomenon described by Lawrence and Lorsch (1967) as "differentiation" into the various functional parts of an organization and the development of a local functional perspective in each part. When sales and research units or engineering and manufacturing units have trouble talking to each other and collaborating effectively, the problem can be viewed essentially as an intercultural one.

If we view labor-management negotiations from this point of view, we can ask whether each group in the negotiation has developed a culture of its own, whether those cultures overlap enough to make mutual understanding possible, and, if not, how enough common culture could be built to make genuine negotiation or problem solving possible. Negotiations in United States companies seem to go faster and produce mutually more satisfactory solutions when there is a shared set of assumptions about the validity of the capitalist system, the rational-legal basis of authority, the openness of the class structure, the Horatio Alger myth, and the value of the product or service being created by the organization.

In multinational organizations such negotiations become even more complex because the intergroup issues get combined with issues of national cultural differences. Thus, negotiation techniques that may work well in one country may be completely unworkable in another country. Assumptions about what the unions want and what worker attitudes they reflect may vary hugely by country, often leading to the erroneous conclusion that if workers are granted codetermination rights, management will automatically lose some of its key prerogatives. In fact, whether management will lose or gain will be a function of both the national culture and the company culture. In many European organizations, increased participation by the labor unions is viewed as positive because worker attitudes are more pro-company in the first place.

The problem of business ethics can be similarly viewed as a cultural issue. What is ethical is, in the first instance, an aspect of a culture, so that if we assume the operation of several cultures within an organization, we can assume that there may be several bases for judging what is ethical (Schein, 1966). Even if a given company has a strong, well-integrated total organizational culture, specifying clear principles, such principles may not apply in other host cultures. For example, in some cultural situations, certain kinds of payoffs between customers and suppliers are seen as a normal exchange in the conduct of business, whereas such payoffs are regarded as bribery or kickbacks in other situations.

Ineffective Meetings and Communication Breakdowns in Face-to-Face Relationships. Even the familiar daily problems of organizational life—the unproductive meeting, the difficulty of getting a point across to a subordinate during performance appraisal, the difficulty of communicating instructions clearly enough to ensure correct implementation, and so on—may be productively analyzed from the cultural perspective. Instead of seeing communication breakdowns as the result of lack of clarity, defensiveness, or semantics, we might recognize that such breakdowns often result from real differences in how people perceive and understand things because of their membership in different cultural units. Instead of seeing semantic problems as "noise" in the system, we might recognize that such problems are inevitable when members of different subcultures try to communicate with each other. Hence, misunderstanding at the face-to-face level should always be treated initially as a cultural issue rather than an issue of individual personality (Hall, 1959; Schein, 1981b).

Experience in meetings and groups teaches all of us how quickly culture forms in even a few meetings. The group forms a language of its own, attaches its own meanings to events, and develops assumptions about itself and its environment that begin to operate as silent filters on perceptions. The effective manager of groups knows that, on the one hand, enough time must be allowed for some group culture to form in order for the group to be effective at all; but, on the other hand, the more the group develops a culture, the more problems it will have in communicating with other groups and the more it may become inflexible in its own operation. Viewing group growth and effectiveness from a cultural perspective gets us past the application of oversimplified standard tools to make meetings more productive or to improve communications.

The last several points are well summarized by Allen (1977, pp. 138-139) in his analysis of research and development organizations:

> The differing cultures of the organizations interpret or structure the problems in different ways; they weigh the solution criteria differently and thus almost guarantee the development of different solutions. Some laboratories, for example, are noted for the conservatism of their designs; others are gamblers and are noted for creative thinking and occasional outstanding breakthroughs. These characteristics, as well as certain of the long-run organizational goals, become ingrained in the members of the organization and thereby provide a conceptual or coding scheme by means of which they categorize their world and communicate about it to others. This common coding scheme develops

in part as a result of the organizational members having experienced over time a series of common experiences and in part by a philosophy developed out of the organization's early experiences or resulting from the influence of a few key individuals. The coding scheme is a common viewpoint manifested in a shared language and a common set of attitudes. It enhances the efficiency of communication among those who hold it in common but can detract from the efficiency of communication with anyone who follows a different coding scheme. Engineers in an organization are able to communicate better with their organizational colleagues than with outsiders because there is a shared knowledge on both ends of the transaction and less chance for misinterpretation. It is amazing to see how misinterpretation can creep into the communication between organizations.

Socialization Failures. Every organization is concerned about the degree to which people at all levels "fit" into it. Organizations will expend considerable effort in training, indoctrinating, socializing, and otherwise attempting to ensure that the "fitting in" is not left to chance (Schein, 1968; Van Maanen, 1976; Van Maanen and Schein, 1979; Ritti and Funkhouser, 1982). When the socialization process does not work optimally, when the new member does not learn the culture of the host group, there are usually severe consequences. At one extreme, if the new employee does not learn the pivotal or central assumptions of the organization, that employee usually feels alienated, uncomfortable, and possibly unproductive. Such feelings may even cause desirable employees to leave the organization. If the new employee learns elements of a subculture that run counter to the pivotal assumptions of the total organization or the managerial coalition that is in power, the result can be active sabotage, or the slowing down of the work of the organization as defined by the coalition in power, leading eventually to stagnation, revolution, or the weeding out of the dissenter.

At the other extreme, if the employee is "oversocialized" in the sense of learning every detail of the host culture, the result is total conformity, leading to inability on the part of the organization to be innovative and responsive to new environmental demands. Optimal socialization can be thought of as learning only those parts of the culture that are essential to the organization's survival and continued functioning.

Because an organization tends to be a conglomeration of subcultures but also has a total organizational culture if it has had enough of a history, the process of cultural learning for the newcomer is complicated and perpetual. On first entering the organization and, subsequently, with each major functional, geographical, or hierarchical move, the person has to learn new subcultural elements and fit them into a broader total view. An analysis of how people manage this process—especially when they move into new settings and groups, where new cultural themes are in conflict with old ones—is crucial to an understanding of both individual outcomes, such as alienation and lack of productivity, and organizational outcomes, such as lack of innovation.

Productivity. As numerous studies of industrial work have shown, work groups form strong cultures, and often such subcultures develop the assumption that work should be limited not by what one is able to do but by what is appropriate to do—"a fair day's work for a fair day's pay" (Roethlisberger and Dickson, 1939; Whyte, 1955; Roy, 1960; Schrank, 1978; Schein, 1980). Sometimes, when the organization is seen to be in trouble or when workers link their own self-interest to that of the company, the norm is toward high productivity (Lesieur, 1958; National Commission on Productivity and Work Quality, 1975), but typically the norm "restricts" output. Until Homans (1950) and others treated such behavior as a sociological phenomenon rather than a characteristic of individual workers, we could not really explain it, because no individual correlates of productivity level could be found that stood up across a variety of situations. But group history and experience could explain not only how the norms arose but the levels at which they were set. In other words, productivity is a cultural phenomenon par excellence, both at the small-work-group level and at the level of the total organization.

Underanalysis and Misunderstanding of Culture

Culture is now a widely used term and is offered as an explanation for many things that go on in organizations. Given this wide usage, the third reason for studying culture is to make our analysis of the concept as precise and accurate as possible. It is very easy to label something as cultural and to rely on our intuitive understanding, because we are all familiar with culture at some level. But such intuitive understanding does not prevent us from misunderstanding and underanalyzing, leading to four kinds of traps: (1) failure to understand the *dynamic consequences* of cultural phenomena, (2) overemphasis on the *process* of cultural learning (socialization) and insufficient emphasis on the *content* of what is actually learned (the actual culture), (3) confusing *parts* of the culture with the cultural *whole,* and (4) confusing *surface manifestations* of a culture with the underlying pattern, or what we might think of as the *essence* or *core* of the culture. These kinds of misunderstanding are, of course, highly interrelated, but we can look at each separately for purposes of analysis.

Dynamic Consequences. Culture is patterned, potent, and deeply embedded in people's thoughts, perceptions, and feelings. It provides an integrated perspective and meaning to situations; it gives group members a historical perspective and a view of their identity. If culture is all this, is it readily changeable, and, more important, should it be changed? Or, to put it another way, the major dynamic consequence of culture is that it stabilizes things for group members. Under what conditions, then, can or should the situation be destabilized in initiating a change process?

Some of the recent writing on organizational culture provides too glib an answer to these questions. For example, Ouchi (1981), in his analysis of Japanese management methods, argues that we should go from the less desirable Type A organization to the more desirable Type Z organization by making people in the organization more "open and trusting." This prescription betrays surprisingly little concern either for the difficulty of producing such a change or for its desirability. Ouchi and others also argue for greater use of "consensus management" in United States companies without giving much consideration to the problem of introducing that style of management into an inherently individualistic culture (Slater, 1970; Evans, 1976; Harris, 1981). The glib prescription misses the point that in Japanese society harmony and subordination of the individual to the group are considered among the highest human values, while in the United States individualism and pragmatism are considered much higher values than group harmony (Inaba, 1981). Groups and teamwork do fit into the United States context if they neither stifle the individual nor undermine efficiency. In fact, the easiest way to sell teamwork to United States managers is to show them that it gets better results than fragmented individual effort (Schein, 1981a).

In a recent book on strategy, Brandt (1981) argues that every organization inevitably goes through a developmental sequence, in which the sixth and final stage involves the "cultivation" of a corporate culture. He further argues that the organization should become conscious of this process and actively manage it. The assumption that the organization has no culture until the late stages of growth and the cavalier statement that one can cultivate a "desirable" culture betray a surprising lack of insight into the dynamics of culture—how it originates, evolves, and stabilizes in the life of an organization.

If we take the concept of culture seriously, we may have to face the possibility that cultural assumptions are virtually impossible to change, or at least we should develop a dynamic theory of change that does justice to the tenacity often exhibited by such assumptions.

Overemphasis on Process Instead of Content. As was indicated previously, a great deal of emphasis has been given in the last several decades to the process of occupational and organizational socialization, but much less effort has gone into describing the actual cultural content of given occupations and organizations. In particular, we lack information on the content of the

culture of different kinds of business organizations, and we lack
theoretical categories for analyzing such content. If one looks at
existing cultural descriptions or methods of studying culture,
one finds that most analysts simply *list* the major categories
that strike them as important. Rarely does one find a theoretical underpinning or rationale for the categories listed. One of
the main reasons for adopting a dynamic evolutionary perspective is that such a perspective generates a logical set of categories for analysis.

Confusing Parts with Wholes. The danger in confusing a
part of a given culture with the whole is that we pick out something trivial and give it too much importance, or that independent observers of the same culture perceive different things and
cannot resolve which is more "true" and/or "important." For
example, when person A encounters the Action Company, he
may be struck by the openness of the environment, the casual-
ness of the clothing worn by employees, the implied informality
of everyone calling everyone else by first names. Person B encountering Action may be struck by the intensity of the work
pace, the level of confrontation among employees, the emotionality that characterizes conversations and meetings. Person A
sees a very open informal culture, B sees a task-oriented, driven
culture; and they have a hard time reconciling their perceptions
unless they both recognize that each is seeing only a part of the
whole. They may even disagree and argue about whose perceptions are correct, not recognizing that both are correct.

We find in written descriptions of organizational cultures
that authors, depending on their purpose and their theoretical
bent, focus on entirely different categories: the company structure, the management philosophy, the personality of founders
and leaders, the organizational climate, the management style,
the functional emphasis, and so on. Each of these elements may
correctly identify one aspect of the organization's culture, but
none of them captures the whole culture. This state of affairs
makes it very difficult to compare and contrast different descriptions of organizations. Because culture pervades everything,
it is very difficult to develop a theoretical rationale for specifying what is the cultural "whole," of which other things are a

"part." One of the main reasons for pushing to the deeper levels of culture is to decipher at those levels the paradigm that provides the "gestalt."

Confusing Symptoms with Essences. The final form of underanalysis is closely related to the previous one but emphasizes the dimension of *depth*. In looking at a culture, one can easily confuse surface manifestations and symptoms with underlying causes, essences, and patterns. Just because the manifest environment of a company feels informal and open does not mean that the actual culture is informal and open. In comparing two companies, one cannot assume that the company that seems more formal and closed processes information less adequately than the company that appears more open and informal.

I remember vividly a confrontation between a German manager and his American colleagues. The Americans were kidding the German about his formal heel clicking, head nodding to superiors, bowing, and shaking hands. They wondered how he ever got any work done what with all the ritual. One day he pointed out angrily to his "informal, open" American friends that when he went to his boss's office every morning he did click his heels, shake hands, and bow; and then, in a completely open manner, he told his boss the *truth* about what was going on in the company pertaining to that day's business. The implication was not lost on his audience that their surface openness often masked their concealing of critical information.

Surface data may, of course, be perfectly accurate. But until we dig deeper, we simply do not know whether what we have observed is just a surface manifestation or a characteristic of how the members of the organization want us to perceive them or whether it reflects deeper patterns in the group. We must be careful not to assume that culture reveals itself easily, partly because we rarely know exactly what we are looking for, partly because underlying patterns are hard to discern, and partly because underlying patterns are so taken for granted that they are likely to be invisible to the insiders as well. As we will see, cultural essences can only be dug out by a joint effort of outsiders and insiders to bring to awareness something that typically has dropped out of consciousness.

Conclusion

Whether we are taking the point of view of the total organization attempting to operate in a complex environment, or the point of view of the individual trying to learn to be productive and satisfied in an occupation or organization, or the point of view of a group engaged in work and/or face-to-face communication, we cannot escape having to analyze at some point the cultural forces involved. Once we demystify the concept of culture and learn to analyze its dynamics, it will aid us enormously in understanding both organizational and individual-level phenomena.

Is there a danger that if culture is pervasive it is also irrelevant? No more so than it is irrelevant for humans to understand how gravity and the atmosphere work. It is precisely the pervasiveness that makes it easy to ignore, however, in that it is hard to get a handle on something that is pervasive. But failing to understand how culture works is just as dangerous in the organizational world as failing to understand gravity and the atmosphere is in the physical/biological world.

Or, to put the matter another way, rather than arguing for the value of cultural analysis, one might well wonder how we can get along without it. And, indeed, we do not get along without it; we manipulate cultural forces intuitively and without awareness. When a manager moves an individual who has a "certain point of view" into a group that needs to "think more like that," we might not initially think of that as culture change; yet, at a certain simplistic level, that is precisely what it is.

Unfortunately, our intuitive understanding often leads to gross oversimplification and outright misunderstanding of cultural phenomena, making our efforts at intervention ineffective or harmful. Therefore, we must also make an effort to understand more precisely what we are dealing with when we deal with cultural phenomena. To enhance that understanding, we need to consider the functions of culture.

3

Functions of Culture in Organizations

A formal definition of organizational culture can tell us what culture is, but it does not tell us why culture arises in a group or an organization in the first place and, more important, why it survives. To understand the dynamics of culture, we must develop a "model" of why basic assumptions arise and why they persist. That is, we must develop theoretically sound answers to questions such as "What does culture do; what functions does it serve?" "How does it originate, evolve, and change?" and "Why is it so difficult to change culture?" Such a functionalist approach helps in the analysis of culture because it provides categories that have immediate relevance for understanding how groups and organizations work. Instead of getting lost in the infinity of cultural phenomena, the researcher and the practitioner can use such dynamic categories as a road map. Furthermore, if we can develop a theory of cultural evolution and cultural change, such a theory will lay a better foundation for whatever aspirations we may have to "manage" culture.

What culture does is to solve the group's basic problems of (1) survival in and adaptation to the external environment and (2) integration of its internal processes to ensure the capacity to continue to survive and adapt (Parsons, 1951; Merton, 1957). To specify these functions more completely, we must list, from an evolutionary perspective, the issues that a group or an organization faces from its origin through to its state of maturity and decline. Although it may be difficult, even sometimes impossible, to study cultural origins and functions in ethnic units whose history is lost in antiquity, it is not at all impossible to study these matters in groups, organizations, or occupations whose history and evolution are available.

Because culture is a dynamic process, the best way to understand it is to draw on group and leadership theory where such theory has dealt specifically with how new organizations form. We must pay special attention to the role of entrepreneurs, founders, and those leaders who manage key organizational transitions, and we must draw on dynamic theories of group development (Schein and Bennis, 1965; Bion, 1959; Bennis and Shepard, 1956; Schein, 1969, 1980, 1983; Rice, 1963; Trist and others, 1963; Cooper and Alderfer, 1978; Alderfer and Cooper, 1980).

The process of culture formation is, in a sense, identical with the process of group formation in that the very essence of "groupness" or group identity—the shared patterns of thought, belief, feelings, and values that result from shared experience and common learning—is what we ultimately end up calling the "culture" of that group. Without a group there can be no culture, and without some degree of culture we are really talking only about an aggregate of people, not a "group." So group growth and culture formation can be seen as two sides of the same coin, and both are the result of leadership activities.

What we need to understand, then, is how the *individual* intentions of the founders, leaders, or conveners of a new group or organization, their own definitions of the situation, their assumptions and values, come to be a *shared, consensually validated* set of definitions that are passed on to new members as "the correct way to define the situation." These intentions and definitions, as they exist consciously or not in the leader's mind, can always be analyzed into an *external* and an *internal* set of issues. The external issues have to do with the leader's and the group's definition of the environment and how to survive in it; the internal issues have to do with the leader's and the group's definition of how to organize relationships among the members of the group to permit survival in the defined environment through effective performance and the creation of internal comfort.

Although these issues are highly interdependent in practice, for purposes of analysis, it is important to note that they reflect very different sets of functional imperatives. The external issues are concerned with survival in what must be assumed to be a *real* environment that is, in part, beyond the control of group members. These external realities define the basic mission, primary task, or core functions of the group. The group must then figure out how to accomplish the core mission, how to measure its accomplishment, and how to maintain its success in the face of a changing environment. But survival over any length of time requires internal integration, and such integration is, of course, aided by external success.

Homans (1950) captured this idea very well in noting that the "external" system—which consists of the physical, technological, and cultural environment—generates activities and interactions, which, in turn, generate sentiments and norms. Once such sentiments and norms have formed, they can be thought of as the "internal" system that now begins reciprocally to influence the external system by also determining activities and interactions. In other words, once culture is formed, it affects how the environment is perceived and dealt with.

However, one must never forget that the environment initially determines the possibilities, options, and constraints for a group, and thus forces the group to specify its primary task or function if it is to survive at all. The environment thus initially influences the formation of the culture, but once culture is present in the sense of shared assumptions, those assumptions, in turn, influence what will be perceived and defined as the environment.

External Adaptation Issues

The issues or problems of external adaptation basically specify the coping cycle that any system must be able to maintain in relation to its changing environment. The essential elements of that cycle are shown in Table 1. Though each step in the cycle is presented in sequential order, any given organization probably works on most of them simultaneously, once it is a going concern (Schein, 1980, 1983, 1984).

Table 1. The Problems of External Adaptation and Survival.

1. *Mission and Strategy.* Obtaining a shared understanding of core mission, primary task, manifest and latent functions.
2. *Goals.* Developing consensus on goals, as derived from the core mission.
3. *Means.* Developing consensus on the means to be used to attain the goals, such as the organization structure, division of labor, reward system, and authority system.
4. *Measurement.* Developing consensus on the criteria to be used in measuring how well the group is doing in fulfilling its goals, such as the information and control system.
5. *Correction.* Developing consensus on the appropriate remedial or repair strategies to be used if goals are not being met.

Consensus on Core Mission, Primary Task, Manifest and Latent Functions. Every new group or organization must develop a shared concept of its *ultimate survival problem,* from which usually is derived its most basic sense of core mission, or "reason to be." In most business organizations, this shared definition revolves around the issue of economic survival and growth, which, in turn, involves the delivery of a necessary product or service to customers. At the same time, society defines as part of the core mission of the economic sector the provision of jobs, so that members of the society have a way to "make a living."

In religious, educational, social, and governmental organizations, the core mission or primary task is clearly different, and what society expects of such organizations as the justification for their existence is different, but every organization must define and fulfill its core mission or it will not survive. The mission typically also involves a deeper sense of *how* to survive in a given environment, where the answer to this question defines more discretely what the group ultimately views its identity to be.

The answer to the question of how to survive usually involves a complex calculus of what the absolute environmental opportunities and constraints are that must be taken into account, and what the internal constraints are beyond which physical survival would not make sense. In other words, under some conditions a group may choose to die rather than to give up its "identity." For example, at one stage in the evolution of Multi, I heard lengthy debates among top managers on the question of whether or not it was legitimate to design products that customers wanted (a marketing orientation favored by some) or whether designs and production should be limited to what some senior managers believed to be "sound" or "valuable" products, based on their conception of what their company had originally been built on. The managers decided that economic survival "at any cost" was not acceptable to them, especially if it meant giving up a company "identity" based on their past technological history.

A similar debate evolved in another company around the question of whether to purchase a company in a different industry. It was not only the economic considerations that were crucial, but deeper questions of "Who are we?" "What are we capable of?" "What do we want to be?"

As a final example, a large packaged-food company had to face the accusation, from consumer groups and nutrition experts, that some of its products—although they tasted good, because of high sugar and artificial flavoring content—had no nutritional value. The accusation raised for the top management not merely an economic question but an identity question: Is this company a food company, or a consumer-oriented edibles company, or both, or neither? At first the company responded to the accusation by attempting to sell more nutritious products, but it found that customers genuinely preferred the cheaper, less nutritious ones. An advertising campaign to sell nutrition did not overcome this customer resistance, nor did lowering the price. Since part of the company's mission was to survive, the pragmatic market-oriented philosophy could be argued more successfully by managers. As a result, the company gradually shifted away from what may have originally been its basic mission.

A useful way to think about ultimate or core mission is to change the question to "What is our function in the larger scheme of things?" Posing the question this way often reveals that most organizations have *multiple functions* and that some of these functions are public justifications, while others are "latent" and, in a sense, not spoken of (Merton, 1957). For example, the manifest function of a school system is to educate. But a close examination of what goes on in school systems suggests several latent functions as well: (1) to keep children (young adults) off the streets and out of the labor market until there is room for them and they have some relevant skills, (2) to sort and group the next generation into talent and skill categories according to the needs of the society, and (3) to enable the various occupations associated with the school system to survive and maintain their professional autonomy. To announce publicly the baby-sitting, sorting, and professional autonomy functions would be embarrassing, but these functions often seem to dominate the activities of school organizations. To admit that some of the organizational decisions of a given school are geared to its own survival would also be embarrassing, and might even be denied because the members of the school system might not be aware of the degree to which their decisions are geared to their own survival.

In business organizations the latent functions include, for instance, the provision of jobs in the community where the business is located; the provision of economic resources to that community, in the form of goods and raw materials purchased; and the provision of managerial talent to be used in activities other than running the business. The importance of these latent functions does not surface until an organization is forced to contemplate closing or moving. Then a number of interest groups—which, in one way or another, were counting on that organization, even though implicitly—suddenly come forward to protest the decision to move or to close.

From this functional point of view, the core mission or primary task can be defined as the task that is at the top of the priority hierarchy. Those priorities can shift as the internal and/ or external environment changes, but at any given moment there is always a priority survival issue; and the resolution of that issue, the solution developed to deal with it, potentially becomes a core cultural element.

Identifying the core mission and goals is usually a part of an organization's process of strategy formation. But those exercises in strategy formulation that start with externally oriented goals and then assess internal strengths and weaknesses may be going at it backward. One needs to understand one's strengths and weaknesses first, in order to get a sense of one's core mission—that is, how one will relate to one's environment. From this sense of mission, one can specify one's goals and then develop more concrete plans (see Beckhard and Harris, 1977). As the members of an organization develop a shared concept of their core mission, and as this concept enables the group to survive in its environment, it becomes a central element of that group's culture and serves as the underlying context in which goals and the means for achieving them can be specified.

Consensus on Operational Goals Derived from Mission. Consensus on the core mission does not automatically guarantee that the members of the group will have common goals. The mission is often understood but not well articulated. In order to achieve consensus on goals, the group needs a common language and shared assumptions about the basic logical operations by which one moves from something as abstract or general as a sense of mission to the concrete goals of designing, manufacturing, and selling an actual product or service within specified and agreed-upon cost and time constraints. For example, in Action there was a clear consensus on the mission of bringing out a line of products that would win in the marketplace, but this consensus did not solve for the senior management the problem of how to allocate resources among different product development groups, nor did it specify how best to market such products.

And it was in the area of marketing that one could see most clearly the lack of semantic agreement on how to think about the marketing function. As a result, management often thought that agreement had been reached on a certain procedure until implementation revealed that different people had assumed different goals for the marketing function. For example, one group thought that marketing meant better image advertising, another group thought it meant developing the next generation of products, while a third group emphasized merchandizing and sales support as the key goals.

In Multi there was a clear consensus on the mission to remain in the pharmaceuticals business because it fitted the broad self-concept of senior management and was profitable, but there was considerable disagreement on what rate of return should be expected from that division and over what length of time its growth and performance should be measured.

Formal studies of organizational goals have revealed that these are sometimes hard to specify, partly because they get confused with the mission or primary task and partly because they reflect compromises among the powerful members or coalitions within the organization (Cyert and March, 1963; March and Simon, 1958; Perrow, 1970; Mintzberg, 1979, 1983). As mentioned, there can be complete agreement on core mission, yet different groups in the organization can derive quite different goals from the mission. Goals can also be defined at several levels of abstraction and in different time horizons. Is our goal to be profitable at the end of next quarter, or to make ten sales next month, or to call twelve potential customers tomorrow? Only as consensus is reached on such matters, leading to solutions that work repeatedly, can we begin to think of the goals of an organization as potential cultural elements.

Consensus on Means. The group cannot perform its primary task unless there is clear consensus on the means by which goals will be met. How to design, finance, build, and sell the product has to be clearly agreed on. From the particular pattern of these agreements, not only the "style" of the organization but also the basic design of tasks, division of labor, organization structure, reward and incentive systems, control systems, and information systems emerge.

The skills, technology, and knowledge that a group acquires in its effort to cope with its environment also become part of its culture if there is consensus on their use. Collectively, all these skills, structures, and processes define what can be thought of as the "means" for accomplishing the organization's goals, and, as can be seen, these means will constitute a large part of the culture if the group or organization has a long history.

In the evolution of its means, a group most clearly defines its boundaries and its rules for membership. For example, an organization that starts with its own vision of what the customer wants, based on an invention by the founder or other key members of the initial group, will build itself around the technological issues of how to design and manufacture what has been invented, giving higher status to these functions than to finance, sales, or marketing. It may come to believe, if that approach is successful, that the ultimate "best" way to operate is to keep engineering and manufacturing in the driver's seat. If such a belief comes to be shared widely and is taught to newcomers, it becomes a part of the organization's culture. In contrast, a company that starts out developing a product that some customers wanted, and hires its research and development personnel to be responsive to customer requirements, will develop a style built around marketing functions. Its top managers, then, might feel justified in firing the whole R & D department if it does not deliver the product that customers want. A young engineer entering these two companies might find them completely different in their orientation toward his work.

The accomplishment of the organization's goals, even though they are directed toward the outside, requires the creation of a structure *inside* the group to make that accomplishment possible. The kind of internal structure that evolves, the way in which roles, resources, and tasks are allocated, will ultimately reflect both the externally oriented intentions of the founders and the internal dynamics of the members. It is this complex interaction between externally dictated purposes and internally evolving interpersonal dynamics that makes it so hard to predict clearly what kind of structure and norms will arise in any given group. But the issues of division of labor; the allocation of tasks, property, and turf; and the design of processes to be used to manage work are always there and must be dealt with.

In Multi the founders believed that solutions to problems result from hard thought, scientific research, and careful checking of that research in the marketplace. From the beginning this company had clearly defined research roles and distinguished them sharply from managerial roles. The norm had developed that one must become an expert in one's own area, to the point where one knows more about that area than anyone else, a norm clearly derived from some of the assumptions of the scientific model on which the company operated. Historically, this link to the culture of science may have accounted, in part, for the assumption that one's area of expertise is one's own property or turf and the feeling that it might be considered insulting to be given advice in that area. It was as if people were saying "If you try to tell me something about *my job*, I will resist and feel threatened, even if you are my boss, unless you have previously held a job very similar to mine, so that you have credibility in my eyes." The defined turf includes one's subordinates, budget, physical space, and all other resources allocated to one. This level of felt autonomy and the formal relationships that developed among group members became their means of getting work done.

In Action, on the other hand, a norm developed that the only turf one really owns is one's accountability for certain tasks and accomplishments. Budget, physical space, subordinates, and other resources are really common organizational property over which one has only influence. Others in the organization can try to influence the accountable manager or his subordinates, but there are no boundaries or "walls," physical space is viewed as common territory, and "sharing" knowledge is highly valued. Whereas in Multi to give ideas to another is considered threatening, in Action it is considered mandatory to survival.

Lack of consensus on who "owns" what can be a major source of difficulty. For example, at one time in Action's history, there was a lack of consensus on the rules for obtaining key engineering services, such as drafting and the use of the model-building shop. Some engineers believed that work would be done in the order in which it was submitted; others believed that it would be done according to the importance of the work, and they often persuaded the service manager to break into the queue to give their work priority. This aroused great anger on the part of those who were waiting their turn patiently and, as might be expected, made the service managers very anxious. The total group eventually had to get together to establish a common set of policies, which, interestingly enough, reinforced the existing pattern and legitimized it. Both engineering and service managers were to do the "sensible" thing, and, if they could not figure out what that was, they were to refer the matter to the next higher level of management for resolution. The policy discussion ended up reinforcing the assumption that, since no one is smart enough to have a "formula" for how to do things, people should use their intelligence and common sense at all times. Ambiguity is considered a reality that must be lived with and managed sensibly.

Feelings around territory, property, and turf also have a biological basis. Few things arouse as much aggression in animals as to have their defined territory invaded. Few circumstances cause as much breakdown of normal behavior patterns as excessive crowding, rendering any private space a physical impossibility (Hall, 1966). In cultures where crowding is inevitable because of shortage of space, the cultural norms develop defensively. Butterfield (1982) notes in his description of China that when one bumps into someone in a crowded bus, one need not even say "sorry," as Westerners would do routinely, because one has only bumped into a "stranger." The same kind of depersonalization operates in the Japanese subway, and, for that matter, in any kind of intense crowding situation.

Division of labor, the allocation of various kinds of roles, can be seen as an extension of the allocation of physical and other kinds of property, since various amounts of status, access to rewards, and certain privileges inevitably accompany the assigned roles. Therefore, how those roles are allocated and the consensus on criteria for allocation not only become the means by which tasks are accomplished but also resolve major *internal* group issues. Because the *means* by which things get done in the external environment become "property" in the internal environment, we often see the means controlling the ends. Changing an organization's structures and processes is often difficult because it involves not only considerations of efficiency and effectiveness vis-à-vis the external task but also the reallocation of internal "property."

Consensus on Criteria for Measuring Results. Once the group is performing, it must have consensus on how to judge its own performance in order to know what kind of remedial action to take when things do not go as expected. For example, in one young and rapidly developing computer company, the evaluation of engineering projects hinged on whether certain key individuals in the company "liked" the product. The company assumed that internal acceptance was an acceptable surrogate for external acceptance. In another computer company, the criterion was completely different. Products had to be built and market tested before it was considered legitimate to mass-produce them. Some companies teach their executives to trust their own judgment as a basis of decisions; others teach them to check with their bosses; still others teach them not to trust results unless they are based on hard data, such as sales or at least market research.

If members of the group hold widely divergent concepts of what to look for and how to evaluate results, they cannot develop coordinated remedial action. For example, senior managers within companies often hold different views of how to assess financial performance; debt/equity ratios, return on sales, return on investment, stock price, and other indicators all could be used. Debates can occur around whether financial criteria should override criteria such as customer satisfaction or employee morale. These debates are complicated by potential disagreements on the correct time horizons to use in making evaluations—daily, monthly, quarterly, annually, or what. Even though the information systems may be very precise, such precision does not guarantee consensus on how to evaluate information.

The potential complexity of achieving consensus on criteria was illustrated in an international refugee organization. Field workers measured themselves by the number of refugees processed, but senior management paid more attention to how favorable the attitudes of host governments were, because those governments financed the organization through their contributions. Senior management therefore checked every decision that was to be made about refugees with virtually every other department and several layers of management, to ensure that the decision would not offend one of the supporting governments. However, this process markedly slowed the making of decisions and often led to "lowest common denominator" conservative decisions. This, in turn, led to great irritation on the part of field workers, who felt that they were usually dealing with crisis situations in which slowdowns might mean death for significant numbers of refugees. They perceived top management as hopelessly mired in what they considered to be simply bureaucratic tangles, and they did not understand the caution that top management felt it had to exercise toward sponsoring governments.

Lack of agreement across the hierarchy on how to judge success—amount of money contributed or number of refugees processed—was the major source of difficulty in improving the overall performance and level of employee satisfaction of this organization. In addition, there may have been basic lack of consensus even on the core mission. Whereas the field workers tended to think of core mission as the survival of refugees, senior management was clearly more concerned with the survival of the total organization, which in its view depended on how it related to the United Nations and to the host governments. Senior management had to decide whether to indoctrinate field workers more effectively on what the core organizational survival problem really was or to live with the internal conflict that the lack of consensus seemed to generate. On the other hand, the younger idealistic field workers could well argue (and did) that to survive as an organization made no sense if the needs of refugees were not met. In this organization, then, one would have to speak of conflicting subcultures or an absence of a total organizational culture with respect to external issues.

In Multi a comparable issue arose in evaluating the performance of different divisions. The high-performing divisions chose to compare themselves internally to the low-performing divisions and were, therefore, complacent about pushing for even higher performance levels. Senior management chose to compare these same divisions to their external competitors in the same product/market space and found that they were underperforming by that criterion. But the tradition of being "one family" made it hard to convince division managers to accept tough "external" standards.

Many organization change programs that are labeled as involving "culture change" actually deal only with this one element of the culture—the measurements to be applied in the future. Thus, new chief executives come in and announce that they will emphasize product quality, or bring costs under control, or get the organization to be more customer oriented. This sometimes sounds like a real change in mission but, on closer examination, turns out merely to be a new focus on how to measure success. From this perspective it is clear that such new signals are only *one* element of culture change. If only the results signals are changed, without concern for mission, goals, and means, very little actual change may come about.

Consensus must be achieved both on the criteria and on the means by which information is to be gathered. For example, in Action there has developed a very open communication system, built around high levels of acquaintance and trust among the members of the organization. This system is supported by a computerized electronic mail network, constant telephone communications, frequent visits, formal and informal surveys and sensing meetings, and two- to three-day committee meetings in settings away from the office. In Action there is a powerful assumption that information and truth are the lifeblood of the organization. In contrast, in Multi there is a tightly structured reporting system, which involves weekly telephone calls, monthly reports to the financial control organization in headquarters, semiannual visits to every department by headquarters teams, and formal meetings and seminars where policy is communicated downward in the organization. In Multi the main assumption appears to be that information flows primarily in designated channels and informal systems are to be avoided because they can be unreliable.

Consensus on Remedial and Repair Strategies. The final area of consensus crucial for external adaptation concerns *what to do* if a change in course is required and *how to do it.* If information surfaces that the group is not on target—sales are off, profits are down, product introductions are late, key customers complain about product quality, or the like—what is the process by which the problem is diagnosed and remedied? If a product fails in the marketplace, does the organization fire the product manager, reexamine the marketing program, reassess the quality of the research and development process, convene a diagnostic team from many functions to see what can be learned from the failure, or brush the failure under the rug and quietly move the good people into different jobs?

In Action the diagnosis is likely to result from widespread open discussion and debate among members at all levels of the organization; after the discussion and debate, self-corrective action often is taken because people now recognize problems about which they can do something. Thus, by the time top management ratifies a course of action and announces it, most of the problem often has already been dealt with. In Multi remedial action is taken locally, if possible, to minimize the upward delegation of bad news. However, if problems surface that are companywide, top management will go through a formal period of diagnosis, often with the help of task forces and other specific processes. Once a diagnosis has been made and remedial action decided on, the decision is formally disseminated through systematic meetings, memoranda, phone calls, and other formal means.

These processes are not limited to problem areas. If a company is getting signals of success, does it decide to grow as fast as possible, does it develop a careful strategy of controlled growth, or does it take a quick profit and risk staying small? Consensus on these matters becomes crucial to effectiveness, and the kind of consensus achieved is one of the determinants of the "style" of the company.

Of particular importance here is the organization's response to "bad news," or information that is threatening to survival. Organizations that have not had periodic survival problems may not even have a "style" of responding to such problems. On the other hand, those organizations that have had survival crises have often discovered in their responses to such crises what their deep-down assumptions and values really were. In this sense an important piece of an organization's culture can be genuinely latent. No one really knows what response it will make to a severe crisis, yet the nature of that response will reflect deep elements of the culture, particularly those elements that have to do with internal integration. For example, many organizations about to go out of business have discovered, to their surprise, high levels of motivation and commitment among their employees. One also hears the opposite kinds of stories, often from wartime, of military units that were counting on high levels of commitment only to find individuals losing their will to fight, seeking excuses to get out of combat, and even shooting their own officers in the back. Crisis situations reveal whether worker subcultures have developed around restriction of output and hiding ideas for improvement from management or whether these subcultures support productivity goals.

In a first-generation company, crises will reveal some of the deeper assumptions of the founder, and, as these become manifested, the culture of the group may be elaborated around them. In one company the founder reacted to poor economic circumstances by massive layoffs of even his closest colleagues. In contrast, in another company the founder in a similar situation put everyone on part-time work and suggested that everyone take a percentage pay cut but made it clear that he valued his people and wanted to retain as many of them as possible. What Kets de Vries and Miller (1984) identify as "neurotic" organizations, whose culture becomes dysfunctional, often arise from a series of such crisis resolutions, which produce a systematic bias in how problems are responded to.

Responses to crises thus provide opportunities for culture building and reveal aspects of the culture that have already been built. From that point of view, this area of organizational adaptation is one of the most important to analyze, understand, and, if possible, manage.

Internal Integration Issues

The process of becoming a group is simultaneously (1) the growth and maintenance of relationships among a set of individuals who are doing something together and (2) the actual accomplishment of whatever they are doing. In real time it is impossible to distinguish these processes, but conceptually they must be distinguished. What keeps a group together, its "reason to be," or what I have called the "external adaptation function," is quite different from the processes of creating that togetherness, processes that make groups capable of accomplishing things that individuals alone cannot accomplish.

What we ultimately end up calling the culture of that group will be influenced both by its external adaptation processes and by its mode of building and maintaining itself, its processes of internal integration. And, as we will see, the internal integration system will both be influenced by and in turn influence the external adaptation system (Homans, 1950). The internal issues that must be dealt with by any group if it is to function as a social system at all are summarized in Table 2.

Developing a Common Language and Conceptual Categories. To function as a group, the individuals who come together must establish a system of communication and a language that permits interpretation of what is going on. The human organism cannot stand too much uncertainty and/or stimulus overload. Categories of meaning that organize perceptions and thought, thereby filtering out what is unimportant while focusing on what is important, become not only a major means of reducing overload and anxiety but also a necessary precondition for coordinated action.

Two children operating a seesaw not only need to be able to signal each other that they want to operate the seesaw together; they also need some verbal or nonverbal means of signaling when to push and when to relax, or how far back to sit if their weight is different, or how fast to move. Members of a

Table 2. The Problems of Internal Integration.

1. *Common Language and Conceptual Categories.* If members cannot communicate with and understand each other, a group is impossible by definition.

2. *Group Boundaries and Criteria for Inclusion and Exclusion.* One of the most important areas of culture is the shared consensus on who is in and who is out and by what criteria one determines membership.

3. *Power and Status.* Every organization must work out its pecking order, its criteria and rules for how one gets, maintains, and loses power; consensus in this area is crucial to help members manage feelings of aggression.

4. *Intimacy, Friendship, and Love.* Every organization must work out its rules of the game for peer relationships, for relationships between the sexes, and for the manner in which openness and intimacy are to be handled in the context of managing the organization's tasks.

5. *Rewards and Punishments.* Every group must know what its heroic and sinful behaviors are; what gets rewarded with property, status, and power; and what gets punished in the form of withdrawal of the rewards and, ultimately, excommunication.

6. *Ideology and "Religion."* Every organization, like every society, faces unexplainable and inexplicable events, which must be given meaning so that members can respond to them and avoid the anxiety of dealing with the unexplainable and uncontrollable.

founding group coming together to create a new organization need to learn about each other's semantic space (even if they start with a common basic language, such as English), in order to determine what they mean by such abstractions as "a good product," of "high quality," produced at "low cost," to get into the "market" "as rapidly as possible." If several members of a group are using different category systems, they not only cannot agree on what to do but they will not even agree on their definition of what is real, what is a fact, when something is true or false, what is important, what needs attention, and so on. Most communication breakdowns between people result from their lack of awareness that they are making basically different assumptions about meaning categories in the first place.

For example, in my role as a consultant to a small family-owned food company, I asked some managers whether, in their daily work, they experienced any conflicts with subordinates, peers, or superiors. Unless I happened to be talking to a particularly disgruntled person, I usually elicited an immediate and flat denial of any conflict whatsoever. This response puzzled me, since I had been called in to help figure out what to do about "severe conflicts" that members of the organization were perceiving or experiencing. I finally realized that I was making two assumptions not shared by the managers I was questioning: (1) that conflict is a general term referring to any degree of disagreement between two or more people; (2) that conflict is a normal human condition and is always present in some degree. My interviewees, on the other hand, had two quite different assumptions: (1) that the word "conflict" refers to a severe disagreement that is difficult if not impossible to reconcile (a different semantic interpretation of the word itself) and (2) that conflict is bad, in the sense that a person who has conflicts is not managing well. Once I realized that different assumptions were at the root of the communication problem, I could change my question to "Tell me about the things that make it easy or hard for you to get your job done." If any evidence of interpersonal "disagreements" began to surface, I made my own assumption explicit: that such disagreements are, in my view, completely normal in organizations. I then often got incredibly vivid and detailed stories of severe "conflicts" and, in subsequent discussions, found that the word itself could be used without further misunderstanding or defensiveness. In this example my clients and I were building a common language for our own work.

To extend the example to the organization, in group meetings I often noted that the chairman got angry with a member who was not contributing and began to draw conclusions about the competence of that member. The chairman assumed (as I learned later by asking about the situation) that the silence meant ignorance, incompetence, or lack of motivation. The silent member, it turned out, was ready to make a presentation and was very frustrated because he was never called on to give it. He assumed that he was not supposed to volunteer, and he began to believe that his boss did not value him. If their different assumptions were not brought to the surface, the danger was that both would validate their incorrect assumption, thus setting up a classic case of a "self-fulfilling prophecy." In this group the absence of a common consensually validated communication system undermined effective action. A total group culture had not yet formed, though various subgroups may already have been operating on shared assumptions, such as "Our boss does not value our contributions."

If we look at this process in an evolutionary sense, we can see that it is the creators of groups who often build the common category system. For example, the founder of a small high-technology company—whose own sense of his mission was to give the world a cheaper, yet technically better product—had to teach his engineers how to design an "optimal" level of elegance and quality into the product. He had to point out in detail what to look for and pay special attention to in the myriad of details involved in design, how to analyze customer responses, how to think about costs, and how to react to feedback from manufacturing and marketing. One might label such teaching as getting across certain "values," but, in fact, the process went much deeper than that. The values were embedded in the conceptual categories themselves, and what was being taught was really a category system, along with the values embedded in the rules of how to respond.

How powerful such categories can become is illustrated by the previously cited computer company, where the shared assumption developed that the best model of a customer was the design engineer himself, since he was a prototype of the user of the product being designed. If the engineer liked his own product, he assumed that others also would like it; and this concept of how to measure product "goodness" was institutionalized in many parts of the company. The term "marketing" came to be associated with taking these "good" products and ensuring that they would get out to the customers efficiently. It was assumed that customers would automatically appreciate the products, and this assumption was repeatedly confirmed in the marketplace. The idea that "marketing" might involve finding out what potential customers would want in the future, and building such criteria into the initial product designs, did not surface until the technology made it possible to reach a less sophisticated computer user. Real communication problems then developed between those groups who were continuing to build sophisticated products, in accordance with one marketing concept, and other groups who were trying to develop completely different notions of marketing. The important lesson to learn is that the disagreement did not involve business judgment but a lack of common language and categories that would make judgment possible.

The basic language used by a group usually has built into it most of the critical conceptual categories needed. Thus, English speakers learn through English words the major cultural categories of the Anglo-Saxon cultural tradition. For example, the word "management" reflects the proactive, optimistic, pragmatic approach that characterizes the American culture. It is a surprise to many Americans that a comparable word does not exist in other languages, such as German. And, even more important, if the word does not exist, the concept also may not exist in the same sense. For example, in German there are words for leadership, leading, and directing; but managing, as Americans mean it, does not readily transpose either as a word or as a concept.

Because new groups always come out of a host culture, it is often difficult to distinguish what is culturally "new" in the new group. Does the new computer company simply reflect its members' culture of origin? The founders will, of course, bring their own prior cultural assumptions to the new situation; but, as the new group begins to experience its own issues of survival and growth and begins to develop its own history, it will develop, in addition, its own language and conceptual categories.

A common language and common conceptual categories are clearly necessary for any other kind of consensus to be established; and consensus on basic concepts and assumptions is necessary because it is the precondition for any communication. Finally, we might note that groups develop language systems not only to build consensus and survive but also as a way of differentiating themselves and giving themselves a sense of identity through the technical jargon that only insiders can understand (Hughes, 1958; Roy, 1960; Van Maanen and Barley, 1984).

Consensus on Group Boundaries; Criteria for Inclusion. If a group is to function and develop, one of the most important areas for clear consensus is the perception of who is "in" the new group and who is "out" or "not in," and by what criteria those decisions are made. New members cannot really function and concentrate on their primary task if they are insecure about their membership, and the group cannot really maintain a good sense of itself if it does not have a way of defining itself and its boundaries.

Initially, the criteria for inclusion are usually set by the leader, founder, or "convener"; but, as the group members interact, those criteria are tested and a group consensus arises around the criteria that survive the test. In a young company, there is often a heavy debate over who should be an owner or a partner, who should have stock options, who should be hired for key functions or be an officer, and who should be ejected because he or she does not "fit." In this debate real personnel decisions are being made, and at the same time the criteria of inclusion are themselves being forged, tested, and articulated so that they become clear to everyone. Such debate also provides opportunities for testing mission statements, goal clarity, and means clarity, illustrating how several cultural elements are simultaneously being created, tested, articulated, and reinforced. One way of determining a group's core assumptions and values is to ask present members what they really look for in new members and to examine carefully the career histories of present members, to detect what accounts for their inclusion in the group. If there is little consensus on what to seek in new members, one must question whether the group as a whole has a single culture or consists only of assorted subcultures.

The Action Company reveals a crucial element of its culture when one inquires about its hiring process. Every new member of the technical or managerial staff must be interviewed by at least five to ten people, and only if that member is acceptable to the entire set is he offered a job. If one asks what the interviewers look for, one finds that intelligence, self-reliance, the ability to articulate clearly, tolerance for ambiguity, and high motivation are all central criteria used in selection, though most of them operate implicitly. What interviewers tend to say when questioned is more vague: "We want someone who will fit in." Once a person has been hired, he is provisionally accepted as a permanent member. If he fails in an initial job assignment, the assumption is made that he is a competent person but was put in the wrong job. In other words, once one is "in," it is difficult to lose that status, even after a series of job failures. In an economic crisis, the company would slow down its rate of hiring but would be reluctant to lay anybody off.

In the Multi Company, prior education is a key criterion. Most of the young technical and managerial staff come from a scientific background, highlighting the assumption that, if one is to succeed in the company, one must understand the scientific base on which it was built. Having an advanced degree, such as a doctorate, is a distinct advantage even if one is being hired into a marketing or managerial job.

Both Action and Multi have difficulty hiring and absorbing what they call "MBAs," by which they mean the all-purpose generalist who does not have a solid technical or scientific background and who might be more concerned with personal ambition than contributing to the technical work of the organization. Behind these perceptions lies the further assumption that "general" management, though necessary, is not the key to success.

One of the immediate consequences of defining who is in and who is out is that differential treatment rules begin to be applied. Insiders get special benefits, are trusted more, get higher basic rewards, and, most important, get a sense of identity from belonging to a defined organization. Outsiders not only get less of the various benefits and rewards but, more important, lose specific identity. They become part of a mass that is simply labeled "not us" or "outsiders" and are more likely to be stereotyped and treated with indifference or hostility.

As organizations age and become more complex, the problem of defining clear boundaries also becomes more complex. More people come to occupy boundary-spanning roles, such as salesmen, purchasing agents, distributors, franchisees, board members, and consultants. In a complex society, individual employees belong to many organizations, so that their identity is not tied up exclusively with any one organization. Locating a "cultural unit" becomes more difficult, since a given organization may really be a complex set of overlapping subcultures (Louis, 1983). But consensus on criteria for membership is always one means of determining whether a cultural unit exists in any given group.

Stratification: Consensus on Criteria for Differentiation of Influence and Power. A critical issue in any new group is how influence, power, and authority will be allocated. The process of stratification in human systems is typically not as blatant as the dominance-establishing rituals of animal societies, but it is functionally equivalent in that it concerns the evolution of workable rules for managing aggression and mastery needs. Human societies develop pecking orders just as chickens do, but both the process and the outcome are, of course, far more complex.

The easiest way to observe this process is to watch a new group, such as a committee or a training group, in the early hours of its life. Much of the behavior of the new members can be explained only if we assume that they are insecure, unsure of their role or position, and, in effect, "testing the social waters." Everyone comes into the new situation with some needs to have influence, but those needs will vary greatly from person to person. Each person will also come into the situation with very different prior or assumed status, and will have varying degrees of power and authority attributed to him or her. The process of group formation will then involve a complex mutual testing around who will grant how much influence to whom, and who will seek how much influence from whom. The founders of the group will, of course, influence this process by initially applying their own criteria and attempting to grant power to the members of their choice. Some members will be given formal positions that have power or authority associated with them, and some rules about how to make decisions will be specified—for example, do we vote, seek consensus, do what the chairman wants, debate everything out? But the process of group formation always involves a certain amount of testing of what the founder may attempt to impose, so that the norms eventually shared are usually a negotiated outcome, not an initially imposed set of rules or guidelines. And, in fact, every time a new member enters the group, some degree of renegotiation must take place in order to determine where the new member fits into the stratification scheme.

The core issue of power distribution derives from the underlying biological nature of the human organism. Culture eventually covers over with a veneer of "civilization" the underlying biological roots of human behavior. But we cannot ignore the fact that all human beings have to learn to deal with their biologically based aggressive feelings, their needs to dominate, control, and master others and the environment. Only when we recognize that cultural norms regarding the handling of aggression help us deal with feelings that might run out of control, endangering us and others, can we understand why those norms are not easily changed. The very process of change may invite a period of instability, where we may fear loss of control, and that fear may keep us committed to whatever cultural assumptions we have, even if another set of assumptions might be more desirable from an objective point of view.

To give but one example, a recent television newscast reported a strike in a midwestern meat-packing plant. The visual coverage showed a group of adult male strikers heaving baseball-sized rocks with all their might at the windshields of the cars of workers who had decided to cross the picket lines. It was a vivid reminder of how easily our aggressive impulses are tapped and how strong the cultural restraints must therefore be to keep our environment more or less safe for ourselves. At the same time, this incident illustrated how culture channels such aggression. Presumably, the integrity of the union was at stake, and the aggressive behavior toward workers crossing the picket line was a measure of how much this integrity was threatened.

Action and Multi differ dramatically in their methods of allocating power. In Action power is derived from personal success and the building of a network of support. Formal rank, seniority, and job description have relatively less influence than personal characteristics and track record. Personal characteristics such as the ability to negotiate, to convince, and to be proved right by circumstance are emphasized. The formal system of status is deliberately deemphasized in favor of an assumption that everyone has a right to participate, to voice an opinion, and to be heard—since, it is assumed, good ideas can come from anyone. But, as previously mentioned, because no one is smart enough to evaluate the quality of an idea by himself, anyone has a right to challenge and debate and, in fact, is obligated to do so. Aggression is thus channeled into the daily working routines but directed at ideas, not people. A further assumption—that once one is in the organization, one is a member of "the family" and cannot really lose membership—protects people from feeling personally threatened if their ideas are challenged.

Multi, in contrast, has a very formal system of allocating power—a system based on seniority, loyalty, and successful performance of whatever jobs were allocated to the person by higher authority. After a certain number of years, an employee acquires a rank, similar to the kind of rank one acquires with promotion in military service or the civil service, and this rank is independent of particular job assignments. Status and privileges go with the rank and cannot be lost even if the employee is given reduced job responsibilities. The working climate emphasizes politeness, formality, and reason. Displays of aggression are taboo, but behind-the-scenes complaining, badmouthing, and politicking are the inevitable consequence of suppressing overt aggression.

Both organizations could be labeled from some points of view as "paternalistic," in that they generate strong family feelings and a degree of emotional dependence on leaders or formal authorities. However, the drastic difference in how the rules of power allocation actually work in these two organizations serves to remind us how vague and potentially unhelpful broad labels such as "autocratic" or "paternalistic" are in characterizing organizational cultures.

Peer Relationships: Consensus on Criteria for Intimacy, Friendship, and Love. Every new group must decide simultaneously how to deal with authority problems and how to establish workable peer relationships. Whereas authority issues derive ultimately from the necessity to deal with feelings of aggression, peer relationship and intimacy problems derive ultimately from the necessity to deal with feelings of affection, love, and sexuality. Thus, cultures develop clear sex roles, kinship systems, and rules for friendship and sex that serve to stabilize current relationships while ensuring procreation mechanisms and, thereby, the survival of the society.

At the new group or organization level, the deeper issues of sex and procreation are typically irrelevant unless we are talking about a family firm that is specifically concerned with keeping succession in the family. Then who marries whom and which children come into the firm are indeed major problems, and the emerging norms of the organization will reflect the assumptions of the founding family about succession (Beckhard and Dyer, 1983). Indeed, one of the most salient features of family firms is that certain levels of intimacy and trust appear to be reserved for family members, creating a kind of dual intimacy system.

As Freud pointed out long ago, one of the models we bring to any new group situation is our own family model, the group in which we spent most of our early life. Thus, the rules that we learned from our own parents for dealing with them and with our siblings are often the initial model we have for dealing with authority and peer relationships in a new group. Because the different members of a new group are likely to have had widely varying experiences in their families of origin, they may start with very different models of what those relationships should be, leading to potential disagreement and conflict on "the right way" to relate to others in the new organization.

If the group's founder is a very dominant person with a very clear model of how these relationships should function, he or she may, over time, be able to impose that model on the other new members. But, even with a strong founder, the outcome is, in the end, a negotiated one, and the norms that gradually evolve in the group will reflect the initial underlying assumptions of a number of the influential members. The leaders of Action believed strongly that good decisions could be made only if everyone was encouraged to challenge authority and if peers were encouraged to debate every issue. The consequence of this belief was that passive and/or dependent behavior by a subordinate was always severely punished, while insubordination was tolerated, and even encouraged, as long as the subordinate was dealing with a task issue. If two peers were having a debate and one of them backed down under an aggressive onslaught, the boss usually would punish the one who backed down rather than the one who behaved aggressively.

Needless to say, there developed a climate of high conflict, high competition among peers, and relatively low levels of intimacy among those peers. Needs for closeness, affection, and intimacy were met off the job. If close friendships led to less confrontation at work, the norms undermined those friendships. The possibility that peers were colluding or making private deals was extremely threatening, leading to intense challenges and probing to ensure that it was not happening. From the point of view of fulfilling its primary task, this organization operated very effectively, but the culture was not one in which people felt particularly comfortable.

As the organization evolved, it developed other norms that created some security and comfort to compensate for the inherent discomfort in the peer norms, primarily norms around a kind of symbolic family membership. As previously noted, it was acceptable for peers to argue and confront each other because in a sense they were members of the family, which provided some kind of ultimate security. Toward outsiders the group usually presented a solid front, and this togetherness provided the intimacy often lacking in internal relationships.

The complexity of cultural patterns is further revealed here if we remember the founders' assumption that confrontation and debate are necessary in order to discover what is ultimately *true*. Particularly in relation to the marketing of their products and services, the founders believed that they did not have any ultimate insight—and, in fact, no one had; hence, the only sensible way to proceed was to bring in bright people and have everyone worrying about the marketing questions. In other words, their theory of truth—built on their understanding of their own technology, the nature of their business, and the nature of their environment—directly influenced their theory of how authority and peer relationships should be organized and managed.

This pattern of assumptions inhibited certain kinds of change. As a consultant I became involved in trying to build "teamwork" among the project managers of the organization, and found surprisingly little support for or skill in working as a team. Early efforts to develop teamwork were based on arguments by top management that the business now needed it, and I, as the consultant, marshaled arguments for why teamwork was theoretically desirable in the situation. There was ample surface agreement; but, whenever an important issue came up, group members always lapsed into highly individualized debating, withheld emotional support, and showed in their behavior a visible lack of support for the idea that teams could be useful and productive.

No progress was made until we began collectively to decipher the sources of resistance—those unconsciously held assumptions about peer relationships, truth, and conflict. Once the underlying cultural pattern had been identified, we could see why the individuals found it difficult to behave as a team. The group members then entered a difficult period of reexamining their original assumptions and, in this process, discovered that certain members were unwilling to adapt to new norms because the old norms, built on individualistic assumptions, were more congruent with their own personal style. The outcome of the whole team-building program, which lasted over a year, was a very selective and limited attempt to build teamwork only for those projects where external requirements for such teamwork were overwhelmingly clear.

Consensus on Criteria for Allocation of Rewards and Punishments. In order to function, every group must develop a system of sanctions for obeying or disobeying the rules. The specific rewards and punishments, and the manner in which they are administered, constitute one of the most important cultural characteristics of a new organization.

Let us look at some examples. In the market-oriented

food company previously mentioned, the norm developed that
a manager who did his job competently could expect to be
moved to another, generally bigger project within approximate-
ly eighteen months. Managers who did not move every eighteen
months began to feel that they were failing. By way of contrast, in the Action Company the norm developed that the de-
signer of a product saw it through from cradle to grave, so a
reward was defined as being allowed to stay with one's product
through manufacturing and marketing all the way to sales.
Being pulled off a project would have been perceived as a punishment. In Multi the key short-run rewards were the personal
approval of senior management and public recognition in the
company newspaper. Longer-range rewards were promotion to
a higher rank or movement to a clearly more important job
assignment. Length of assignment to a given job could mean
that the person was either dead-ended or doing such a good job
that he or she was not replaceable. Action used bonuses, stock
options, and raises as signals of good performance, whereas
Multi relied much more heavily on symbolic nonmonetary rewards.

The reward system usually reflects other important cultural themes, and rewards acquired can be treated as acquired
social "property." Thus, a bonus or a stock option can be translated into acquired property, whereas approval on the part of
the boss or a formal promotion can be translated into social
property or status. The rules by which status is acquired and
held therefore become very important to understand.

The reward system, viewed as a dynamic process, usually
has both short- and long-range time horizons. Many of the
short-range aspects concern the organization's performance in
its defined external environment—getting a product out, reducing inventory, cutting costs, and so on. Ultimately, such organizational performance has to be translated into the individual
performances of different people in their different roles. A system of short-run incentives and rewards usually develops to
maximize the performance of the actors in those roles. Longer-
range aspects of the reward system have to do with "track records," "potential," and other aspects of contribution that are

assumed to be a cumulation of continued high performance. In most organizations short-run rewards and longer-range rewards are different (for example, a financial bonus versus a promotion).

When studying the culture of an organization, one must investigate the reward system because it reveals fairly quickly some of the important rules and underlying assumptions in that culture. Once one has identified what kinds of behavior are "heroic" and what kinds of behavior are "sinful," one can begin to infer the beliefs and assumptions that lie behind those evaluations. The manner in which heroic and sinful behaviors are rewarded and punished then provides further evidence about those underlying assumptions.

Religion and Ideology: Consensus on How to Manage the Unmanageable and Explain the Unexplainable. Every group inevitably faces some issues not under its control, events that are intrinsically mysterious and unpredictable, and hence frightening. At the physical level, such events as natural disasters and the weather require "explanation." At the biological level, such events as birth, growth, puberty, illness, and death require one to have a theory of what is happening and why. In a culture heavily committed to reason and science, there is a tendency to treat everything as explainable; the mysterious is only as yet unexplained. But until science has demystified an event that we cannot control or understand, we need an alternative basis for putting what has happened into a meaningful context. Religion can provide such a context, and can also offer justification for events that might otherwise seem unfair and meaningless. Religion explains the "unexplainable" and provides guidelines for what to do in ambiguous, uncertain, and threatening situations. Those guidelines usually specify and reinforce what is considered heroic and desirable and what is considered sinful and undesirable, thus creating an "ideology" that ties together into a coherent whole the various assumptions about the nature of human nature, the nature of relationships, and the nature of society itself. Ideology can be seen as a set of overarching values that can serve as a prescription for action vis-à-vis other groups and the broader environment, especially in areas that are difficult to explain and manage. In a society that is dominated by religion, ideology merges with religion. The more the society is based on reason, logic, and science, the more ideology has a secular base and comes to be clearly distinguishable from religion.

The organizational equivalent of this general cultural process tends to occur around critical events in the history of the organization, especially ones that are difficult to explain or justify because they were not under organizational control. Organizations are capable of developing the equivalent of religion and/or ideology based on the manner in which such critical events were managed. Myths and stories develop around the founding of the company, times when the company had a particularly difficult time surviving or an unusual growth spurt, times when a challenge to core assumptions and values brought about a rearticulation of those assumptions and values, and times of transformation and change.

For example, in Action certain individual contributors and managers are associated with getting the company out of trouble whenever a severe crisis occurs. Also, certain processes are viewed almost superstitiously as "the way" to get out of trouble. One such process is to bring together a task force under the leadership of one of these heroic managers and give that task force complete freedom for a period of time to work on the problem. Sometimes consultants are brought in with the same kind of faith that "something constructive" will happen as a result of the presence of the outsider.

In a study of the introduction of computerized tomography into hospital radiology departments, it was observed that if the computer went down at an awkward time, such as when a patient was in the middle of a scan, the technicians tried all kinds of remedial measures, including the proverbial "kicking" of the machine. If the computer resumed operating, the technician carefully documented what he or she had just done and passed on this "knowledge" to colleagues, even though there was no technical or logical basis for it. In a real sense, this was superstitious behavior, even in a realm where explanation was possible (Barley, 1984a).

An organization's "ideology" in this context can be any of several things. Sometimes it is the conscious component of the total set of assumptions that make up the culture. Sometimes it is a set of rationalizations for essentially unexplained or superstitious behavior. Sometimes ideology reflects ideals and future aspirations as well as current realities and, thereby, functions as a guide and incentive system to members. Ideologies often have statements about the core mission, the goals, the preferred means for accomplishing them, and the preferred set of relationships among organizational members.

Ideologies often are partially stated in formal company documents as the key values of the organization. They are likely to be embodied in company charters, annual reports, and orientation and training materials, but in this form they are often merely a list of values and may not even make up a coherent ideology. Only when there are stories supporting the values and when the underlying assumptions behind the values are articulated can one determine what the substance of the ideology really is.

Stories and myths about how the organization dealt with key competitors in the past, how it survived a downturn in the economy, how it developed a new and exciting product, how it dealt with a valued employee, and so on, not only spell out the basic mission and specific goals (and thereby reaffirm them) but also reaffirm the organization's picture of itself, its own theory of how to get things done and how to handle internal relationships (Mitroff and Kilmann, 1975, 1976; Dandridge, Mitroff, and Joyce, 1980; Dyer, 1982; Ouchi, 1981; Pettigrew, 1979; Wilkins, 1983; Martin, 1982; Koprowski, 1983). For example, a story widely circulated in one high-technology company is that during a severe recession no one was laid off because management and hourly people alike were willing to work shorter hours for less pay, thus enabling the company to cut its costs without cutting people. The lesson to be derived is the affirmation of strong values around people (Ouchi, 1981). A similar story is told in Action about the "rehabilitation" of a key engineer who was associated with several important projects, all of which failed. Instead of firing him, the company—reaffirming its core assumption that if someone fails, it is because he is mismatched with his job—found an assignment for him in which he could succeed and once again become a "hero." Buried in this story is also the assumption that it is individuals who count and that any person whom the company has hired is by definition competent.

A story from another high-technology company concerns an engineer who was sent to the West Coast to fix some equipment. He caught the midnight plane but was not able to get together luggage or clothing. The repair took a week, requiring the engineer to buy clothing, which he duly charged to the company. When the accounting department refused to approve the charge, the engineer threatened to quit. The company president heard about it and severely punished the accounting department, thereby reaffirming the company's dedication to technical values and to its highly motivated technical employees.

Through stories, parables, and other forms of oral or written history, an organization can communicate its ideology and basic assumptions—especially to newcomers, who need to know what is important not only in abstract terms but by means of concrete examples that can be emulated.

The Anxiety Reduction Function

So far we have concentrated on the functions of culture that represent positive organizational learning. Groups or organizations have internal and external issues to cope with; they learn how to cope with them; and the perceptual, cognitive, and emotional responses that are learned form the basic culture. But culture does more than solve external and internal problems. It serves the basic function of reducing the anxiety that humans experience when they are faced with cognitive uncertainty or overload. That is, for each of the issues defined above, humans would experience high levels of anxiety if they could not sort out from the mass of stimuli those that are important and those that are not. Once we learn how to think about our primary task; have goals, means, and information systems; and agree on how to communicate, relate to each other, and conduct our daily affairs, we also have a system for sorting out from the mass of input the things that must be attended to, and a set of criteria for reacting to them.

Cultural assumptions can be thought of as a set of filters or lenses that help us to focus on and perceive the relevant portions of our environment. Without such filters and lenses, we would experience overload and uncertainty. Once we have cultural solutions, we can relax to some extent, and one reason why we resist culture change is that it is inherently anxiety producing to give up the assumptions that stabilize our world, even though different assumptions might be more functional. In other words, culture not only solves external survival and internal integration problems but, once acquired, also reduces the anxiety inherent in any new or unstable situation.

Conclusion

Ultimately, what makes it possible for people to function comfortably with each other and to concentrate on their primary task is a high degree of consensus on the management of the issues discussed in this chapter. If internal issues are not settled, if people are preoccupied with their position and identity, if they are insecure, if they do not know the rules of the game and therefore cannot predict or understand what is going on, they cannot concentrate on the important survival issues that may face the organization.

The core problem for any organization is how to work simultaneously on its primary task and on its problems of internal integration. The internal integration and external adaptation issues are intertwined and interdependent. The environment sets limits on what the organization can do, but within those limits not all solutions will work equally well. What solutions are feasible is also limited by the characteristics of the members of the group.

The culture that eventually evolves in a particular organization is thus a complex outcome of external pressures, internal potentials, responses to critical events, and, probably, to some unknown degree, chance factors that could not be predicted from a knowledge of either the environment or the members. What I have tried to do in this chapter is to identify the common issues faced by every new group, recognizing that the manner in which those issues are dealt with will result in a unique outcome.

4

Content and Levels of Culture

Assumptions arise in many areas, some of them more superficial and peripheral than others. Thus, my assumptions about the right way to do things are more superficial than my assumptions about ultimate goals, the right things to do. My assumptions about the right way to treat authority figures are more superficial than my assumptions about human nature. The deeper levels of assumptions are the more general ones, dealing with more ultimate issues, from which the more superficial ones can be deduced. But this is not to say that superficial assumptions are unimportant. The right way to do things and the right way to treat authority figures are extremely important issues in day-to-day affairs, but the culture cannot be really understood if we lack insight into the deeper levels.

If one is to diagnose these deeper levels, one needs typologies or dimensions for analysis. The categories discussed in this chapter and the dimensions used to analyze them are arbitrarily chosen from various typological studies of cultures. I have also added some dimensions that I have found particularly necessary for the understanding of companies with which I work. The major source is Kluckhohn and Strodtbeck's (1961) massive comparative study of a number of cultures in the United States Southwest. But the dimensions I will discuss only partially reflect the dimensions used in that study, since my own experience and observation have led to new dimensions and alternative ways of conceptualizing the dimensions discussed by Kluckhohn and Strodtbeck. The dimensions I will review are shown in Table 3.

Table 3. Basic Underlying Assumptions Around Which
Cultural Paradigms Form.

---

1. *Humanity's Relationship to Nature.* At the organizational level, do the key members view the relationship of the organization to its environment as one of dominance, submission, harmonizing, finding an appropriate niche, or what?
2. *The Nature of Reality and Truth.* The linguistic and behavioral rules that define what is real and what is not, what is a "fact," how truth is ultimately to be determined, and whether truth is "revealed" or "discovered"; basic concepts of time and space.
3. *The Nature of Human Nature.* What does it mean to be "human" and what attributes are considered intrinsic or ultimate? Is human nature good, evil, or neutral? Are human beings perfectible or not?
4. *The Nature of Human Activity.* What is the "right" thing for human beings to do, on the basis of the above assumptions about reality, the environment, and human nature: to be active, passive, self-developmental, fatalistic, or what? What is work and what is play?
5. *The Nature of Human Relationships.* What is considered to be the "right" way for people to relate to each other, to distribute power and love? Is life cooperative or competitive; individualistic, group collaborative, or communal; based on traditional lineal authority, law, charisma, or what?

Humanity's Relationship to Nature

In every group there will evolve a deeply held view of whether nature, the perceived total environment, can be subjugated and controlled (the Western tradition), whether nature must be harmonized with (the assumption of many Oriental religions and societies), or whether one must subjugate oneself to nature (the assumption of some Southeast Asian religions and societies). The organizational counterpart of this core assumption is the group's view of its relationship to its defined and perceived environment within the larger host culture. Does the group view itself as capable of dominating and changing its environment; does it assume that it must coexist in and harmonize with its environment by developing its proper niche; or does it assume that it must subjugate itself to its environment and accept whatever niche is possible (Thompson and McEwen, 1958; Thompson, 1967; Duncan, 1972)? In a sense this is the organizational counterpart of what has been described for the individual by the concept of "locus of control" (Rotter, 1966; Brislin, 1983). Just as individuals vary in the degree to which they feel they have control over their own fate, so do organizations vary in this regard.

Which assumption an organization makes is obviously one of the deepest levels of its strategic orientation. At this level we are talking about the assumptions underlying an organization's "primary task," "core mission," or "basic functions," whether manifest or latent. If the organization's assumption about itself at this level is out of line with environmental realities, it may sooner or later face a survival problem. Therefore, when organizations examine their strategy, they focus heavily on initial assumptions about the environment and attempt, as much as possible, to validate those assumptions before deciding on goals and means.

The basic issue is how correct the assumptions are, not how grandiose they are. If a very large corporation or government decides that it is the major factor in the environment and can, in effect, create and control its own environment, it can validly develop a monopolistic strategy, while another company in that same arena may decide that its only option is to work in those areas that are left over by becoming highly adaptive and responsive. Either assumption can lead to adequate survival and growth, but either one can also lead to difficulties if it turns out to be wrong.

Organizational health, then, can be thought of as the organization's ability to assess accurately whether its initial assumptions about its relationship to the environment are continuing to be accurate as it and the environment evolve. The organization's "adaptive coping cycle" then becomes crucial in maintaining "health" (Schein, 1965, 1980). It must develop the ability to (1) obtain valid information, (2) import it to the right places in the organization, (3) make the necessary transformations in strategy, goals, and means, and (4) measure outcomes.

Assumptions about the relationship between the organization and its environment not only deal with basic dominance/submission issues but also with areas of focus. That is, the organization may make assumptions about whether the most relevant dimensions of the environment to be taken into account are technological, political, economic, or sociocultural. Not every aspect of the environment will be given equal attention by a given organization. Those aspects that are attended to and around which assumptions form will crucially shape the organization's world view and thus become a core element of its culture.

For example, both Action and Multi view themselves as *technologically* dominant, in the sense that they hold deep assumptions about the technological superiority of their products. One of the resulting problems in both organizations is that they have a relative inability to assess clearly their position in the marketing environment. To become more market oriented is, for both of these organizations, essentially a cultural shift that is not easily made because it may mean the abandonment of a core assumption around technological superiority or the recognition that this element of the environment is no longer the most relevant for ultimate survival.

The Nature of Reality and Truth

A key part of every culture is a set of assumptions about what is "real" and how one determines or discovers what is real. These assumptions will, of course, relate to the above assumptions about humanity's relationship to nature, but the focus now is on how members of a group take an action, how they determine what is relevant information, and when they have enough of it to determine whether to act and what to do.

For example, as I have already pointed out several times, in Action reality is defined by pragmatic criteria of whether things work. If an objective test is impossible or too difficult to construct, the idea is debated to see whether it stands the test of being subjected to severe critical analysis. In Multi much more emphasis is given to research results from the laboratory and to the opinions of those considered wise and experienced. But the ultimate criteria used depend on the type of information needed or the type of decision being made.

Levels of Reality. All groups differentiate in some way the following areas:

1. *External Physical Reality*—those things regarded as empirically determinable by objective or, in our Western tradition, "scientific" tests. For example, if two people are arguing about whether or not a piece of glass will break, they can hit it with a hammer and find out (Festinger, 1957). If two managers are arguing over which product to introduce, they can agree to define a test market and establish criteria by which to resolve the issue. On the other hand, if two managers are arguing over whether or not to give corporate funds to a political campaign, both would have to agree that the conflict is not resolvable at the external physical level of reality. Different cultures have different notions of what constitutes "external physical reality." In many cultures what we would regard as the "spirit world," which is not real to us, would be regarded as externally real. Vivid examples of how ambiguous the borderline can be are provided in Castaneda's (1968, 1972) descriptions of his experiences with the Indian shaman Don Juan and in the controversies that surround research on extrasensory perception.

2. *Social Reality*—those things that members of a group agree on as being matters of consensus, not externally testable. Many political opinions, as well as assumptions about the nature of people, life, and the afterlife, fall into this category. Probably the most important set of such beliefs has to do with group boundaries and assumptions about "us" and "them." As one can see in international conflicts, there

is no way to test who is right about a given political conflict; hence, negotiation becomes very difficult. The bad
joke about the naive diplomat who tells the Arabs and the
Israelis to settle their differences in a good Christian manner makes the point well. One of the reasons why business
decisions are often difficult to make and why management
is a complex activity is the lack of consensus on whether a
given decision area belongs in the realm of physical or social reality. If an organization is to have coherent action,
there must be shared assumptions about which decisions
are scientifically resolvable and which ones are based on
consensual criteria—such as "Let the most experienced person decide" or "Let's decide by majority vote." Notice that
the consensus must be on the criteria, not necessarily on
the ultimate substance of the decision.

3. *Individual Reality*—the things that a given person has learned
from experience and that, therefore, have a quality of absolute truth to that person. But that truth may not be shared
with anyone else. When we disagree at this level, it becomes
very hard to move forward until we can articulate clearly
what our actual experience base is. We must also have some
kind of consensus on whose experience we are willing to
trust. In a traditional, "lineal" society, based on hierarchical
authority, if the "elder statesman" speaks, we take his experience as valid and act as if what he says is objectively
true. In a pragmatic, individualistic society, the attitude
might well be "Prove it to me."

What is defined as physical, social, and individual reality
is itself the product of social learning and hence, by definition,
a part of a given culture (Van Maanen, 1979b). But cultural
norms have less importance in the area of physical reality,
which operates by natural laws as discovered by the scientific
method. Where cultural assumptions become crucial is in the
area of social reality, or what Louis (1981) calls "intersubjec-
tive" reality, as distinct from universal objective reality or individual subjective reality. In fact, the bulk of the content of a
given culture will concern itself primarily with those areas of
life where objective verification is not possible and where, there-

fore, a social definition becomes the only sound basis for judgment. It is in this area that we are most susceptible to discomfort and anxiety if we do not have a common way of deciphering what is happening and how to feel about it.

Every group must develop some consensus on how to reach truth, depending on its basic concept of what truth is. In a scientifically based pragmatic society, we tend to seek an open marketplace of ideas and look for objective criteria. If those are not available, the group may legitimize open argument and debate as a way of resolving differences. Only those ideas or "facts" that survive debate are treated as "true" or worthy of acting on. In a more collectivist group-oriented society, the process of arriving at truth is very different. In Japan, for instance, something is regarded as "true" or "valid" only if it survives a consensus process that provides an opportunity for everyone to examine its implications for the group as a whole, to ensure that the implied action will not be harmful to the group.

In a similar vein, Hall (1977) distinguishes between "high-context" and "low-context" cultures. This distinction closely parallels Maruyama's (1974) contrast between "unidirectional" and "mutual causal" paradigms. In the low-context, unidirectional culture, events have clear universal meanings; in the high-context, mutual causality culture, events can be understood only "in context," meanings can vary, categories can change, and causality cannot be unambiguously established. Though this distinction has more meaning when one compares civilizations or large ethnic units, it has utility for groups as well. For example, Action is a high-context culture, in which the meaning of words and actions depends on who is speaking and under what conditions. Managers know each other well and always take into account who the actors are. When a senior manager is observed publicly punishing a subordinate for something "dumb" that he did, this may mean simply that the subordinate should have consulted a few more people before going off on his own. If the manager doing the punishing is a newcomer to the company, the observers may judge that the subordinate is in deep trouble. In Multi, by contrast, messages tend to have the same meaning no matter whom they are coming from.

Moralism-Pragmatism. The dimension I have found most

useful for comparing business organizations is an adaptation of England's (1975) moralism-pragmatism scale. In his study of managerial values, England finds that managers in different countries tend to be either pragmatic, seeking validation in their own experience, or moralistic, seeking validation in a general philosophy, moral system, or tradition. For example, Europeans tend to be more moralistic while Americans tend to be more pragmatic. If we apply this dimension to the basic underlying assumptions that a group makes, we can specify different bases for defining what is "true." We then come up with a dimension closely resembling the typology of authority first spelled out by Weber (1947; see also Schein, 1980):

1. Pure dogma, based on tradition and/or religion.
2. Revealed dogma—that is, wisdom based on trust in the authority of wise men, formal leaders, prophets, or kings.
3. Truth derived by a "rational-legal" process, as when we establish the guilt or innocence of an individual by means of a legal process that acknowledges from the outset that there is no absolute truth, only socially determined truth.
4. Truth as that which survives conflict and debate.
5. Truth as that which works, the purely pragmatic criterion.
6. Truth as established by the scientific method, which becomes, once again, a kind of dogma.

This dimension not only highlights the basis on which truth is determined but also can be related to "uncertainty avoidance" (Hofstede, 1980) or "tolerance for ambiguity" (Adorno and others, 1950). Managers and employees in different countries and different companies vary in the degree to which they are comfortable with and can tolerate uncertainty and ambiguity. Some researchers (Pascale and Athos, 1981) argue that higher tolerance levels in certain managerial areas are associated with more effectiveness.

From the point of view of this analysis, one needs to determine not which position along any of these dimensions is the correct one but what underlying assumptions are held by members of a group and whether there is consensus on those assumptions. If such consensus does not exist, it is questionable whether the group has any culture at all, inasmuch as this dimension underlies communication and consensus on all the other issues described.

Action has high consensus that reality is defined by pragmatic criteria and debate. In my consultation work with Action, for instance, I was never asked for a recommendation; if I gave one, it was usually overridden immediately by various ideas from the client, which were then debated among the members. The company is comfortable with ambiguity and has its own system of pragmatically moving toward action alternatives. In Multi I was always asked what I *knew* from my other consulting experience and what I would recommend. I was treated as a scientist who was bringing some knowledge to the organization, and I often found that my recommendations were implemented exactly. On the other hand, if what I recommended conflicted with another cultural element, as when I suggested more lateral communication, the recommendation was dismissed outright. Multi does not tolerate ambiguity well and operates much closer to the moralistic end of the dimension.

Assumptions About Time. Every culture makes assumptions about the nature of time and has a basic orientation toward the past, present, or future (Redding and Martyn-Johns, 1979). For example, Hall (1959, 1966, 1977) points out that in the United States most managers view time as "monochronic," an infinitely divisible linear ribbon that can be divided into appointments and other compartments, but within which only one thing can be done at a time. If more than one thing must be done within, say, an hour, we divide the hour into as many units as we need and then do one thing at a time. Time is a valuable commodity that can be spent, wasted, or made good use of; but once a unit of time is over, it is gone forever. In contrast, some cultures in southern Europe and the Middle East regard time as "polychronic," a kind of space defined more by what is accomplished than by a clock, and within which several things can be done simultaneously. Even more extreme is the Asian concept of time "as phases, rather circular in form. . . . One season follows the next, one life leads into another" (Sithi-Amnuai,

1968, p. 82; quoted in Redding and Martyn-Johns, 1979). The manager operating by this kind of time "holds court" in the sense that he deals simultaneously with a number of subordinates, colleagues, and even bosses, keeping each matter in suspension until it is finished. Relationships may be more important than efficiency; therefore, rapid completion of a task or punctuality may not be valued as highly as they are in the United States (and a United States manager can become impatient and frustrated when, for no discernible reason, he must wait outside someone's office for an unknown length of time). Yet polychronic time concepts do exist in United States organizations. A doctor, for example, may simultaneously see several patients in adjacent offices, and a foreman usually is totally available at all times to all his machine operators. Again, what is crucial here is not which concept of time we use but the degree of consensus among group members on which concept is appropriate to use at a given time.

Monochronic time assumptions have implications for how space is organized. If one has to have appointments, one requires areas in which they can be held, thus requiring desks or offices and the opportunity for privacy. Since monochronic time is linked with efficiency, one is concerned with using it effectively; time can be wasted, saved, or well used; and its efficient use requires a space layout that allows a minimum of wasted time. Monochronic time controls human behavior and is, therefore, well suited to situations that require highly coordinated actions ("Synchronize your watches!"). Monochronic time, because it facilitates coordination, is well suited to the management of large systems. Polychronic time assumptions require open areas, easy access, and comfort, to permit longer periods of contact. "Holding court" is effective for building relationships and for solving complex problems where information is widely scattered and highly interactive, so that all channels must be kept open at all times. Polychronic time is therefore more suitable for the early stages of an organization and for smaller systems. Privacy in this situation is handled by proximity and softness of voice, not by retiring to closed areas.

Another dimension of time on which group members need consensus has to do with the size of relevant units in relation to given tasks (Jaques, 1982). Do we measure and plan for things annually, quarterly, monthly, daily, hourly, or by the minute or the second? What is considered accurate in the realm of time? How many minutes after an appointed time can one show up and still be considered "on time"? What are the time-tables for certain events, such as promotions? How much time should be spent on a given task, and what is the length of a feedback loop? What is our planning horizon, what Jaques calls the axis of intention, in days, months, years?

As Lawrence and Lorsch (1967) noted years ago, one of the reasons sales and R & D people have trouble communicating is that they work in totally different time cycles. In their comparative study of several types of organizations, Lawrence and Lorsch observed that the length of the time horizon depended on the kind of work one was doing. For salesmen the time horizon involved the completion of a sale, which could take minutes, hours, days, or weeks. But, in general, even their longer time horizons were much shorter than those of the research people, for whom a one- or two-year horizon was normal. In other words, research people would not get closure, in the sense of knowing that they had a good product, until a much longer period of time had gone by. The implication for communication was clear: When the salesman said that he wanted a product "soon" and the research man promised the product "soon," they might be talking about completely different things and not realize it.

In Action one constantly hears complaints from the sales department that engineering is not getting the products out "on time." If one talks to engineering, one is told that the product is on schedule and doing just fine. Each function gets angry at the other. Neither recognizes that the judgment being made of what is "on time" differs because different frames of reference are being used. Action and Multi differ in their overall time horizons, probably because of the underlying technologies and markets they are in. In Multi the slow deliberateness of the research process seems to have spilled over into the management process. Things are done slowly, deliberately, and thoroughly. If a project is going to take several years, so be it.

Time horizons differ not only by function and occupa-

tion but by rank. The higher the rank, the longer the time horizon over which a manager has discretion (Jaques, 1982). Different norms about time arise, therefore, at different rank levels.
Senior managers assume that one must plan in cycles of several
years, whereas such an assumption may not make sense to the
middle manager or the worker, whose time cycles are daily,
weekly, or monthly.

Another important dimension is the time orientation of
different groups. Kluckhohn and Strodtbeck (1961), in their
comparative study of several cultures, found that some were
predominantly oriented toward the past (traditional China),
some toward the present (Spanish Americans in the United
States Southwest), and some toward the near-term future (contemporary United States). The implications for communication
are clear. A manager who is oriented to the future may propose
a *new* way of doing things to a subordinate who is oriented to
the past. They will obviously have difficulty agreeing on a
course of action. Unless they understand each other's assumptions, they will not know why they are having difficulty, and
each may view the other as "unreasonable."

Assumptions About Space. Space has both a physical and
a social meaning (Van Maanen, 1977). That is, for coordinated
social action to occur, one must share assumptions about the
meaning of the placement of physical objects in an environment, and one must also know how to orient oneself spatially
in relation to other members of one's group. Placement of oneself in relation to others symbolizes social distance and membership. For example, Hall (1966) points out that in United
States culture there is high consensus on four kinds of "normal
distance," and within each of these there is consensus on what
it means to be "very near" or "very far":

1. *Intimacy Distance.* Contact and touching are being "very
   near"; six to eighteen inches is the range for being "far."
2. *Personal Distance.* Eighteen to thirty inches is being near;
   two to four feet is being far. This is the range within which
   we have personal conversations with another individual
   even if we are in a crowd or at a party. This distance permits normal or soft tone of voice to be used.

3. *Social Distance.* Four to seven feet is near; seven to twelve feet is far. Social distance defines talking to several people at once, as at a dinner party or a seminar; it usually involves some raising of the voice, less personal focus on an individual.

4. *Public Distance.* Twelve to twenty-five feet is near; over twenty-five feet is far. At this distance the audience is defined as undifferentiated; we raise our voice even more or use a microphone.

Feelings about distance have biological roots. Animals have clearly defined "flight distance" (the distance that will elicit fleeing if the animal is intruded upon) and "critical distance" (the distance that will elicit attacking behavior if the animal is intruded upon). Conditions of crowding not only elicit pathological behavior in subhuman species but are one of the most reliable ways of eliciting aggression in humans. Hence, most cultures have carefully defined rules about how to define personal and intimate space through the use of a variety of cues to permit what Hall calls "sensory screening." We use partitions, walls, sound barriers, and other physical devices, and we use eye contact, body position, and other personal devices to signal respect for the privacy of others (Goffman, 1959; Steele, 1973, 1981).

We also learn how to manage what Hall calls "intrusion distance"; that is, how far away to remain from others who are in personal conversation without interrupting the conversation, yet making it known that one wants attention when appropriate. In some cultures, such as ours, intrusion occurs only when one interrupts with speech (one can stand close by without "interrupting"), whereas in other cultures even entering the visual field of another constitutes a bid for attention and hence is seen as an interruption. In these cultural settings, the use of physical barriers such as closed offices has an important symbolic meaning—it is the *only* way to get a feeling of privacy (Hall, 1966).

At the organizational level, one can clearly see that Action and Multi have contrasting assumptions about space. Action has opted for completely open office landscaping, with partitions low enough to permit everyone to see over the tops; in

Multi the offices are arranged along corridors and have heavy doors that are kept shut. As one walks around Multi, one rarely sees anyone. In one European company that has an office lay-out similar to Multi's, lights installed on the outside of offices signal to potential visitors whether the person inside is willing to be interrupted. It would be inconceivable in that organization to keep one's door open.

Organizations develop different norms of who should have how much and what kind of space. In most organizations the best views and locations are reserved for the highest-status people. Some organizations use space allocation as a direct sta-tus symbol; size of office, quality of furniture in the office, and even the quality of the wall decoration are determined on the basis of rank. In contrast, Action, which aggressively tries to re-duce status and privileges, reserves the good locations, such as corners, for conference rooms; and high-status people are ex-pected to take inside offices, so that clerical and secretarial peo-ple can work on the outside, next to windows.

Where things are located, how they are built, the kind of architecture involved, the decorations encouraged or allowed, the furnishings—all the things that provide the visual environ-ment—will vary from one organization to the next and may well reflect deeper values and assumptions held in the larger culture and by the key leaders. The positional and distance cues used by members to define situations and relationships similarly reflect deeper assumptions. Unless there is consensus on such assump-tions, group members will not know how to orient themselves and define their relationships to each other, thus undermining communication and any kind of concerted group action.

The Nature of Human Nature

In every culture there are core assumptions about what it means to be "human," what our basic instincts are, and what kinds of behavior are considered "inhuman" and, therefore, grounds for ejection from the group. Kluckhohn and Strodt-beck (1961) note that in some societies humans are seen as basi-cally evil, in others as basically good, and in still others as mixed or neutral, capable of being either good or bad. Closely related are assumptions about how perfectible human nature is: Is our goodness or badness intrinsic and do we simply accept what we are, or can we through hard work or faith overcome our badness and earn our salvation?

In every culture there are also core assumptions about the relationship of the individual to the group; these assumptions reflect ultimately the concept of "self." Redding and Martyn-Johns (1979) point out that Western and Asian societies have strikingly different core concepts of the "self"; most notably, Asians are less focused on differentiating the individual from the group and, therefore, put less emphasis on self-actualization as a core personality process. In some cultures the self is compartmentalized, so that work, family, and leisure involve different aspects of the self; in other cultures the self is more of a whole, and even the idea of separating work from family does not make any sense. Hofstede's (1980) comparative study reinforces this point in identifying "individualism" as one of the core dimensions along which countries differ. For example, countries such as the United States, Australia, and the United Kingdom come out highest on this dimension, while Pakistan, Colombia, and Venezuela come out lowest.

At the organizational level, the core assumptions about the nature of human nature—that is, how workers and managers are viewed—will, no doubt, reflect the more basic assumptions of the host culture, but each organization will also build up its own elaborations of such assumptions. And the broader cultural assumptions may leave a great deal of latitude in that human nature may be considered highly variable.

In our Western tradition, human nature is generally regarded as proactive; humans are seen (except by some religious groups) as intrinsically neither good nor bad; and, more important, humans are assumed to be perfectible if they do the right things (such as "work hard"). In any case, the individual is ultimately responsible and is the basic unit of society. As McGregor (1960) has noted, within this broad framework an important second layer of assumptions distinguishes how the individual regards other individuals. The Theory X person assumes that

people are lazy and must, therefore, be motivated and controlled; the Theory Y person assumes that people are basically
self-motivated and therefore need to be challenged and channeled, not controlled.

If we take McGregor's typology as a broad one, defining
the extremes of idealism and cynicism about employee motivation, we can see a further layer of assumptions about such motivation in the historical development from "rational-economic"
assumptions to "complex" assumptions (Schein, 1965, 1980).
Early theories of employee motivation were almost completely
dominated by the assumption that the only incentives available
to managers are monetary ones, because the only essential motivation of employees is economic self-interest. The Hawthorne
studies (Roethlisberger and Dickson, 1939) launched a new
series of assumptions, what I have called "social" assumptions:
that employees are motivated by the need to relate well to their
peer and membership groups and that such motivation often
overrides economic self-interest, as illustrated in restriction of
output, which clearly reduces take-home pay (Whyte, 1955).
Subsequent studies of work and the effects of the assembly line
introduced another set of assumptions: that employees are self-
actualizers who need challenge and interesting work to provide
self-confirmation and valid outlets for the full use of their talents (Argyris, 1964). Motivation theorists, such as Maslow
(1954), organized these varying assumptions into a hierarchy: if
the individual is in a survival mode, economic motives will
dominate; if survival needs are met, social needs come to the
fore; if social needs are met, self-actualization needs are released.

Most current theories are built on still another set of assumptions—namely, that human nature is complex and malle-
able and that one cannot make a universal statement about human
nature; instead, one must be prepared for human variability.
But this variability makes it essential for organizations to develop some consensus on what their assumptions are, because
management strategies reflect those assumptions. Both the incentive and the control systems in most organizations are built
on assumptions about human nature, and if those assumptions

are not shared by members of the organization, it becomes difficult to plan any coherent systems.

The initial assumptions adopted by members may well reflect the personal biases of the founders/owners of an organization, since they will tend to select associates who share assumptions similar to their own. These assumptions then become embedded in the incentive, reward, and control systems of the organization, so that new members of the organization are motivated to share those assumptions or, if they cannot share them, to leave the organization.

In Action, as noted previously, the core assumption about human nature is that individuals are self-motivated and capable of responsible and creative decision making. The core assumption in Multi is more difficult to decipher, but there are strong indications that individuals are viewed ultimately as "good soldiers," who will perform responsibly and loyally and whose loyalty will be rewarded by the organization. It is expected that individuals will do their best in whatever is asked of them, but loyalty is ultimately assumed to be more important than individual creativity. One gets the sense that in Action the individual is ultimately more important than the organization and that in Multi the organization is ultimately more important than the individual. In each case it is assumed that the members of the organization are motivated accordingly.

The Nature of Human Activity

Kluckhohn and Strodtbeck (1961) note that cultures make different assumptions about how to act, and these assumptions reflect their assumptions about human nature and about the fundamental relationship of the group to the environment. At one extreme is a "doing orientation," which correlates closely with (1) the assumption that nature can be controlled and manipulated, (2) a pragmatic orientation toward the nature of reality, and (3) a belief in human perfectibility. This is the predominant orientation of the United States and is certainly a key assumption of managers in the United States, reflected in the World War II phrase "CAN DO" and in the stock American phrases "getting things DONE" and "let's DO something about it." The notion that "the impossible just takes a little longer" is central to United States business ideology. I chose the pseudonym Action for the organization I have repeatedly referred to because this assumption is one of the most deeply held in that organization. When there is a difficulty, do something about it, solve the problem, involve other people, get help, but do something, don't let it fester.

The doing orientation focuses on the task, on efficiency, and on discovery, what some authors have identified with the Greek god Prometheus (Morris, 1956). Handy (1978) describes two types of organizations that assume a basic activity orientation. The first type is linked to Athena and focuses on the *task* activity; the other is linked to Zeus and focuses on the building of useful *relationships*—on enhancing one's position of influence through actively building political alliances and developing personal charisma.

At the other extreme is a "being orientation," which correlates closely with the assumption that nature is powerful and humanity is subservient to it. This orientation implies a kind of fatalism: since one cannot influence nature anyway, one must become accepting and enjoy what one has. Handy (1978) describes this kind of organization as Dyonisian. It has an existential orientation that focuses more on the here and now, on individual enjoyment, and on acceptance of whatever comes.

A third orientation, which lies between the two extremes, is "being-in-becoming," referring to the idea that the individual—through detachment, meditation, and control of those things (for instance, feelings and bodily functions) that can be controlled—must achieve harmony with nature. This orientation emphasizes self-development, self-actualization, fulfilling one's potential. The focus is on what the person *is* rather than what the person can *accomplish.* In short, "the being-in-becoming orientation emphasizes that kind of activity which has as its goal the development of all aspects of the self as an integrated whole" (Kluckhohn and Strodtbeck, 1961, p. 17). Handy has identified this orientation with Apollo and speaks of an Apollonian organization as one that emphasizes hierarchy, rules, clearly defined roles, and other means to help people curb and control their "natural" impulses and desires and, thereby, reach a state of perfection. Implicit in this view is a theory of human nature as well: that basic impulses are dangerous and must be controlled.

One element of activity orientation that is not dealt with explicitly in the Kluckhohn typology but is increasingly important today has to do with underlying assumptions about the nature of work and the relationships between work, family, and personal concerns (Schein, 1978). One assumption would be that work is primary; another, that the family is primary; another, that self-interest is primary; and another, that some form of integrated lifestyle is possible and desirable both for men and for women (Schein, 1978; Bailyn, 1978, 1982). If members of a given organization have different assumptions about the nature of work activity and its relative importance to other activities, those differences will manifest themselves in frustration and communication breakdowns.

How activity orientation is linked to sex roles also must be examined. Hofstede (1980) found in his survey a basic dimension labeled "masculinity"; this dimension reflects the degree to which, in a given country, male and female roles are clearly distinguished. Countries that come out highest on his combined index are Japan, Austria, and Venezuela; countries at the lowest end are Denmark, the Netherlands, Norway, and Sweden. The United States is near the middle of the distribution on this measure.

Activity orientation assumptions underlie managerial styles of decision making. A high degree of consensus among managers about the "correct" way to think about problems and to act on them can then become a deeply embedded cultural assumption, reflecting the assumptions of leaders and the actual experience of managers. Some theorists are using Jungian theory to develop typologies of managerial archetypes, which can then be used to classify various organizational assumptions (Mitroff, 1983).

The Nature of Human Relationships

At the core of every culture will be assumptions about the proper way for individuals to relate to each other in order to make the group safe and comfortable. When such assumptions are not widely shared, we speak of "anarchy" and "anomie" and think of novels such as Golding's (1958) *Lord of the Flies,* which dramatizes what happens to human beings who do not have a clear consensus on how to relate to each other.

Whereas the previous assumption areas dealt with the group's relationship to the external environment, this set of assumptions deals more with the nature of the group itself and the kind of internal environment it creates for itself. This area has received the most attention from organization theorists and has spawned the most varied typologies of organizational phenomena. However, assumptions about relationships, while crucial, are not the only important assumptions that underlie a group's ability to function. Each of the areas reviewed previously is equally important; and as I have pointed out, sets of assumptions are interrelated.

Assumptions about relationships must solve the problems of (1) power, influence, and hierarchy and (2) intimacy, love, and peer relationships. Such assumptions will, of course, reflect the even more basic assumptions about the nature of human nature. For example, if we assume that humans are inherently aggressive, we will develop a society built around controls of such aggression and relationship assumptions such as "One must take care of oneself" or "One must compete, but compete fairly." If we assume that humans are inherently cooperative, the assumptions about relationships might well emphasize how to cooperate to accomplish external goals. Assumptions about relationships, therefore, will directly reflect or be coordinate with assumptions about human nature, the nature of the external environment, and the nature of truth and reality.

If one looks at cultures around the world, obvious differences appear in assumptions about how people relate to each other and what the basic relational units are. Some cultures are what Kluckhohn and Strodtbeck call "individualistic" and

Havrylyshyn (1980) calls "individual-competitive" (the United States, for example); other cultures are "collateral" or "group cooperative" in emphasizing that the group is more important than the individual (Japan, for example); still other cultures are "lineal" in that they emphasize hierarchy and tradition as bases of authority (some Latin countries, for example).

Hofstede's (1980) dimension of "power distance" identifies a related variable. He notes that countries vary in the degree to which people in a hierarchical situation perceive greater or lesser ability to control each other's behavior. People in high power-distance countries, such as the Philippines, Mexico, and Venezuela, perceive more inequality between superiors and subordinates than people in low power-distance countries, such as Denmark, Israel, and Austria. If one looks at the same index by occupation, one finds higher power distance among unskilled and semiskilled workers than among professional and managerial workers, as would be expected.

At the organizational level, assumptions about relationships will, of course, reflect the assumptions of the wider culture, but they become elaborated and differentiated. The founder/leader may believe that the only way to run an organization is to give individual tasks, hold individuals accountable for performance, and minimize group/cooperative work because that would only lead to "lowest common denominator" group solutions. Another leader might emphasize cooperation and communication among subordinates as the best means of solving problems and implementing solutions. These two leaders would develop quite different working styles, which would be reflected ultimately in the organization's processes, reward systems, and control systems.

Action and Multi differ dramatically in this regard. Action reduces power distance between superiors and subordinates as much as possible, building on the assumption that good ideas can come from anyone at any time. Senior managers are always available and willing to talk to anyone about any issue, constrained only by the practicalities of time. A senior manager in R & D recently left the organization for a bigger and better job, only to return three months later with the comment "In the

new company, I had an idea for a new product and was told
that I would have to talk first to my boss, then to the director
of R & D, and then to the senior vice-president. In Action if I
have an idea, I go straight to the president and we kick it
around. This is the kind of place in which I want to work." In
contrast, Multi values hierarchy, formality, and protocol. One
does not approach people informally. Meetings and conferences
have to be well defined, have a clear purpose accepted by all,
and be planned with rank and appropriate deference in mind.
During my consulting visits, I saw only people who had specifically requested some time around some agenda that they were
concerned about. It would not have been appropriate for me
to drop in on people or to strike up conversations in the executive dining room beyond the minimal cordialities.

Most of the typologies proposed in this area focus on the
degree of "participation" considered appropriate in the basically
hierarchical system of organizations. Perhaps the most general
theory here is Etzioni's (1975), which distinguishes between (1)
coercive systems, (2) utilitarian systems, and (3) systems based
on goal consensus between leaders and followers. In the coercive system, members are alienated and will exit if possible; in
the utilitarian system, they will participate according to norms
of "a fair day's work for a fair day's pay"; and in the normative
consensus system, they will be morally involved and identify
with the organization. Assumptions about peer relationships can
be derived from these systems. In the coercive system, peer relationships develop as a defense against authority; in the utilitarian system, they evolve around the work group and typically
reflect the kind of incentive system that management uses; and
in the normative system, they evolve naturally around tasks and
in support of the organization.

At a more specific level, the typologies developed emphasize the degree of absolutism of authority: (1) autocratic, (2)
paternalistic, (3) consultative or democratic, (4) participative
and power sharing, (5) delegative, and (6) abdicative, which
implies delegating not only tasks and responsibilities but power
and controls as well (Likert, 1967; Harbison and Myers, 1959;
Bass, 1981; Vroom and Yetton, 1973; Tannenbaum and

Schmidt, 1958). Some typologies add a dimension of "professional" or collegial relationships in an organization where individuals have broad vested rights and a "moral" orientation toward organizational goals, such as in professional partnerships in law or medicine (Jones, 1983; Shrivastava, 1983).

These organizational typologies deal much more with aggression, power, and control than with love, intimacy, and peer relationships. As was shown with the Etzioni typology, one can often derive what the assumptions about peer relationships must be from those made about power relationships, but those assumptions often remain implicit.

Dimensions for analyzing human relationships can also be usefully drawn from Parsons' (1951) "pattern variables." He enumerates the following role relationships in a social system:

1. *Emotionally charged or emotionally neutral.* Are relationships in the system emotionally charged, as in a friendship; or is an attempt made to minimize emotionality, as in a purely professional relationship?
2. *Diffuse or specific.* Do individuals relate to one another along many dimensions, as with family members; or are the relationships limited to a single dimension, as with a salesman-customer relationship?
3. *Universalistic or particularistic.* Are the same broad criteria applied to all members of a given role or status (for example, to all sales managers), or are specific criteria applied to given individuals on the basis of their individual situation (for example, "Jones should get a special bonus because he has had a tough territory," or "Smith gets let off the hook on something he messed up because he has a physical handicap," or "Shirley gets to work a good territory because she is the president's niece")?
4. *Ascription or achievement oriented.* Are social rewards, such as status and rank, assigned on the basis of what the person is by birth or family membership or on the basis of what the person has actually done?
5. *Self- or collectivity oriented.* Are an individual's actions

ultimately related to individual self-interest or to a larger collective unit?

Using these variables, we would say that relationships in the Action Company are emotionally charged, specific, particularistic, highly achievement oriented, and self-oriented; in Multi they are emotionally neutral, specific, somewhat though not totally universalistic, somewhat mixed on ascription versus achievement, and also mixed on self- versus collectivity orientation. Clearly, achievement counts at Multi, but ascriptive criteria—such as residence in the community where the company operates, the right family background, and the right level of education—also are considered. Clearly, people are assumed to be ambitious, but the good of the company also is taken into account—more than it is at Action, where the assumption seems to be that if everyone does the correct thing—that is, makes his best individual effort—that will turn out to be best for the company as a whole.

These and other dimensions identify the specific areas where consensus is needed if the organization is to function smoothly. Consensus in these areas then becomes a deep layer of the culture and surfaces only when someone challenges or violates one of the assumptions. For example, an American manager brought up with strong beliefs in achievement as the basis for status could not cope with the fact that a family firm into which he had moved as a general manager was completely dominated by assumptions of ascription, particularism, and emotional diffuseness. Tasks were assigned on the basis of who was who, decisions were made on the basis of who liked whom, and promotions were clearly reserved for family members.

There are, then, many typologies in organization theory for the analysis of human relationships. Each of these focuses on various elements of relationships and thus identifies possible areas of study for organizational culture. Two key reminders are in order: (1) The culture is always much more than just the assumptions about human relationships. (2) Assumptions about relationships are interconnected with assumptions about human nature, human activity, and the nature of reality, space, time, and the environment.

Cultural Paradigms—Interrelated Sets of Assumptions

The final and, perhaps, most difficult aspect of the analysis of assumptions has to do with the degree to which they come to be interlocked into "paradigms" or coherent patterns. Not all assumptions are mutually compatible or consistent with each other. If there is a cognitive drive for order and consistency in the human brain, we can assume that human groups will gradually learn sets of assumptions that are compatible and consistent. If we observe inconsistency and lack of order, we can assume that we are dealing with an as yet unformed culture or that we are observing a conflict among several cultures.

To illustrate what I mean by consistency, if we believe or assume that problems are ultimately solved through individual effort and that individuals are the ultimate source of ideas and creativity, we cannot simultaneously hold the assumption that the best kinds of relationships between members of an organization are collaborative consensual ones. If we believe that ultimately relationships between workers and organizations are either coercive or utilitarian, and that there can never be a common interest between them, then we cannot simultaneously believe in participative management theories, because these theories assume that workers want to contribute to the welfare of the organization.

If a group assumes that the correct way to survive is to conquer nature (that is, to manage its environment aggressively), it cannot simultaneously assume that the best way for members to relate to each other is by passively seeking harmonious relationships. Kluckhohn and Strodtbeck (1961) illustrate the paradigm notion at a higher level in asserting that Western culture is oriented toward the mastery of nature, holds an active optimistic view of man as perfectible, views society as built on individualistic competitive relationships, and has an optimistic future orientation built on a notion of progress. To this we could add a pragmatic scientific view of truth and reality, a monochronic view of time, a view of space and resources as being infinitely available, and a view of authority relationships as "rational-legal" in the sense that power should go to those who have the expertise and are elected or appointed by a process that rests on the democratic principle of "consent of the governed." In the business realm, we expect relationships to be emotionally neutral, universalistic, specific, and achievement oriented (Newman, 1972).

Organizational cultures may not develop to the point of fully articulated paradigms, but when we speak of "strong" cultures, what we probably have in mind is some degree of such articulation. For example, in his analysis of the GEM Corporation, Dyer (1982) notes that it operates on several interlocking assumptions, which give it its particular character: (1) Truth comes ultimately from individuals. (2) Individuals are responsible, motivated, and capable of governing themselves. (3) Truth can ultimately be determined only through debate and conflict (which requires a great deal of "fighting" and testing of ideas in groups and meetings). (4) Members of the organization are a family who accept and like each other and will take care of each other. Assumption 3 cannot safely be implemented without assumption 4, and one hears from members of the organization some concern that they are losing their "family feeling" and, as a consequence, are beginning to confront each other less; therefore, they fear, they may be compromising the quality of some of their solutions to problems. The Action Company operates by assumptions very similar to these, and they can be contrasted to what might be inferred to be the paradigm in Multi: (1) Truth comes ultimately from older, wiser, better-educated, and more experienced members. (2) Individual members are capable of and willing to give commitment and loyalty to the organization (the "good soldier" assumption previously mentioned). (3) Relationships are basically hierarchical (lineal), but work/task space is clearly compartmentalized and allocated to members as their own niche or turf to manage and own. (4) Members of the organization are a family who will take care of each other.

These examples indicate that cultural paradigms are far

more than some of the typologies of organizations that one finds in our literature. Many of these typologies take a single assumption dimension (such as those discussed earlier), develop several types along that dimension, and then call the types "archetypes." In fact, those archetypes often ignore other dimensions of assumptions and, therefore, fail to test whether or not there are coherent paradigms operating. Two autocratic companies may differ dramatically in their view of time, space, truth, relationships to nature, and activity, just as two bureaucratic organizations may differ dramatically from each other on these dimensions. In fact, one of the reasons why organization theory may not have progressed further than it has is that most of the typologies which are published tend to be unidimensional.

To conclude: Unless we have searched for the pattern among the different underlying assumptions of a group and have attempted to identify the paradigm by which the members of a group perceive, think about, feel about, and judge situations and relationships, we cannot claim that we have described or understood the group's culture. At the minimum we should take each of the assumption areas described in this chapter and attempt to answer systematically whether or not real consensus exists among group members in that area. We can then decide that there is no culture or a weak culture, or culture conflict between several groups. But unless we push to this level of analysis, we should not make any statement about culture at all. Superficial statements run the risk of losing the very meaning of the concept of culture or trivializing it to a point where the concept becomes no more valuable than the concept of values or norms.

5

How to Uncover
Cultural Assumptions
in an Organization

It is one thing to define basic cultural essence as the pattern of assumptions that underlie what people value and do; it is quite another thing to determine what that underlying pattern of assumptions actually is. Anthropologists have various ways of "deciphering" a culture, and some of these involve complex methods of analysis of the observable artifacts, particularly the spoken language and other signs (Frake, 1964; Spradley, 1979; Barley, 1983). The basic approach I propose here is better described as an iterative "clinical" interview, a series of encounters and joint explorations between the investigator and various motivated informants who live in the organization and embody its culture. My assumption is that only a *joint* effort between an insider and an outsider can decipher the essential assumptions and their patterns of interrelationships (Evered and Louis, 1981; Schein, 1984). This joint effort may involve quite elaborate and extensive data-gathering activities and may include some of the more formal methods that anthropologists propose. As I will describe later in the chapter, such methods also may include formal interviews, analysis of artifacts, and group inter-views to get at insiders' perceptions. The final determination of the cultural "essence" must then be a *joint* effort, for two basic reasons:

1. *To avoid the subjectivity bias.* The outsider cannot ex-perience the categories of meaning that the insider uses, because he has not lived long enough in the culture to learn the seman-tic nuances, how one set of categories connects to other sets of categories, how meanings are translated into behavior, and how such behavioral rules apply situationally. What the newcomer learns at entry reveals surface layers of the culture; only when inner boundaries are crossed is the member told what really goes on and how to think about it (Schein, 1978; Van Maanen and Schein, 1979). Furthermore, the outsider inevitably imposes his own categories of meaning onto observed events, and these interpretations are incorrect to an unknown degree. The in-sider can correct the misinterpretations by hearing how the out-sider interprets events. But they need to talk it out explicitly, so that the misinterpretation can be observed and corrected.

2. *To overcome internal invisibility.* The insider cannot tell the outsider what the basic assumptions are and how they are patterned, because they have dropped out of awareness and are taken for granted. The insider can become aware of them only by trying to explain to the outsider why certain things that puzzle the outsider happen the way they do, or by correcting interpretations that the outsider is making. This process requires work on the part of both the insider and outsider over a period of time. The nature of this work can be likened to trying to bring to the surface something that is hidden but not concealed deliberately. It is so taken for granted that it escapes notice, but it is perfectly visible once it has surfaced into consciousness.

Revealing the Cultural Paradigm:
Joint Exploration Through Iterative Interviewing

The ten steps involved in the method proposed here are listed and described in the following paragraphs. Many of the methods advocated by corporate culture analysts (Schwartz and Davis, 1981; Kilmann, 1984; Peters, 1980; Pettigrew, 1979; Silverzweig and Allen, 1976; Tichy, 1983) seem to assume that if one just asks the "right" questions initially, one can decipher the culture. In the model suggested here, however, there are no initial "magic questions" or correct things to observe, and the outsider cannot decipher the culture by himself, no matter how many data he has. The theoretical categories discussed in the previous chapters can alert the investigator to the areas where observations should be made, but such categories should not be used as a guide to questioning prior to exposing oneself to the culture in a natural way.

1. *Entry and Focus on Surprises.* The interested outsider enters the organization or group to be deciphered and begins to experience the culture, both actively through systematic observation and passively through encountering "surprises" (Louis, 1980)—things that are different from what the outsider expects. In Action, I was most surprised by the high level of interpersonal conflict, which seemed to be immune to my interventions. In Multi, I was most surprised by the fact that my communications did not circulate freely. Both of these proved to be important symptoms or artifacts of deep cultural assumptions.

2. *Systematic Observation and Checking.* The outsider engages in systematic observation to calibrate the surprising experiences as best he can and to verify that the "surprising" events are indeed repeatable experiences and thus likely to be a reflection of the culture, not merely random or idiosyncratic events.

3. *Locating a Motivated Insider.* The outsider must now find someone in the culture who is analytically capable of deciphering what is going on and who is motivated to do so. It is the *insider's* motivation to obtain some kind of help or clarity that makes this a "clinical" rather than an ethnographic approach. Often the insider initiates the project by seeking help of some kind and then becomes involved as a participant in unraveling aspects of the culture (Schein, 1969). In Action and Multi, such persons were initially the clients who brought me into the system. Subsequently, additional resources for mutual exploration surfaced in the personnel and training departments. It turned out that some of the internal consultants and some of the people in the training department themselves wanted to dis-

cuss my observations with me, so they provided a natural vehicle for further deciphering.

4. *Revealing the Surprises, Puzzlements, and Hunches.* Once a relationship has been established with the insider, the outsider can reveal his observations, surprises, reactions, and even his own projections, theories, and hunches about what is going on in the culture. Often such revelations are "set up" by the insider with routine questions such as "What do you think of our company, now that you have been here for a while?" If the insider does not provide a natural setting for revelation of reactions, the outsider must be able to create such a setting. Specifically, the outsider must assess the insider's readiness to hear observations that may sound judgmental and to deal with them in a nondefensive manner. How the outsider reveals his observations is also crucial. I generally avoid abstractions and generalizations; instead, I stick very closely to my own personal reactions to events, thereby allowing the insider to consider the possibility that my idiosyncrasy rather than a cultural force is operating. In Action maybe I am just supersensitive to interpersonal conflict in groups and there is nothing significant in it; in Multi maybe my not having my memos circulated reflects my own need for prominence, not some cultural phenomenon in the company. This form of communicating also minimizes the risk of the insider's becoming defensive if the observation hits a sensitive spot.

5. *Joint Exploration to Find Explanation.* The insider attempts to explain to the outsider what the surprising event means, or, if the outsider has a hunch, the insider elaborates on or corrects the outsider's interpretation. Both parties now have to probe systematically for the underlying assumptions and the patterns among them. At this point the theoretical categories, the issues that every group must face (as outlined in Chapter Three), and the categories of basic assumptions (as outlined in Chapter Four) become relevant as a mental checklist to ensure that all of the cultural terrain is being covered. That is, both people must relate the observations to the various theoretical categories to see where there is most clearly a connection and where the data clearly reveal an underlying assumption. In this

process the outsider must assume the role of a clinical interviewer who is helping the insider search in his own mind for the deeper levels of explanation that can help both persons decipher the basic assumptions of the culture. Since the essential data are in the insider's head, the process must be designed to bring out these data, which the insider takes for granted. The outsider must be sensitive to how best to probe without arousing defensiveness, inducing superficial explanations, or exhausting the insider to the point of wanting to terminate the relationship.

In practice this activity usually takes place when both parties are relaxed, maybe at the end of a consulting day or over a meal, or at a session deliberately designed to be diagnostic. In Multi, I have spent countless hours with a young professional internal consultant and trainer, talking out my own frustrations in working with the company and having him provide a necessary cultural framework for understanding what is happening, adding data where relevant from his own experience. It is where our experiences are identical that we know we are dealing with a real cultural issue. In Action much of the clarification came from another process that happened to be available. The company was using other consultants in various parts of the organization, and we all met periodically to compare notes on what was happening and to decipher assumptions in a group context. With five or six of us sharing our experiences at Action, we could calibrate more accurately what the major cultural assumptions seemed to be.

6. *Formalizing Hypotheses.* The output of step 5 is explanations that make sense, stated in the form of underlying assumptions, but these assumptions can be taken only as hunches about the culture at this point and must be formalized into hypotheses. Both the insider and the outsider must determine what further data would constitute a valid test of whether such an assumption is operating. Such data might be in the form of operational values that should be derivable from the assumptions, or actual behavior that one should be able to observe if the assumption holds. The theoretical categories described in Chapter Four for analyzing basic assumptions can serve as guidelines for things to look for in trying to explain surprises and

other observations. In a sense they provide theoretical tools that the insider and outsider can use to build a "model" of the culture.

7. *Systematic Checking and Consolidation.* Through new interviews or observations, the interested insider and the outsider now search for new evidence. At this point systematic interviewing of informants may be in order, since the outsider now has some idea of what questions to ask. In the initial stages of encountering the culture, the outsider would have such a vast array of possible things to ask about that he would hardly know where to begin. At this point in the process, the outsider knows enough to know where to look, what to look for, and whom to ask. Questionnaires, content analysis of documents, stories and other artifacts, formal interviews, systematic observations, and all the other techniques of gathering social data now become highly relevant.

8. *Pushing to the Level of Assumptions.* One of the most difficult steps in the deciphering process comes when one must go beyond the articulated values and attempt to understand the deeper layer of assumptions behind them. Such probing probably cannot be successfully undertaken outside one's own culture. That is, if I am an American investigator, I probably can decipher the culture of an American company, but I could never fully decipher the culture of a French, Japanese, or Latin American organization unless I had lived in those countries for some time. The essence of this step, then, is to take the confirmed hypothesis and attempt to state clearly what assumption is operating and how that assumption affects behavior. In Action, I have begun to understand what it means to fight over an idea in the search for truth in an uncertain world, and it no longer makes me uncomfortable. I understand the rules of the game. In Multi, I understand what it means to want to solve one's own problem, to be the expert and to seek help only from other experts, so I am no longer surprised at the kinds of questions I am asked and the kinds of problems I am involved in. I know when my own behavior fits the culture and when it is countercultural.

9. *Perpetual Recalibration.* As new data surface, and as

the outsider becomes better acquainted with the culture, he can refine and modify the model of the culture that he has begun to construct, and he can test that model on other interested insiders. But they must be interested and analytical, because otherwise they may not recognize the assumptions by which they operate. Worse, they may get defensive if they feel that a judgment is being made or embarrassed that their behavior has been "exposed." In other words, a correct view of the culture is not necessarily readily accepted by the uncritical members of that culture because they may not like the assumptions they operate by or because the assumptions are simply too complicated to comprehend.

I have had counterproductive experiences both in Action and in Multi when I attempted to lecture to insiders about their culture, even if they requested the lecture. Clearly, they were sometimes not ready to have their culture analyzed. On the other hand, culture discussions of this sort provide important new data that permit recalibration. Just as in group training or therapy, resistance to interpretations provides important data, so in cultural analysis the reaction of people to cultural descriptions provides important further data on what the culture is all about.

10. Formal Written Description. As a final test of our understanding of the assumptions of a given organizational culture, it is necessary to write down the assumptions and to show how they relate to each other in a meaningful pattern—to articulate the paradigm. It is very easy to assume that we understand and have an intuitive feel for what is going on, but unless we can clearly write out what we think we feel, we cannot tell whether we really understand and whether anyone else could understand. The written analysis would undergo perpetual modification as new data arise, but some description is an essential step in the method of deciphering.

The interested insider can go over the written description as a further test of accuracy, but it is not at all clear that making such a written description generally available is helpful. The whole issue of when and how one reveals a culture to the group members requires further clinical diagnosis. How the cultural data are used, then, is a function of what problems the client system wishes to address.

In Multi the cultural description became relevant when we were diagnosing forces that would aid or hinder the Redirection Project, but until then it remained only an interesting bit of data, which I shared with the internal consultants and the manager of management development. In Action there is so much internal preoccupation with the culture already that my role has been more that of a clarifier, sharpener, and implications tester. For example, I once asked, "If your culture really assumes that every individual must think for himself, how is that consistent with your wish to have senior management make decisions and push them down the system?"

Interview Methodology

If one is going into a new organization, how does one interview a willing informant to begin to get at cultural assumptions? Such interview information would supplement the immediate data that the outsider would obtain from his own encounters with the organization, and, of course, each interview is itself an encounter to be deciphered in accordance with the preceding steps. But general interview data and focused interview data can be helpful in structuring the initial encounters.

The basic idea is to get a historical reconstruction of how the group solved its major problems of external adaptation and internal integration and which kinds of solutions worked repeatedly and became embedded. To get at this, I ask about the critical incidents in the history of the group, using the categories in Chapter Three, Tables 1 and 2, as a private mental checklist to make sure that everything has been covered.

The interview should take the informant through the history of the unit being studied, in order to discover key historical events and the manner in which they were handled:

1. *Let's go back over the history of your organization. Can you tell me when it was founded and describe the events that occurred at that time?*

   a. Who was involved? (Try to locate the important found-
       ing figures or leaders who might have been the real cul-
       ture creators, and find out what their values, biases, as-
       sumptions, and goals were.)
   b. What were the critical problems in getting started?
       (Try to find out what the survival issues were and how
       they were handled.)
   c. Were there specific goals that emerged? Ways of work-
       ing? Key values that emerged early?
2. *What was the next critical incident that occurred?* (A critical incident is any major event that threatened survival, or
   caused reexamination or reformulation of goals or ways of
   working, or involved membership or inclusion issues. To
   discover a critical incident, the interviewer might ask the re-
   spondent to recall events that caused problems for which
   the organization had no ready solution, or events that challenged existing norms and solutions (such as an act of insubordination), or anything interpersonal that was unusual
   or tension provoking and required some kind of response.)
   a. Tell me how people were feeling about what was hap-
       pening. Were they anxious or angry or delighted or
       what?
   b. What was done? Who did anything? (Here the inter-
       viewer tries to elicit—in detail—the nature of the re-
       sponse and the key actors who were responsible for the
       response. If an informant says, for example, "We were
       faced with a cutback, but instead of laying people off,
       we went to all of us working fewer hours and taking a
       pay cut," the interviewer might ask: "Who thought of
       this idea?" "How was it implemented?")
   c. What was the meaning of the response? What goals, val-
       ues, and assumptions were implied or explicitly stated
       in the response?
   d. What happened? Did the response work? How did peo-
       ple feel subsequently? Did the response continue? (The
       interviewer then asks questions about the next crisis or
       critical event, around which the same series of ques-
       tions would be asked again.)

Analysis of Interview Responses and Observational Data

As one elicits incidents, feelings, what was done, and how it worked, one should try to elicit or imagine the underlying values and assumptions that may be involved in the responses and begin to look for patterns in them. This is the analytical activity that accompanies steps 5 and 6 in the sequence described at the beginning of this chapter. We cannot argue that we are dealing with a cultural element until we see some repetition of response, some behaviors, values, and assumptions that clearly are shared and continue to be used in new situations. So one needs to elicit enough history to begin to see the pattern.

Other Sources of Cultural Data

How much can one infer from an analysis of artifacts, such as the structure of the organization, its information and control system, and its announced goals, charters, mission statements, myths, legends, and stories? Because such data are often used, their strengths and weaknesses must be briefly discussed here.

Organizational Structure. The problem with inferring culture from an existing structure is that one cannot decipher what the underlying assumptions were that initially led to that structure. The same structure could result from different sets of underlying assumptions. For example, when we discover a highly centralized structure in an organization, what can we infer about the leaders' assumptions: (1) that this is the right way to organize for the primary task, or (2) that they have a monopoly on truth, or (3) that key positions have to be protected for their friends and relatives, or (4) that people cannot really be trusted (Theory X) and therefore must be tightly controlled, or (5) that only hierarchical relationships and clear lines of authority make it possible to run *any* organization? Or is the structure a tradition based on historical evolution, resulting from assumptions made by earlier managers? Or is there another possible inference that we haven't even thought of?

If deciphering the implicit "meaning" of a given organizational structure is a problem for the culture analyst, it could also be a problem for the employee who lives within the structure. McGregor's (1960) big insight in his analysis of Theory X and Theory Y was that if a structure implies a certain assumption about human nature, people may begin to adapt to that structure by behaving in the manner they are "expected" to behave. In other words, if the founder is cynical about people and builds an organization and a control system that implies an inability on the part of employees to motivate or control themselves, those people soon "get the message" that they are not trusted and either leave if they cannot stand that kind of environment or adapt by acting the way the system expects them to. But what if the leader is not cynical, and is using high centralization and tight controls for other reasons or because he is perpetuating a tradition? We then have the danger that the message which the structure sends is not at all the intended message.

Given that humans cannot stand too much ambiguity and uncertainty, and therefore need an organizational structure as a primary vehicle for stabilizing relationships both hierarchically and among colleagues, all organizations develop some system of roles and statuses to permit tasks to be allocated in a clear manner and to permit the members to develop stable expectations of each other. Structure thus reduces anxiety and makes organizational life predictable and stable. But, because the inferring of assumptions from structure is difficult, both the insider and the outsider must check carefully what the actual assumptions are and avoid premature attribution or projections.

In summary, the structure of an organization serves important functions and thereby becomes a key element of the culture. But the cultural content—what the structure actually implies in the way of assumptions about the task, the people, and relationships—must be carefully deciphered, not glibly assumed. Two organizations with identical structures could have totally different cultures. And two similar cultures could develop, at least in the short run, different structures. For instance, two radiology departments introduced computerized tomography at about the same time, but one became highly centralized while the other became highly decentralized (Barley, 1984b).

An Organization's Formal Information and Control System. If what is highlighted in the information and control system is actually attended to by key managers, the system reflects the culture. But we have all seen organizations where the formal system and the informal processes of management bear little relationship to each other. In fact, in some organizations managers actively ridicule their control system as something that the "accountants" or "financial boys" have cooked up but that is largely irrelevant to really managing the place. On the other hand, the formal systems are clearly an artifact of the culture and therefore reflect something. At the minimum they may reflect the fact that one of the subcultures within the organization is working at cross-purposes with other parts of the culture. The nature of this conflict can serve as a useful starting point for diagnosing the strains within the larger culture. What I am suggesting is that the explicit formal system cannot be taken at face value. It clearly has messages embedded in it, but until one observes what managers actually pay attention to, one does not know what the messages really are.

And, to complicate matters, the original intentions reflecting one set of assumptions may turn out to be quite different from their effects and the assumptions that people infer. In either case, the messages that such systems and procedures carry are implicit. If one organization is programmed to do recurrent things on a daily basis while another one operates on a monthly basis, this certainly sends important signals about time assumptions, but what are those assumptions? If one set of procedures requires an employee to get approval from two levels of management before something moves forward, while another procedure requires only the employee's signature, this certainly sends different signals about assumptions of what he can and cannot do or can be trusted with. But as with structure, unless one examines the historical origins and the intentions of the creators of the systems and procedures, one does not really know what those assumptions are.

An example from Multi will make this point clear. Multi operates worldwide; therefore, central policies and procedures covering travel from headquarters to various regional units have been formulated. In order to take a trip, a member of the headquarters personnel organization must get approval from his own boss and from his boss's boss. When I first learned about this, it

struck me as the kind of artifact that clearly supported the
strong *hierarchical* assumptions of the organization, and I further assumed that it reflected a lack of willingness to delegate.
Why not give people a travel budget and make them live within
it? When I raised this question with several senior managers, I
uncovered a totally different set of reasons for the existence of
the policy. Apparently, the company had for years given complete freedom to its headquarters personnel. As a result, travel
to the regional units was so frequent that the regional line managers felt as if they were doing nothing but entertaining headquarters visitors. Attempts to impose budgets did not curb the
amount of visiting of the regions. It was in reaction to the
strong frustration of the *regional* managers that higher management imposed what amounted to a travel ban, which really signaled to the organization that the regions were more important
as organizational units than the staffs in the central headquarters organizations. In order to ensure that the regions were
properly supported, the headquarters staff had to be curbed.

What seemed a repressive policy on travel proved to be a
cultural artifact rich in information about headquarters field
relationships, attitudes toward delegation, and changing priorities as the company evolved. But only after investigation was I
able to decipher what the artifact actually reflected and how it
should be interpreted. My suspicion is that most organizational
procedures have rich cultural histories of this sort, and one will
not understand the meaning of those procedures until their histories have been analyzed and deciphered.

As a final point, we need to observe that some of the
most potent messages carried by systems are embedded in the
technological processes themselves rather than in the psychological meaning of these processes. For example, the introduction
of computer-based information or decision support systems involving the placement of a terminal on each manager's desk, so
that he has access to all information anywhere in the system, is
based on several process assumptions that may or may not be
shared in the organization:

1.   That important information is carried in the reports put

into the computer system (versus face-to-face probing of what is going on).

2. That the same information should be available to all levels of management (versus being the private property of each job holder, as in Multi).

3. That access to *more* information will improve the management process (versus reducing managerial access to only those items of information that are deemed crucial to managing a given function or area, where *less* would be considered better).

4. That instant access on the part of everyone to all information will improve the management process (versus introducing systematic time delays, so that given levels can have access to information before other levels get it).

If the culture of the organization is built on assumptions different from the ones that are implicit in a given technological process, that process either will not be adopted or will be subverted. In any case, one could not infer the culture from the existence of the process.

Myths, Legends, Stories, and Charters. Many of the published analyses of culture limit themselves to the analysis of the explicit artifacts, such as stories and organizational credos. While it may be possible to determine how stories about founders and the charters and credos of their companies *reinforce* their assumptions, one cannot infer those assumptions from such data alone. One cannot assume that what is in the stories and charters is anything more than the espoused values, and these may or may not match with actual assumptions that operate. The same caution must be applied to the content of materials that are to be transmitted to newcomers and to the myths and legends that arise in every organization to help everyone remember important values (Martin, 1982; Mitroff and Kilmann, 1975, 1976; Smith and Simmons, 1983).

The origin and the function of organizational "stories" are not at all clear, but some themes have been identified. Stories often communicate the values and beliefs of founders or other central characters in the organization who have become symbolic role models. The stories are often prescriptive and can thus become direct vehicles of indoctrination. On the other hand, in an organization with many subcultures or conflicting coalitions, stories can become a means of spreading a counter-culture or of revealing inconsistencies or absurdities in the main culture. In an illuminating paper, Martin and Siehl (1983) analyze the key values of General Motors as seen in an official history and as seen by the disenchanted John DeLorean (Wright, 1979). The point of most of DeLorean's stories is to make the company look ridiculous and ineffective.

Sometimes stories are used to idealize former leaders, even though the idealized behavior is no longer relevant in the present. In this case the point of the story is not only to communicate a value but also to give employees a sense of pride and something to identify with. For example, in a large European company, it was said that an employee went to one of the important past leaders who built the company into its leadership position, and opened the conversation with "Herr Doctor Schmitt." Schmitt immediately interrupted the employee and said, "I am not a doctor," at which point the employee excused himself and said, "Herr Director Schmitt." Schmitt again interrupted and said, "I am not a director; I am an entrepreneur, and I *employ* directors." What comes through in the story is not only the personality of this early leader, but the prestige hierarchy that one must learn if one works in this organization. Entrepreneurial behavior is assumed to be the key to success.

Explicit statements of creeds, philosophies, and charters make the espoused message explicit, reflecting the leader's intentions to get a certain message across. But we cannot assume that these consciously articulated messages necessarily reflect what may be more implicit cultural themes, either because the leader is not aware of them, or is conflicted about them, or is deliberately trying to displace some implicit themes with more consciously explicit ones that fit his intentions better.

Closely related to published philosophies and creeds are published recruiting brochures, employee orientation handbooks, initial indoctrination and training materials, videotapes, and other artifacts that attempt to get across to newcomers what some key elements of the culture of the organization are. Such materials are more likely to exist in companies that are past their "youth," that have developed enough of an espoused value system to be able to articulate it, but such materials also exist in first-generation companies in the form of letters from the founder, videotapes of the founder, and other materials that bring founding principles and values to the newcomers.

In conclusion, organizational artifacts are better used to check one's hypotheses about basic assumptions than to decipher what those assumptions are in the first place.

Group Interviews to Elicit Positions on Specific Dimensions

If the goal of the cultural analysis is to give insiders a quicker insight into their own culture without going through the formal process of analysis by an outsider or a joint team, I have used some form of group interview or discussion. I often ask groups of interested insiders, working with or without me, to diagnose where they fall along a given cultural dimension. Such an activity would typically have to be preceded by a lecture/seminar on the general concept of culture as underlying taken-for-granted assumptions, and by illustrations of the specific dimensions discussed in Chapter Four. The group members then select one or more dimensions to analyze and go to work with the aid of one of the following focused sets of instructions.

This technique is useful because the group provides the stimulus to bring out what is ordinarily hidden, and outsiders attending the discussion can observe the behavior of group members from the point of view of the very assumption being analyzed. In other words, where opportunities to make unobtrusive ethnographic observations do not exist, one can still observe a great deal of the culture in action by creating and observing group meetings at which cultural issues are discussed. Each of the following examples of instructions should be treated as a first approximation, to be refined according to the particular needs in a given organizational situation.

Dimension 1:
Organization's Relationship to its Environment

What are the organization's basic assumptions about itself?

1. Basic Identity and Role: Who are we (type of product, service, market, customer); what is our core mission or ultimate function in society, our "reason to be" or our justification for survival?
2. Relevant Environments: What and who are the relevant environments we must relate to because they represent constraints and threats, on the one hand, and opportunities, on the other hand?
    a. Economic
    b. Political
    c. Technological
    d. Sociocultural
    e. Other
3. Position vis-à-vis Those Environments:
    a. Dominant and in control
    b. In harmony with, symbiotic
    c. Dominated by, must find and adjust to own niche

Analytical Method to Be Used in Group Discussion

1. Reconstruct and analyze organization's history by identifying all major crises, crucial transitions, and other times of high emotion.
2. For each event identified, reconstruct how management at that time defined identity/role, relevant environments, and position.
3. Locate patterns and themes across the events analyzed.
4. Cross-check patterns and themes against current strategic criteria.
5. Articulate the assumptions that underlie actions taken.
6. Check these assumptions against current behavioral data.

Dimension 2:
Nature of Reality and Truth, Basis for Decisions

What are the organization's basic assumptions about reality?

1. Physical, Social, and Subjective Reality: In the organization's view, which decision areas belong in the domain of physical reality (externally verifiable by objective criteria—matters of fact)? Which belong in the domain of social reality (verifiable only by consensus—matters of opinion, custom, dogma, principle)? Which belong in the domain of subjective reality (verifiable only by subjective experience—matters of personal opinion, bias, taste)?

2. Criteria of Verifiability—Moralism-Pragmatism: Within a given domain, how do we determine when something is "true" or "real" and, hence, can serve as a basis for taking action?

   a. Tradition—"It has always been done this way."
   b. Religious/moral dogma—"This is the *right* way to do it."
   c. Revelation by wise men or authorities—"Our president wants to do it this way." "Our consultants or experts recommended that we do this."
   d. Rational/legal process—"We take this kind of decision to the marketing committee and do what they decide."
   e. Conflict resolution, open debate—"We thrashed it out in three different committees, tested it on the sales force, and the idea is still sound, so we will do it."
   f. Trial and error, what works—"Let's try it and see."
   g. Scientific test—"Our research shows that this is the way to do it."

Analytical Method to Be Used in Group Discussion

1. Identify a set of decisions that involved strategic issues and high conflict prior to resolution.

2. Classify the decisions according to whether they were judged to fall in the realm of physical or social reality.
3. Identify for each set the kinds of criteria that made people feel that a decision could finally be reached.
4. Look for the pattern and themes in these criteria.
5. Articulate the basic assumptions underlying the criteria.
6. Check the conclusion against current behavioral data in the organization.

Dimension 2A: The Nature of Time

What are the organization's basic assumptions about the nature of time and how time is structured (these often reflect the host culture's concepts of time)?

1. Direction of Focus
   a. Orientation toward the past
   b. Orientation toward the present
   c. Orientation toward the future
2. Basic Concept
   a. Linear, monochronic
   b. Polychronic
   c. Cyclical
3. Size of Relevant Units, Length of Cycles

Analytical Method to Be Used in Group Discussion

1. Identify and analyze some recent decisions in terms of whether prime importance was given to what was done in the past, what is being done now, or what can be done in the future.
2. List all major systems and procedures used in the organization and determine the length of recurring cycles for each.
3. How much variation is allowed around targets and deadlines? How much time elapses before one is "late" for an appointment? "Late" in delivering a product? "Late" in meeting a deadline?
4. How long are appointments?

5. Does the organization use time clocks, time sheets, other time records?
6. For each of the domains above, look for common themes from which assumptions could be inferred, and then check those assumptions against current behavioral data.

Dimension 2B: The Nature of Space

What are the organization's basic assumptions about the nature of space, how available is it, how is it to be structured, and what are its symbolic meanings?

1. Availability
   a. Infinitely available
   b. Available but constrained
   c. Highly unavailable
2. Uses of Space as a Symbol
   a. How is space utilized to symbolize status and power?
   b. How is space utilized to symbolize peer relations, how is it allocated as turf or "property," and is it utilized to maintain privacy?
3. Norms of "Distance"
   a. Appropriate distances for formal and informal status relationships
   b. Appropriate distances for intimate and friendship relationships
   c. Appropriate distances for meetings, relationships with outsiders, and so on

Analytical Method to Be Used in Group Discussion

This area does not lend itself easily to formal analysis via specific questions. The suggestion would be for the group to review its own experience in many different organizational situations to get a feeling for how space is used and what assumptions underlie it. Most members will have learned these assumptions, and it is a matter of sharing experiences to bring them to the surface. The preceding outline can be used as a guide for organizing the discussion.

Dimension 3: The Nature of Human Nature

What basic assumptions are held about human nature, and how are they applied to our own organization at the employee and managerial levels?

1.   Basic Human Nature
     a.   Humans are basically "bad" (lazy, antiorganization, self-seeking).
     b.   Humans are basically "good" (hard working, committed, generous, pro-organization).
     c.   Humans are basically neutral (mixed, variable, capable of being good or bad).
2.   Mutability
     a.   Humans are basically fixed at birth and must accept what they are. If possible, they may be able to compensate for being innately "bad" by their deeds.
     b.   Humans are mutable and perfectible.

Analytical Method to Be Used in Group Discussion

1.   Identify organizational heroes and villains, successful people and failures, and compare the stories told about them from the point of view of what is said about their "human nature."
2.   Analyze recruitment, selection, and promotion criteria.
3.   Analyze performance appraisal criteria: What are people looking for, what kinds of comments are written down, what seems to be valued and not valued?
4.   Analyze reward and control system for the implicit assumptions that underlie how things are processed (for example, frequent checking up implies that one does not trust people, which, in turn, implies that one thinks that people are not trustworthy).
5.   Look for the common assumptions across the preceding domains.
6.   Check assumptions identified against current behavioral data.

Dimension 4: The Nature of Human Activity

What is assumed to be the proper and natural stance of humans vis-à-vis their environment?

1. Proactive, "Doing" Orientation: Humans *over* nature, act to solve problems, nothing is impossible, fight, win, try (Promethean).
2. Reactive, "Being" Orientation: Humans *subordinate to* nature, accept fate, relax and enjoy what is inevitable (Dionysian).
3. Harmonizing, "Being-in-Becoming" Orientation: Humans *in* nature, full development of own talent as natural, perfect oneself (Apollonian).

Analytical Method to Be Used in Group Discussion

1. Identify a set of problems faced by the organization in its history where the primary source of the problem was outside forces that acted as barriers or constraints to what the organization wanted to do.
2. What were the approaches advocated for dealing with the problem? Did they reflect primarily one of the preceding approaches?
3. What approaches were actually adopted? Did they reflect primarily one of the preceding approaches?
4. What assumptions were implicit in the approaches adopted?
5. Check the assumptions identified against behavioral data.

Alternate Method That Might Be Used

1. Identify former leaders, founders, and heroes in the company history. What assumptions did they hold about their stance toward nature?
2. Identify currently successful and unsuccessful members of the organization. What differences in assumptions seem to characterize the two groups?
3. Check assumptions identified against current behavioral data.

Dimension 5: The Nature of Human Relationships

What are the organization's basic assumptions about how relationships should be conducted so that basic human needs for love and aggression are constructively managed? Or what assumptions underlie the basic rules for the management of (1) power, control, and influence and (2) intimacy and affection?

1. Human Relationships: What is the ultimate basis for structuring all human relationships?
    a. Lineality—tradition, hierarchy, family
    b. Collaterality, group cooperation—group consensus and group welfare
    c. Individuality, competition—individual rights and individual welfare
2. Organizational Relationships: What is the ultimate basis for structuring organizational relationships? There are many typologies in this area, based on power distribution, involvement, how work is structured, how conflict is resolved, and the nature of the organizational mission itself. The power distribution issue is probably most central.
    a. Autocracy—based on assumption that leaders, founders, owners, or those who have power have the right and duty to exercise it.
    b. Paternalism—based on assumption of autocracy and on assumption that those in power are obligated to take care of those not in power.
    c. Consultation—based on assumption that all levels have relevant information to contribute but power remains in the hands of the leaders or owners.
    d. Participation—based on assumption that information and skill at all levels are relevant to organizational performance; hence, power must be shared as appropriate.
    e. Delegation—based on assumption that power must be placed where information and skill reside but that accountability remains in managerial roles.
    f. Collegiality—based on assumption that organization members are partners who share full responsibility for total organization.

Analytical Method to Be Used in Group Discussion

1. Identify a group of important recent decisions and examine whether they were made by individuals, groups, or both, and how power was exercised in the decision-making process.
2. Examine organizational stories and legends about heroes and villains, to discover how such people related to other people in the organization.
3. Examine critical incidents, such as instances of insubordination, to determine how the organization deals with violations of authority norms.
4. Look for themes in the decisions, stories, and events to identify the underlying assumptions.
5. Check assumptions against current behavioral data.

Conclusion

I have not found a reliable, quick way to identify cultural assumptions. Sometimes such assumptions are obvious at the outset; sometimes they are highly elusive, even after months of study; and sometimes one must conclude that there are no shared assumptions working across the organization because of a lack of shared history.

The only safe approach is triangulation; that is, checking each bit of information obtained against other bits of information until a pattern finally begins to reveal itself. In this process the dialogue of the insider and the outsider is crucial. An important part of such triangulation is to test one's insights by seeing how members of the organization respond to one's own behavior and interventions. As Lewin (1952) noted long ago, if one wants to understand a system, one should try to change it. The spirit of that dictum underlies action research and diagnostic activities in all human systems and is especially relevant to the diagnosis of cultural elements.

Can one use questionnaires or other more formalized tests? Given the approach I take to culture, the answer must clearly be "no." At best what one would get with such an instrument is some of the espoused values of group members. If these were then treated as an artifact to be deciphered along with other artifacts, one is probably on safe ground; but if one took the data to be a measure of the culture in the sense of underlying taken-for-granted assumptions, one would be skating on very thin ice indeed, and, worst of all, would not know how thin the ice actually was.

As I have repeated often, culture does not reveal itself easily. It is clearly there, but to articulate it and describe it requires great patience and effort.

6

Ethical Problems
in Culture Studies
and Interventions

If an organization is to understand its own strengths and weaknesses, and if it is to make informed strategic choices based on realistic assessments of external and internal factors, it must study and understand its own culture. But this process is not without its problems, risks, and potential costs. Basically, three kinds of risks must be assessed.

1. The analysis of the culture could be incorrect. The analysis of what the basic assumptions are and how they fit into a pattern and paradigm may be wrong and, if so, may give the decision maker incorrect data on which to base decisions. If decisions are made on the basis of incorrect assumptions about the culture, serious harm could be done to the organization.

2. The organization might not be ready to receive feedback about its culture. The analysis may be correct, but the insiders may not be prepared to digest what has been learned about them. If culture is like character, and functions in part as a set of defense mechanisms to help avoid anxiety and to pro-

137

vide positive direction, self-esteem, and pride, then various conditions might make an organization reluctant to accept the cultural truth about itself. Psychotherapists and counselors constantly must deal with resistance or denial on the part of patients
and clients. Similarly, unless an organization's personnel recognize a real need to change and feel psychologically safe enough
to examine data about the organization, they will not be able to
hear the cultural truths that inquiry may have revealed. A potentially even more dangerous risk is that the group will achieve
instant insight and will automatically and thoughtlessly produce
changes in the culture (1) that some members of the organization may not want, (2) that some members may not be prepared for and, therefore, may not be able to implement, and (3)
that may not solve the problem.

One reason people avoid therapy is that they are not
ready for the insights that therapy inevitably brings with it. Insight produces change automatically because certain illusions
and defenses can no longer be used. If culture is to the organization what character is to the individual, then insight into one's
own culture may remove defenses that had been operating, and
on which the organization had been relying. To study a culture
and reveal that culture to the insiders, then, can be likened to
an "invasion of privacy," which under many conditions is not
welcome. Therefore, the student of culture should make the client system fully aware that there are consequences to having
one's culture laid bare, so to speak.

One company, for example, "discovered" through self-
study and with the aid of outside consultants that it "assumed
that people are motivated and will put in a fair day's work for a
fair day's pay." The company measured output, not number of
hours on the job, and generally held an idealistic view of human
nature. During a period of economic decline, it was confronted
with its idealistic assumptions about employees and, because
productivity had become a problem, was ready to make a
change. Its managers decided that idealism was no longer ten-
able and that they had better get control of the situation. They
installed time clocks and had industrial engineers study the behavior of the workers to make sure that productivity could be

controlled and maximized. Once the new procedures were installed, the workers concluded that the company had really changed for the worse, lost some of their motivation, began to resent the time clocks and tried to figure out how to cheat them, and generally kept their productive effort to the minimum that they could get away with.

This kind of sad tale is usually associated with the advent of hard-nosed managers who come in with different styles, but in this case the only intervention was the clear exposure to the members of the company of how idealistic their culture was. Because they were frightened of the economic downturn, they were not able to perceive accurately that their culture was still a viable way of dealing with economic adversity and that they did not need to institute radical changes. They might have been better off not knowing what their culture was.

3. The organization could be made more vulnerable through having its culture revealed to outsiders. If a correct analysis of the culture of an organization becomes known to outsiders, because it either is published or simply is discussed among interested parties, the organization may become vulnerable or put at a disadvantage, since data that would ordinarily remain private now may become public. For various reasons the members of the organization may not want their culture laid bare for others' viewing. If the information is inaccurate, potential employees, customers, suppliers, and any other categories of outsiders who deal with the organization may be adversely influenced.

Here again the analogy to "character" is useful, in that we clearly would not publish an accurate personality profile of a living individual unless that person, for reasons of his own, wanted such a publication. If it is important to the scientific community to have such material published—for instance, if psychiatrists or clinical psychologists want to inform their colleagues about the cases they have treated—the cases must be sufficiently disguised to ensure the absolute anonymity of the person being reported on. Paradoxically, business organization cases are rarely disguised, even though those cases often include revealing details about an organization's culture. If the organization fully understands what it is revealing, and if the information is accurate, no harm is done. But if the case reveals material that the organization is not aware of, such publication can produce undesirable insight or tension on the part of members and can create undesirable impressions on the part of outsiders. If the information is not accurate, then both insiders and outsiders may get wrong impressions and may base decisions on incorrect information.

Obligations of the Culture Analyst

If the above risks are real, then who should worry about it? Is it enough to say to an organization that we will study your culture and let you know what we find and that nothing will be published without your permission? If we are dealing with surface manifestations, artifacts, and publicly espoused values, then the guideline of letting members clear the material seems sufficient. But if we are dealing with the deeper levels of the culture, the assumptions and the patterns among them, then the insider clearly may not know what he is getting into, and the obligation shifts to the outsider as a professional, in the same way that it would be the psychiatrist's or counselor's job to make the client genuinely aware of what the consequences are of proceeding into an investigation of personality or character.

The analyst of a culture undertakes a professional obligation to understand fully what the potential consequences of an investigation are. Such consequences should be fully spelled out before the relationship reaches a level where there is an implied psychological contract that the outsider will give feedback to the insiders on what has been found out about the culture.

Examples to Illustrate Dimensions of the Problem

So far I have identified risks and indicated who must be responsible for assessing those risks. But do we have any evidence on potential costs, on what might actually happen if we investigate organizational cultures, give feedback, and publish results? We know what can happen in the individual realm, and we have plenty of experience from action research projects undertaken under the broad label of "organization development" of the effects of giving back to a system data about itself, but we have relatively limited experience in the culture realm. The following examples, drawn from my own experiences, indicate some of the dimensions of the problem and the potential costs involved.

Example 1. A clear example of projecting wrong assumptions occurred at a meeting of managers of a company that prided itself on taking into account the feelings and preferences of its personnel and their families. The managers were discussing succession in several key jobs, including the job of president. At one point in the discussion, a person was selected to become head of the international division—a job that could lead eventually to the position of executive vice-president and ultimately president. The personnel vice-president and one other group member, however, had talked to this individual and knew that he did not want to move overseas because of the critical age of his children. At this point the president entered the discussion and said, "Let me talk to him. Maybe I can explain the situation to him more clearly." My own reaction at this moment was one of dismay because this apparent attempt at persuasion seemed to me a clear violation of the company's principle that personal feelings should weigh heavily in these decisions. Clearly, others in the group felt the same way; one or two challenged the wisdom of the president's intervening, on the grounds that it would put too much pressure on the individual.

The president then explained his logic, and it is at this point that a deeper assumption emerged. The president said: "I understand that we should not pressure him to take the job if he does not want it, *and if he understands fully what he is giving up.* I want to explain to him that we consider the international VP job a crucial stepping stone, that we consider him the logical candidate to move up the ladder, and that we will be forced to move him off the ladder if he does not take this job. We don't have time to develop him in an alternate fashion, and he may not realize the consequences of rejecting the offer. But if he understands and still feels that he should reject it, we will respect that decision and look for another candidate."

The deeper assumption, then, was that a key executive must be given full organizational information and allowed to make a choice. If he knew that he was in line for the presidency, he might want to reassess the family priorities and consider moving. The implied assumption was that the *individual* is the only one who can ultimately make the choice. Had the group simply moved him off the ladder, it would have made the choice for him. My initial assumption about this company's assumptions was way off the mark, as it turned out.

Example 2. At one company where I was functioning as a consultant, I was invited to attend the annual meeting and to discuss with the total group my observations of the company's culture. I tried to be objective and neutral in my analysis, but at one point I likened certain aspects of that culture to a military model. Several members of the group, who were themselves former military men and who loved the army, took offense at what they viewed as a derogatory depiction of the army (though I believed I had been neutral in my statements). Their perception that I misunderstood and had challenged one of their values led to an unproductive argument about the validity of the cultural description and to some degree of discrediting of the consulting project. Ever since this event, I have felt that my relationship with these individuals is "strained" and that the larger goals of the project have been undermined.

What did I learn? There are several possible lessons. The most obvious one is that the outsider should never be "lecturing" insiders on their own culture because one cannot know where the sensitivities will lie and one cannot overcome one's own subtle biases. Perhaps if I had stated each of my points carefully as hypotheses or questions for them to react to, I might have avoided this trap.

Second, I learned that my analysis plunged the group members into an internal debate that they were not prepared for and that had multiple unanticipated consequences. The people who objected to my analogy revealed some of their own biases at the meeting in ways that they might not have intended to, and comments made later suggested that some people were "shocked" because so-and-so had revealed himself to be a such-and-such kind of person.

The analogy itself, likening aspects of the organization's functioning to the military, unleashed feelings that had more to do with the larger culture in which the organization operated and brought in a whole set of irrelevant feelings and issues. Many people in the group were made very uncomfortable by the "insight" that they were indeed operating like the military, because they had either forgotten this aspect or had illusions about it. My comments stripped away those illusions.

Third, and perhaps this point is the most important one, I learned that giving feedback to an individual is different from giving feedback to a group, because the group very likely is not homogeneous in its reactions. My "lecture" on the culture was well received by some members of the group, who went out of their way to assure me that my depiction was totally accurate. Obviously, this segment of the group was not threatened by what I had to say. But with others I lost credibility, and with still others I created enough threat to unleash defensiveness, plunging the group into an uncomfortable new agenda that had to be managed. The full consequences of this "incident" remain to be assessed.

Example 3. Where the preceding example focused on internal consequences, this example focuses on external ones. I was teaching in a management school as a visiting faculty member and accidentally discovered that a case being used by a colleague in his course dealt with a company I was familiar with. I read the case and found that it created a totally wrong impression of that company along several important cultural dimensions, but no one was aware of this or, for that matter, cared. Unfortunately, the areas where wrong impressions were created made the company seem an unattractive place to work, and the students who were using the case were potential recruits to that company. I did some informal checking among students and found that their attitudes were indeed subtly influenced and that several had sentiments along the line of "I would never work at a place like that." Such a reaction is perfectly reasonable if the data on which it is based are accurate. But the data were not accurate, and neither the company nor the faculty member using the case knew that they were not accurate. The only way to prevent undesirable consequences in this case would have been to disguise the company name and data sufficiently to make it impossible for students to get actual impressions of an actual company from the case.

Example 4. A student with whom I am acquainted interviewed a large number of managers and observed the behavior in a company in order to decipher and describe its culture. The study was carefully done; in the final write-up, the organization was fairly well disguised; and insiders pronounced the description "accurate." But, they asked, "Couldn't you say it in a way that would not make us look so bad?" It should be noted that the evaluation of "looking bad" was entirely, as in example 1, the reaction of only some insiders. The write-up simply reported objectively without evaluating.

One of the managers who did not like the report discovered, well after this project had been launched with complete insider approval, that a company policy formulated within the last year prohibited the publication of case studies about the company—probably for reasons of avoiding inaccurate impressions, along the lines of the events of example 2. Several insiders, who felt that they had an obligation to the student, fought to have the description released; but several other insiders were sufficiently nervous about the description, even though it was completely disguised, that it took several months and many rewrites before they felt relatively comfortable about the paper.

When the insiders approved this project, they did not know what the cultural description would actually look like; they had no way of assessing whether they should approve it. Since they did not have a particular need to gain insight into their own culture at this point in their history, the actual confrontation with the data was for some members of the company uncomfortable. Truths were spelled out that were better left implicit or buried; and the fact that outsiders probably would not recognize the company was small comfort, since everyone knew that other insiders would immediately recognize the company.

The availability of the description in written form became a de facto intervention in this company's functioning because it articulated many thoughts, values, and assumptions in ways that they had never been articulated before, and the company had not contracted for anything other than giving a student permission to interview and observe. Whether, on balance, the intervention will have been helpful or harmful remains to be seen. What is clear, however, is that a good description of the culture, made available in written form, is an intervention.

Some Implications

Several implications suggest themselves. First of all, since organizations have high visibility in society today, a description of an organization's culture makes public the deeper underlying aspects of that organization at a time when it is still very much part of the scene. We should not do this lightly, and we should have a clear picture of what our motivation is when we do it. Organizational research of any sort is an intervention, and the ethics of research should first of all be the ethics of intervention (Schein, 1969, 1980). We should be guided by the values of the clinician and recognize that organizational research, particularly on such a sensitive issue as organizational culture, requires a clear understanding between the client and the researcher that satisfies ethical principles of intervention, such as protection of the client's welfare (Schein, 1980, chap. 13).

The researcher/interventionist should know as much as possible about the potential consequences of the project and ensure that those consequences are communicated to the client. Where the consequences are better understood by the researcher than the client, the researcher should make a highly responsible decision not to engage in projects that could be harmful to the client.

What if we want to analyze a culture in order to show up

some of its undesirable consequences? Here the principle of adequately disguising the organization seems to solve the problem. But suppose we want a given organization to be embarrassed or want to show up some malevolent aspects of an organization to which we are opposed. Here the analogy would be to the psychiatrist who wants to publish a character analysis of a person considered "evil." Under what conditions can we name the company and describe the undesirable consequences of its culture? For scientists/interventionists the answer would probably be "never." But we know that we develop passions and sometimes act as political animals. In such instances we should at least not hide our political activities under the umbrella of science. In fact, we would have to be very careful not to let our feelings about "good" or "bad" aspects of a given organizational culture destroy our objectivity in analyzing that culture.

In the current fad of trying to figure out why some Japanese companies are seemingly outproducing their American counterparts, I get the feeling that I am reading more about evaluations of organizational cultures than I am about the facts of those cultures. To give but one example, the debate about the supposed benefits of Ouchi's (1981) Theory Z type of company has completely obscured the fact that the current descriptions of the culture of a Theory Z organization have not gone beyond the artifactual and value level. We know that such companies have lifetime employment and that they care about people, but we do not know, in the company examples cited, the underlying assumptions on which the policies, practices, and values are built. Should this make us nervous? Yes, because one can build lifetime employment on the assumption that employees are "owned" by the company, to be done with whatever the company pleases to do with them—an assumption that was not uncommon in strongly paternalistic companies in the early part of this century. The consequence sometimes was that the employee became, in effect, a prisoner, because leaving meant "disloyalty" and would lead to his being blackballed from the company forever (or even blacklisted so that others in the industry might not hire him).

To evaluate an organization, it is important to spell out

the underlying assumptions accurately and not to settle for surface manifestations, which could reflect very different assumption sets. On the other hand, if one is against certain practices,
one must be careful not to attribute to the organization assumptions that fit one's biases but may be completely wrong.

Conclusion

The culture of an organization is not easy to define, and
the strength of a culture will vary with a number of circumstances. In our effort to define the culture, we may discover
that no single set of assumptions has formed as a deep-down
paradigm for operating or that the subgroups of an organization
have different paradigms, which may or may not conflict with
each other. Furthermore, culture is perpetually changing, so
that the cultural researcher must be willing to do perpetual
searching and revising.

Even if we begin to have an intuitive understanding of an
organization's culture, we may find it extraordinarily difficult
to write down that understanding in such a way that the essence
of the culture can be communicated to someone else. We have
so few examples in our literature that it is even hard to point to
models of how it should be done. But when we see the essence
of a culture, the paradigm by which people operate, we are
struck by how powerful our insight into that organization now
is, and we can see instantly why certain things work the way
they do, why certain proposals never get bought, why change is
so difficult, why certain people leave, and so on. Few concepts
are so powerful in the degree to which they help us decipher
what may be a very opaque area. It is the search for and the occasional finding of this central insight that make it all worthwhile. Suddenly we understand an organization; suddenly we
see what makes it tick. That level of insight is worth working
for, even if, in the end, we can share it only with colleagues.

7

How Culture Forms:
Theoretical
Perspectives

One of the most mysterious aspects of organizational culture is how it originates. How do two companies with similar external environments and founders of similar origins come to have entirely different ways of operating five or ten years later? Equally mysterious is the evolution of culture and the degree to which culture at times seems to resist change. Why do some cultural elements survive even though they seem to serve no useful purpose, and why do they sometimes survive in the face of intense efforts by leaders and/or group members to change them? In order to get at these historical factors, we need some concepts and theories that tell us where to look for cultural origins and that explain cultural dynamics.

Central to this analysis will be a synthesis of group dynamics theory, leadership theory, and learning theory. *Group dynamics* and *open-systems* theory, as developed in the Lewinian framework at leadership workshops (Schein and Bennis, 1965; Bradford, Gibb, and Benne, 1964; Cooper and Alderfer,

1978; Alderfer and Cooper, 1980) and as developed at the Tavistock Institute by Bion and others in the application of psychoanalytical models to groups and organizations (Jaques, 1955; Bion, 1959; Colman and Bexton, 1975; Miller and Rice, 1967; Rioch, 1975; Wells, 1980), provides important insights on how group members interact with each other and with their leaders. I will label this area "sociodynamic" theory. Leadership theory and research give us insight into how founders, entrepreneurs, owners, and leaders create and embed their own assumptions in groups and organizations. Learning theory, especially the models dealing with cognitive learning and anxiety reduction, provides principles that help to explain why some solutions are stabilized while others disappear.

Sociodynamic Theory

Group dynamics theory—built on detailed observations of training groups, therapy groups, and working groups—has revealed underlying interpersonal and emotional processes that help to explain what we mean when we say "A number of people *share* a common view of a problem and develop a *shared* solution." We need to understand what is meant, in this context, by the concept of "sharing" and to be able to explain the learning mechanisms involved in the adoption of a solution to a problem. All definitions of culture involve the concept of shared solutions, shared understandings, and consensus; yet it is not at all clear how human sharing comes about.

Before tackling the dynamics of "sharing," let us examine some of the issues that new groups face. The distinction consistently made between external survival issues and internal integration issues has its origins in the observation that the individual entering a new group initially defines the other new members as his external environment. Each individual must survive and remain personally integrated while facing other people who make up what is initially not a cohesive group but only a collection of individuals brought together for some purpose (Schein and Bennis, 1965; Schein, 1969). The first and most important point to understand, then, is how each individual comes to feel that he is a member of the group in the first place and how each member resolves the core conflict between the wish to be enveloped by and fused with the group, thereby completely losing personal identity, and the wish to be completely autonomous and free of the group, thereby potentially becoming estranged from and losing potential membership in the group.

Individual Needs Versus Group Concerns

The individual in a social context has basically three primary needs (Schutz, 1958; Schein, 1969; McGrath, 1984):

1. *Inclusion, Identity.* Every person entering a new group needs to know whether he is "in" the group or out of the group and needs to develop a viable role or identity within the group. The viable identity that is sought is often a paradoxical "compromise" between total engulfment by the group and total estrangement from the group. Until the person experiences congruity between what he believes is expected of him and what he believes he can deliver, he will be preoccupied, anxious, and not entirely able to pay attention to the group's external tasks. Instead, his emotional energy will be channeled into a personal problem of survival in the new social situation.

2. *Control, Power, Influence.* Every person entering a new group needs a certain amount of influence and control, deriving from deeper, more primitive needs to master the environment. In a sense this need reflects the autonomy and mastery side of the core conflict, the need to feel powerful and appropriately independent of others while still retaining membership in the group.

3. *Acceptance and Intimacy.* Every person entering a new group needs to feel a certain amount of personal acceptance above and beyond the basic need for inclusion. This need reflects the other side of the core conflict, the need to belong in a deeper sense, to be engulfed by the group and to achieve the basic security that comes with that.

Insofar as these interpersonal needs reflect the basic human needs for security (inclusion), mastery of the environment (influence and control), and love (acceptance and intimacy), they operate as powerful dynamic sources of (1) anxiety and preoccupation when thwarted and (2) positive energy when in the process of being fulfilled. Every member of a new group, even the founder of the group, is struggling to fulfill his own needs in these areas, and this struggle militates initially against any coherent group action. In a sense the new group does not exist as a functioning group capable of fulfilling its mission until the members have learned that they can fulfill their individual needs to some degree by means of belonging to the group. Only then can they shift their attention to the group as a psychological object with its own identity and needs. The first and most powerful experience of "sharing" thus comes with the discovery that every member has similar feelings of anxiety and alienation.

Of course, individuals have other group identities that they bring from prior memberships: family, occupation, neighborhood, friendship groups, prior employers, and so on. But in a *new* configuration, new identities must be built and mutually accepted before the new group will develop a culture of its own. In fact, it is because individuals bring multiple prior cultural experiences and roles to any new group that problems of identity, control, and intimacy arise in the first place. If individuals faced new situations with only one role repertory and only one set of prior cultural learning, they would not experience the anxiety that comes from having to make choices in new situations.

Individual Coping Styles

Groups vary immensely in the kind of culture they develop. This variation cannot be explained by environmental factors alone because many groups with very similar environments have developed very different cultures. Instead, we must seek the ultimate explanation for these variations in a complex interaction of the personalities of leaders, members, and circumstances. Not all personality theories are equally relevant to an understanding of group phenomena. But since the emotional issues faced by members have their roots in basic human needs, we can postulate that a personality theory will be relevant to group formation to the extent that it deals with those basic common needs. Several such theories or models are reviewed in this section.

Emotional Coping Styles. The adaptation made by Wallen (1963) of basic psychoanalytical theory (Horney, 1945) provides one useful framework for this line of thinking. Wallen postulated that all of us have a basic problem in dealing with our biologically rooted feelings of aggression and love. He observed that people differ from each other in their capacity to express their aggressive feelings and their loving, tender feelings, leading to three basic types of coping styles:

1. *Sturdy Battler:* comfort in expressing aggressive, controlling feelings but discomfort with and suppression of affection. The group member using this style copes with anxiety by actively testing the interpersonal environment, by fighting, competing with, controlling, challenging, and resisting other members and especially authority figures in the attempt to sort out his own identity. Such a person would be labeled as basically "counterdependent" in the group context and as "moving against people" in Horney's terms.

2. *Friendly Helper:* comfort in expressing affection and tender feelings but discomfort with and suppression of aggression. The group member using this style copes with anxiety by creating close relationships with other members, supporting, helping, and making alliances with others, and leaning on authority in the attempt to sort out his own identity. Such a person would be labeled as basically "dependent" in the group context and as "moving toward people" in Horney's terms.

3. *Logical Thinker:* comfort with procedures, rules, and group processes that rule out the expression of either aggressive or loving emotions, based on discomfort with expressing any emotions in the group context. The group member using

this style copes either by means of withdrawing, passivity, and feigned indifference to what is going on in the group or by actively promoting nonemotional processes, such as logic, procedure, and formal rules. A person using this style seeks well-defined formal roles, and would be seen as "moving away from people" in Horney's terms.

Every person has the capacity to use each of these styles, depending on the situation, but most people develop characteristic styles on which they lean when they become anxious in the interpersonal context. If one thinks of the above styles as the three tips of a triangle, one can locate one's stylistic bias by noting where in the triangle one would characteristically fall.

How does this model help us to understand emerging group culture? First of all, it helps us to understand why a set of people coming from the same host culture would still have difficulty arriving at consensus in a new group situation. The Wallen theory assumes that members using any given style are cognitively tuned to certain categories of interpersonal information and that other categories are threatening to them.

The "sturdy battler" type is tuned toward locating in other members those who are strong and who are weak, those who can be controlled and who will be controlling, those who have authority and therefore need to be fought or watched, and those who are winning and who are losing. Sturdy battlers are threatened by too much affection, by the possibility that they will lose their ability to fight. They will, therefore, always attempt to create a group world in which one can test oneself against others and gradually determine a workable "pecking order."

The "friendly helper" type is tuned toward locating in other members those who are warm and who are cold, those who are helpful and who are not, those who are supportive and those who are threatening. Friendly helpers are threatened by too much aggression, by the possibility that they will not be accepted or liked or will be overwhelmed by feelings of hostility. They will, therefore, attempt to create a group world in which people can work closely together, be supportive, and like each other.

The "logical thinker" type is tuned toward locating in other members those who think clearly and those who are fuzzy, those who are accurate and who are inaccurate, those who are structured and who are not, and those who are oriented toward procedures and those who are not. Logical thinkers are threatened by any degree of emotionality in the group setting because they are afraid that they will be overwhelmed by their own feelings of aggression or love. They will, therefore, try to create a group world in which logic, structure, and procedure dominate, in which feelings are irrelevant and can be legislated off the agenda.

As was stated earlier, every person has the capacity for each type of emotional response and coping style, but, other things being equal, each of us tends to gravitate toward certain characteristic styles, especially when we are under tension. These styles, learned in earlier cultural settings, are then brought into new situations, where they initially are likely to cause communication problems and to slow down group formation *because each type, in the effort to create the perfect group world, will threaten each of the other types.*

If the external task demands working together, the group members gradually learn through interaction what each other's biases are and how to accommodate to them. Some members may find that they cannot get their own needs met and may leave the group. Those who remain will gradually develop common conceptual categories and a language geared to mutual understanding and acceptance. However, if a group is trying to function on a common task while members still have difficulty understanding and accepting each other's different emotional styles, it will be difficult to accomplish anything. Too much emotional energy will go into coping with interpersonal anxiety reduction.

On the other hand, variations in personal style can begin to aid the group in accomplishing its task. The group, as a working entity, will need the energy and initiative that are often supplied initially by the members who feel most comfortable being aggressive. When external demands produce stress and frustration, the group will need the emotional "glue" to stick together that is often supplied by the members who feel most comfortable with tender, supportive feelings. And the group will need the procedures, problem-solving processes, and structure that are often supplied initially by the members who most need to create structure in order to control feelings. Evidence that each style is needed comes from efforts in training workshops to create homogeneous groups and the discovery that such groups begin to differentiate themselves into the three types on their own.

One of the paradoxes and complexities of group formation is that the very things that are initially difficult for each individual member to deal with, the diversities of style, become at a later stage in the group a source of strength for certain kinds of task accomplishment. But such stylistic differences do not help to explain in a dynamic sense how group movement toward effective work and the sharing of assumptions actually takes place. The second model helps us to understand such movement.

Degrees of Intrapsychic Conflict Around Emotional Issues. Around the issues of managing aggression and managing love, one can assume that different members entering a new group situation will have different degrees of intrapsychic conflict—that is, they will be more or less "hung up" on these issues —because current situations will trigger defensive responses that worked in earlier life situations. The degree of "conflictedness" around authority issues ultimately reflects each person's experience with his own parents and the degree to which childhood feelings of dependence and counterdependence have been worked through. Similarly, the degree of "conflictedness" around intimacy issues will reflect childhood experiences of acceptance and rejection by parents and other primary groups.

Klein (1959) observed that adult behavior in groups recreates certain key elements of infant behavior vis-à-vis the mother, leading to characteristic defensive maneuvers. It is necessary to understand such maneuvers if one is to decipher some of the events that occur in groups. Specifically, the problem for the infant is that the mother is both a source of gratification (when she provides food and love) and a source of frustration (when she withholds food or love). She appears and disappears unpredictably from the infant's point of view and is therefore necessarily viewed with ambivalence. As the child's ego develops, this ambivalence is itself a source of anxiety and discomfort, since it is painful and unsafe to recognize one's own hostility. Because of the growing abstraction capacity of the human brain, the child can cognitively *split* the mother into a good mother and a bad mother. The perceived bad mother can then be repressed and her characteristics can be projected onto other people, who can then be hated. Whereas hating the mother is unsafe, hating someone else who has "bad" characteristics can be safe and even socially acceptable.

In organizational authority situations, the counterpart dynamic occurs when we feel that our boss has both good and bad aspects. Our own ambivalence toward that boss makes us anxious and uncomfortable, leading to the repression of the negative feelings, the projection of the bad qualities onto another person or boss, and the subsequent experiencing of the negative feelings toward this other person. Such a defensive maneuver is often encouraged in social institutions by defining one authority figure as the benign one, the good captain in the military, and another as the hated taskmaster, the master sergeant in the military (Jaques, 1955). In group situations this mechanism is evoked because groups are in many respects recapitulations of the "mother" in that one can be totally dependent on a group and merge oneself with others. The core conflict between being engulfed or being estranged, being too much in or too much out of the group, can be seen and felt as a symbolic recapitulation of the problem of growing independent of one's mother.

Because other group members, by virtue of their different sociological statuses and personal styles, remind us of our past relationships, they become projective screens for the unconscious fantasies and needs that are brought out in the new group situation. The roles that evolve in new group situations, therefore, reflect both the individual's own predispositions and the projections that other members make onto that individual.

The process of "getting acquainted," "testing the waters,"

and "finding one's place in the group" can now be seen as a highly complex interaction involving both conscious and unconscious elements, both rational assessments of the situation and irrational projective identifications elicited by one's own unconscious needs and the characteristics of particular other people in the group. The stereotyping that often goes on in early group meetings, seeing men as the more aggressive and women as the more affectionate members, can be understood as the result of such unconscious impulses; because the impulses are unconscious, these stereotypes are hard to break. We have all observed how quickly women in committees are assigned maintenance roles and how hard it is for them to develop aggressive, dominant roles.

Other group phenomena related to the mechanisms of splitting and projective identification are the *reciprocal* role relationships that can evolve between members. A more dominant person who is made anxious by his uncertainty represses that uncertainty and projects it onto a less dominant member. The less dominant member is made anxious by his assertive tendencies, represses them, and projects them onto the more dominant member. Now the dominant member can safely deplore the "hesitant" conduct of the less dominant one, who can reciprocate by admiring the "certainty" of the more dominant one. Each is comfortable because each is gaining what he wants out of the role relationship. Such mutual role support in problem-solving groups can lead to the suppression of necessary information and opinion—as happened, according to Janis (1972), in the decision process leading to the Bay of Pigs invasion.

The defensive mechanisms used "interactively" among group members reflect both the tendency of certain members to have certain things attributed to them and the tendency to attribute certain things on the basis of one's own conflicts. Thus, using the Schutz (1958) typology of interpersonal needs, we can identify in any new group situation those members who are conflicted around authority and will react by being either overdependent or counterdependent and those members who are conflicted over intimacy issues and will react by being either overpersonal or counterpersonal. Others in the group will be less conflicted in one or the other of these two areas, and it is they who will play the key roles in helping a group move away from an area that has produced paralysis or painful conflict. The less conflicted member produces such movement through the surfacing of implicit or tacit assumptions, which can then be tested against reality, as will be described later in the chapter.

Cognitive Styles. Variations in cognitive style arise because people grow up in different cultures, which themselves make very different assumptions about the nature of the universe, truth, human nature, and human relationships. Individuals initially vary in the cognitive assumptions they bring to a new group situation, and attempt to establish common frames of reference. This process is clearly central to understanding cultural origins in the new group.

Probably the best theory for the analysis of these phenomena is Jung's (1923) because it takes in both the cognitive and the emotional components. On the cognitive side, the key distinctions have to do with (1) the preferences a person develops for how to obtain information from the environment, the dimension of *intuition* versus *sensation,* and (2) the way that information is dealt with once it is internalized, the dimension of *thinking* versus *feeling* and the dimension of *perceiving* versus *judging.*

The *intuitive* person prefers to trust inner psychic resources for data, while the *sensing* person prefers always to rely on external data sources; the *thinking* person prefers to process data by means of logical processes and formal procedures, while the *feeling* person prefers to trust impulses and emotional responses as a basis for decisions; the *perceiving* person prefers to make decisions only after carefully examining all aspects of the situation, while the *judging* person prefers to make a decision quickly and get on with the next problem.

When we are in a new situation, we attempt to construct our social environment in accordance with our cognitive stylistic preference (McKenney and Keen, 1974; Keen, 1977; Mitroff, 1983; Srivastva and Associates, 1983). This process is initially quite unconscious because we are not likely to be aware of our own cognitive biases. Only as others frustrate us do we begin to examine how our styles vary.

The tendency to want to create an ideal "world" in accordance with one's style can be demonstrated in the workshop environment when participants are given a Jungian inventory, such as the Myers-Briggs Type Indicator (Myers, 1975), and divided into homogeneous groups on the basis of stylistic preferences. When each group is then asked to design its preferred type of organization, the different groups invariably come up with totally different designs, reflecting their own personal styles. For example, a group with members who strongly prefer to gather data by "sensing" and to process it by "thinking" will structure itself hierarchically, define clear roles, and generate time limits for everything; in contrast, a more "intuitive," "feeling" group will wish to have a low-structure, open-ended set of meetings to permit free exchange of ideas and mutual support among members. Mitroff (1983) uses this typology to develop organizational "archetypes": (1) bureaucratic (sensing/thinking), (2) matrix, R & D (intuitive/thinking), (3) familial (sensing/feeling), and (4) organic/adaptive (intuitive/feeling). Each of these types expects a different kind of "ideal" world.

Sociodynamic Issues in the Group

The theoretical strands reviewed previously emphasize what the individual brings to the group situation in the way of emotional and cognitive issues. But the group as an evolving entity can be analyzed as a total unit, and for certain purposes such an analysis is necessary to bring out some of the subtler forces in culture formation.

Work and Emotionality. In the early stages of group life, where anxieties run high, one can expect higher levels of ambivalence and projective identification, leading to regressive group "moods" or mental states. In observing therapy groups, Bion (1959) noted that the "work" of the group, the therapeutic task, could be displaced by different emotional states or moods that could sweep the whole group. The group could be at one time acting rationally and purposefully toward the accomplishment of a task, the group analogue to the Freudian "ego" functions, and at another time get overwhelmed by common feelings reflecting earlier regressive emotional states. Since the emotionally dominated, seemingly irrational behavior could not easily be explained by overt group events, Bion postulated that the group was acting "as if" something else under the surface was going on, "as if" it was making an assumption that fitted the emotional needs of the moment. Several such emotional states and their corresponding inferred basic assumptions were identified by Bion.

One such assumption is the *dependency assumption.* If the group is frustrated and unable to move forward in its primary task, a condition especially likely during the early stages of group formation, it may regress to a dependent state and act collectively "as if" the "leader" knew exactly what to do and would tell everyone how to proceed. This state is analogous to the early childhood condition of dependence on a powerful parent who always knew what to do, thus validating the assumption. The emotional state can be shared because everyone in the group has had the same childhood experience and reservoir of primitive feelings. Common feelings of dependency are thus likely to be one of the first and most important *shared feelings* in any new group.

The essence of this emotional state is the seeking of safety and security through finding one individual who will protect the group. The mechanisms of splitting and projective identification aid this process by projecting all good things onto the person to be depended on and all bad things onto a scapegoat, usually another member. If the group has a formal leader, convener, or chairman, that person may become the focus of these feelings. If the group is leaderless, it will seek a strong individual to lean on.

If such an individual is found, one has the basis of a charismatic movement or cult, where members can perpetuate their dependent state and lose themselves as individual entities by merging with the larger whole. In reality a leader of this sort is rarely available. The disappointment experienced by group members and the consequent frustration, combined with the interventions of those members who are less conflicted in this area and hence less likely to project onto the leader, sooner or later produce some form of reality test, which reveals the falseness of the tacit or unconscious assumption: "Our leader really does not know what to do and, in reality, is not the perfect being we hoped for." The disconfirmation of the assumption may be cathartic and permit the group to go back into a work mode, or it may precipitate another regressive assumption to deal with the resulting anxiety.

A second assumption observed by Bion is the *fight-flight assumption*. If dependency does not work, if the leaders keep disappointing the group members, and if the anxiety brought about by insecurity continues, an alternative emotional state may develop. This emotional state—a state of anger and panic, leading to strong anti-intellectual feelings and needs for instant action—is based on the assumption that the group must preserve and protect itself, either by actively fighting someone or by fleeing from someone (Rioch, 1975). Whereas the dependent state is characterized more by feeling lost and paralyzed, the fight-flight state is characterized more by feeling threatened and mobilized for action. In this emotional state, the collective action is primary, and the individual will be sacrificed for the good of the group. Leadership is necessary and will be sought out, but only if it helps the group take action by defining a target to be attacked or fled from. The group may act impulsively by rejecting the disappointing leader, by collectively walking out, or by some other symbolic act of challenging authority; but the action is collective, based on a common feeling, and thus may represent for the group the first and, perhaps, most important *shared action*. Once common action has been taken, the group as a group has been defined, and all members who took part in the action are, by definition, in the group as of that moment. Since the collective action is often based on aggression, even if the decision is to flee, it is likely to lead to powerful emotional learning and shape the group's future action tendencies according to how the collective action worked out.

Finally, Bion observed a *pairing assumption,* where a preoccupation with relationships among some members of the group dominated the whole group's attention. The group seemed to feel that somehow, through the pairing of two members of the group, things would get better. It was as if the group were meeting for the purpose of "reproduction"—to bring forth a new leader, savior, or messiah, or at least a new idea or plan of action that would reduce the frustration and sense of failure. Rioch (1975, p. 27) gives a good description: "When this basic assumption is operative, the other group members are not bored. They listen eagerly and attentively to what is being said. An atmosphere of hopefulness pervades the group. No actual leader is or needs to be present, but the group, through the pair, is living in the hope of the creation of a new leader, or a new thought, or something that will bring about a new life, will solve old problems, and bring Utopia or heaven or something of the sort."

This positive mood sometimes results from the catharsis and relief of having overcome the despair of dependency or the frustration of unsuccessful fight or flight. The group has done something together, proven itself capable of joint action, and is therefore in a euphoric and omnipotent mood. What distinguishes this mood from the optimism that accompanies actual work accomplishment is its hopeful, unrealistic, Pollyannish quality—things will get better somehow, someone will come along and show us the way. The mood is positive and thus keeps the group from the despair of dependence or the anger and hatred of fight-flight, but only as long as the unborn leader does not arrive. Once the new solution is seen not to work, thus dashing the basic assumption, the other feelings will return.

Underlying the pairing assumption may be a deeper assumption, identified by Turquet (1973) as the *fusion* assumption, which I would paraphrase as "We are a great group who can do anything." Implicit in this assumption is the denial of any internal differences among members, an illusion of everyone's liking everyone else, and a positive striving to merge oneself with the group, based on the euphoria resulting from some shared action.

If the group is dominated by either the fusion or the pairing assumption, it is again vulnerable to unrealistic aspirations. At this point reality will be injected by those members who are less conflicted around intimacy issues. By bringing the implicit assumption to the surface and exposing it to a reality test, the group can face up to the fact that it is not perfect, is not homogeneous, and may not be capable of creating a perfect solution. Reality then means getting back to work on the painful task of group building and addressing whatever the external primary task is.

If the group is not in one of the emotional states described, if it is acting on the assumption that it has met to work and is able to work, it is outwardly directed and reality oriented. If it goes into one of the emotional states, it becomes inwardly directed and dominated by regressive fantasies. In such a state of consciousness, the group always tries to seduce the formal leader away from the primary task or work functions of the group, and the leader must then be sensitive to two potential traps: (1) allowing himself to be seduced into the emotional state or (2) trying to get the group to work when, in fact, it is not able to work. One of the most difficult roles that leaders fulfill is to deal with this dilemma and to help the group out of regressive emotional states.

Because Bion's categories deal with regressive emotional states, one may question whether they apply in practice to groups other than the therapy groups with which he dealt. In working with various groups in organizations, I have observed the same phenomena as Bion describes, especially in response to feelings of lack of accomplishment or failure to meet targets; and it is clear that total organizations can develop such common moods if environmental conditions produce feelings of threat, frustration, and anger.

Stages of Group Growth. Some group theories concentrate on successive stages (Bennis and Shepard, 1956; Bradford, Gibb, and Benne, 1964; Tuckman, 1965; Tuckman and Jensen, 1977; Durkin, 1981); others view the group as perpetually dealing with its underlying emotional issues but not necessarily in a set sequence or evolutionary developmental form (Bion, 1959; Cohen and Smith, 1976; Hare, 1976; Gustafson and Cooper, 1979; Wells, 1980; McGrath, 1984). Both views have validity in that certain issues seem to take priority in the formation of the group, but all the issues continue to act simultaneously once they have surfaced, even if they have been

dealt with. Any given issue is capable of resurfacing and dominating the group's attention at any stage. Group life is therefore
better represented by a *paradoxical* model, in which oppositions
and conflicts are perpetually present, than by a *conflict resolution* model, in which conflicts are worked through to a final
solution (Watzlawick, Weakland, and Fisch, 1974; Madanes,
1981). The stages and their attendant core conflicts can be described as follows:

> *Stage 1: Confrontation of dependency/authority issue.*
> The group, in coming together as a group, must deal
> with the issue of who will lead; who will have how
> much authority, power, and influence; and who will be
> dependent on whom. The group must resolve this issue
> in order to be effective in solving its external environ-
> ment problems and to create a comfortable internal en-
> vironment, as previously noted. The nature of the reso-
> lution forms the deepest layer of cultural assumptions.
> Therefore, even if the authority issue resurfaces later,
> there is already a prior set of solutions available to be
> tested.
>
> *Stage 2: Confrontation of intimacy, role differentiation,
> peer relationship issues.* If the group is feeling success-
> ful in its first efforts to deal with the authority issue, it
> is likely to fall into the "fusion" assumption and to
> make euphoric and unrealistic assumptions about how
> good a group it is and how much all the members love
> each other. To surmount this assumption—to develop a
> realistic appraisal of who likes whom, who can accept
> whom, who can do what kinds of work on behalf of
> the group—is a formidable task that now will occupy
> the group through successive levels of confrontation
> throughout the remainder of its life. Assumptions gov-
> erning peer relationships will be the next major cul-
> tural layer to be formed.
>
> *Stage 3: Confrontation of creativity/stability issues.* As
> the group learns to deal with its problems, to accom-
> plish its mission, and to build an internal system that is

safe and comfortable, it begins to face the problem of institutionalization and bureaucratization. When everything was a first effort, creativity and innovation were valued; but as success mounts, creativity can become itself a source of disruption and anxiety. The paradox now is that the group cannot succeed without continued ability to create and innovate, but neither can it feel comfortable with abandoning old solutions in the service of innovation. The cultural assumptions already adopted now can become a constraint and barrier to further growth. The dilemma at this stage is how to maintain adaptiveness without feeling too threatened internally.

Stage 4: Confrontation of survival/growth issues. As the group matures and continues to interact with a dynamic external environment, it will sooner or later discover whether its culture can provide the solutions to new survival problems. And at that stage the question arises of whether the group serves important functions and should survive or whether it should allow itself to die, or be terminated, so that a more adaptive set of solutions can be created by a new group.

Catalytic Marker Events or Critical Incidents. How do basic assumptions become explicit, how are new insights about the group gained by members, how do new common understandings come to be created, and how are norms formed? If one carefully reconstructs a group's history, one finds that all these things happen around events that are experienced in retrospect as "critical," in the sense that they involved high levels of emotionality and/or clear cognitive redefinitions. Such events are later remembered as marker events in the history of the group. These critical moments may not even be noticed at the time, but they can be reconstructed historically and the feelings associated with them can be resurrected. A given incident or event is initially perceived as "critical" when it arouses feeling or new insight in the group members, but the degree to which it actually *becomes* "critical" in the history of the group depends on the kind of response that the group makes to the event and the longer-range consequences of that response. Thus, major obstacles, sources of anxiety, threats, and opportunities provide the emotional stimulus, and what the group does about the situation becomes the critical or marker event, especially if the response is successful—that is, if it solves a problem or reduces anxiety.

Group members often forget such critical events and then cannot reconstruct how things came to be the way they are; but once the event is brought back into memory, it is often captured and stabilized in the form of a story about the group or some of its members. It then becomes a legitimizing piece of the culture, both to explain to members how things came to be and to teach the implicit or explicit lessons to new members. One of the roles of leadership is to capture group history in this way and to state it for the group in a form that makes it possible for group members to understand themselves (Pfeffer, 1981).

This point was illustrated in the early history of the engineering-based Action Company. Implicitly it was well understood that the engineers in the company were the high-status people and that finance and administration were merely service roles. But no one could articulate clearly how the norms around these roles had been developed until a group of us pieced together some of the critical incidents in the company's history. One such incident concerned the engineer who had to travel on short notice to the West Coast to fix a computer, and submitted a bill for a suitcase and some clothes on his expense account. When the accounting department refused to pay the bill, the engineer reported its action to his boss, who brought it up at a meeting. As a result, the senior division manager severely chastised the accounting department for its short-term bureaucratic thinking.

In the Action Company, the emphasis on being totally responsible and thinking for oneself became an implicit norm as a result of many incidents where managers overtly and publicly punished subordinates who were not completely on top of their own job or who acted thoughtlessly. What made such actions "critical incidents" is the fact that they often occurred in meetings where many others were present and that the criticism was often accompanied by fairly high levels of emotion.

As a result of early efforts to stabilize the group environment and make it safe for all members, norms and standards arise and, ultimately, are consensually accepted and enforced. These norms and standards form one building block of what will become the culture of the group if the group exists long enough and has enough common critical experience. Such standards will usually focus on the underlying issues of inclusion (boundaries), authority, intimacy, and roles.

To understand how norms arise in the first place, one must be able to reconstruct the history of the group. Usually one will find that the norms arose from marker events or critical incidents. That is, in response to a dilemma confronting the group, someone initiated a position or line of thought or stated a value; the rest of the group ratified that response through overt agreement or silence; and the response solved the problem. One of the things that make norm formation nearly invisible is that much of the group ratification occurs through silence. That is, no one disagrees overtly; hence, the assumption is made that everyone agrees, and the norm is on its way to becoming stable and taken for granted. The two incidents reported above illustrate how overt reaction to some behavior sets a direction and creates a norm. In both of those companies, the silent ratification process was also highly visible in that managers learned through the absence of response from their boss or peers that they were acting in accordance with the correct norms.

An initial assessment of the strength and complexity of a group's "culture" can then be obtained if one looks at that group's norms—their number, stability, and interconnectedness. The critical events that the group has to deal with provide opportunities for testing whether the norm is operating and, if so, become the basis for strengthening the underlying assumptions that support the norms. For example, to the extent that employees in the Action Company are rewarded for thinking for themselves, even if that involves occasional insubordination, they will strengthen their unconscious implicit assumption that the individual is the ultimate source of creativity and action in the organization.

If a group has had too short or uneventful a history, it will also have very little of what we are defining here as "culture," even though each individual member may have strong cultural assumptions based on his other group identities. In a young organization, one will therefore be more likely to find cultural diversity, or pockets of culture where interaction has been high and critical incidents have provided the basis for norm formation and testing in subgroups.

Shared Understanding. "Shared" understanding means that the members of the group recognize a particular feeling, experience, or activity *as common.* That presumes at least a common communication system, though it can be nonverbal, in which signals mean the same thing to each member (Van Maanen, 1979b). Given the common communication system, what then produces the feeling or experience of sharing can be any of the following kinds of group events:

1. *Common Anxieties:* the empathic discovery early in the life of the group that other members have the same anxieties and tensions as the new member.
2. *Common Emotional Responses:* the discovery of common emotional responses to some highly provoking external stimulus, usually a strong external threat. The strong bonds that arise in wartime probably result from the intense common responses to the anxieties felt by people under threat.
3. *Common Overt Action:* joint activity to deal with the emotionally provoking situation. Such joint activity physically demonstrates the concrete boundaries of the group, since one must either participate or not. If the physical activity is emotionally involving as well and members recognize common emotional responses in each other, the experience of sharing is strengthened. If the members must help each other in the activity and thereby demonstrate commitment to each other, that also strengthens the experience of sharing. Thus, one thinks of the powerful effects of joint

physical ordeals, dangerous safaris, and other activities that require cooperative effort to be successful.

4. *Common Emotional Release:* joint activities that have symbolic meaning and emotional release associated with them. Such activities—for instance, joint sacrifices, ritual hunting and killing of outsiders, and scapegoating—introduce a still greater level of felt "sharing." If the joint activities involve the emotional release of normally inhibited and possibly inappropriate feelings, such as in a lynch mob, then the shared bond is not only in the action and the feeling at the time but in the later feeling of shared guilt and shame. Though the feelings would be less intense, the joint experience of winning a sale over a competitor or succeeding in a very risky business venture would be functionally equivalent.

5. *Common Emotional Regression:* joint emotional release or expression in such activities as drinking bouts, dancing, singing, games, and athletic contests. These activities increase the feeling of sharing because there has been a joint release from social restraints, a mutually licensed regression to earlier and more intense feelings, and, therein, a greater degree of self-disclosure to others, which now makes all the members more vulnerable to each other. Thus, interdependence feelings come to rest not only on what we have shown we can do *for* each other in joint problem-solving activities but on what we can do *to* each other by virtue of what we have learned about each other's more private selves.

Sharing is a complex multifaceted process that rests on many kinds of events in the group's life. When we define a cultural element as a *shared* consensus on some issue, we are presuming a long and intense history of events of the kind described above, not a superficial agreement. When people with different interpersonal styles, emotional makeups, and cognitive styles interact, they cannot build shared meanings out of the immediate interaction. It takes time and common experience to build a communication system in which all parties have the same sense of the "meaning" of events.

Leadership Theory

Leadership theory is a vast domain, much of which is not relevant to the issues of concern here. However, studies that have attempted to understand the relationship of the leader to the group and the effect of a leader's personality and style on group formation are highly relevant to the understanding of how cultures form and evolve.

Leadership and Group Tasks. Most group and leadership theories develop distinctions parallel to the internal and external group issues discussed in Chapter Three. Specifically, they distinguish between external task-oriented leadership functions and internal group-oriented ones. For example, Benne and Sheats (1948) classified leadership functions as *task* functions ("initiating," "giving information," "giving opinions," "summarizing," and "testing for consensus") and *group building and maintenance* functions ("supporting," "harmonizing," "setting and testing standards," and "gate keeping"—that is, controlling the communication flow inside the group). Bales (1950; Bales and Cohen, 1979), in his extensive experimental studies of small groups, derived *task* functions and *socioemotional* functions, and he observed that different leaders fulfilled these two functions. This finding suggests that given individuals in leadership roles might be more predisposed and able to help the group in one or the other area and that, therefore, most groups would need more than one kind of leadership.

In the Ohio State leadership studies (Hemphill, 1950; Stogdill and Coons, 1957; Fleishman, 1973; Bass, 1981), two basic dimensions of leadership were observed: (1) *initiating structure* (creating and managing external task activity) and (2) *consideration* (paying attention to and helping to manage internal relationships). Similarly, Fiedler (1967) distinguished between leaders who see great differences in task effectiveness among their subordinates (*task orientation*) and leaders who see their subordinates as very similar (*relationship orientation*).

In the Michigan studies (Likert, 1961, 1967), a distinction was made between *production*-centered and *relationship*-centered first-line supervisors, and this distinction is reflected in Blake's "managerial grid" model as two dimensions—concern for *production* and concern for *people*—along which a given leader can place himself (Blake and Mouton, 1964).

In longitudinal studies of the development of managers (Schein, 1978), young managers noted that they did not have the self-confidence to aspire to general management jobs until they had acquired *three* kinds of competence: (1) *analytical competence,* to recognize and formulate problems to be worked on (the equivalent of external task concern); (2) *interpersonal competence,* to build and maintain various kinds of relationships and groups; and (3) *emotional competence,* to handle the emotional demands of the managerial role itself.

What all this means is that one cannot separate the process of leadership from the process of building culture, that the very issues identified as the problems around which culture is eventually evolved or learned are the issues identified as leadership functions in most theories. One might go so far as to say that a *unique* function of "leadership," as contrasted with "management" or "administration," is the *creation and management of culture.* At the same time, all leaders are influenced by their own prior cultural learning. Furthermore, once leaders have created a culture, they may well become constrained by that culture and find that they no longer can lead the group into new and creative avenues. A complex interplay of creative and constraining forces operates both inside the leaders and in the group. The resolution of such potentially conflicting forces becomes, then, one of the central tasks of leadership.

Leadership and Group Style. The assumptions of the leaders or founders of a group, the authority relationships formed in the group, and the manner in which leaders and members interact at an emotional level will determine both the evolutionary stages of the group and its cultural "style." Sometimes such stylistic biases, by virtue of their extremity or inappropriateness to external environmental conditions, could be labeled maladaptive or "neurotic," in the sense that they become self-defeating. In training or therapy groups, the group leaders are typically trained to be aware of their own emotional predispositions to lead the group into inappropriate behavior and to fall into regressive group moods. In groups that are formed for the explicit purpose of fulfilling a task, however, a danger exists that the founders/leaders will not be aware of emotional traps or their own emotional biases. Thus, they might precipitate emotional crises without even being aware of it, and not know how to react to the crisis once it has been precipitated. For example, some entrepreneurs, because of their self-confidence and self-centeredness, unwittingly encourage high levels of dependence among their subordinates but are unprepared to deal realistically with such dependence. If they disappoint their subordinates and precipitate a fight-or-flight reaction, such leaders may be unprepared for the level of anger and resistance that they then encounter from their subordinates. Such disappointment is almost certain to occur for at least two reasons: (1) The leader cannot possibly live up to the fantasies that members have about powerful parental authorities. (2) The leader will inevitably expect more than a passive-dependent response from subordinates and, when they do respond in this fashion, will urge them to behave more independently—thereby making them even more anxious, angry, and confused. The more he threatens them, the more likely they are to regress.

Studies of the psychodynamic makeup of leaders also reveal that the defensive biases of leaders can result ultimately in "neurotic" organizations, ones that cannot accurately assess external and internal realities and that function, therefore, on partial data, projections, and fantasies (Zaleznik, 1974; Zaleznik and Kets de Vries, 1975; Kets de Vries and Miller, 1984; Maccoby, 1976; Levinson, 1968; Jaques, 1951, 1955; Bion, 1959; Wells, 1980). The most thorough analysis of how leader/subordinate relationships can lead to such neurotic adaptations is provided in Kets de Vries and Miller's typology:

1. The *paranoid* style, based on pervasive suspicion and mistrust of others, leads to a preoccupation with intelligence and control activities, centralized power, a reactive mode of

developing strategy, high vigilance both externally and internally, an emphasis on diversification, and an internal climate of cynicism, conservatism, and caution.

2. The *compulsive* style, based on fear of being at the mercy of unexpected events and not in control of things that may affect the organization, leads to a compulsive preoccupation with detail, perfectionism, a heavy emphasis on ritualized and formalized controls and procedures, formal policies, tight hierarchies, carefully thought-out and rigidly implemented strategies, a fixation on established activities (to the detriment of innovation), and a climate of dominance and submission.

3. The *dramatic* style, based on an inordinate need to gain attention and to impress the people who count most, leads to narcissistic preoccupation, excessive expression of emotion, a craving for activity and excitement, exploitation of others, superficial and often bold decisions, high risk taking, unclear organizational structures or processes that unleash constant change programs, and a climate of ambiguity.

4. The *depressive* style, based on a feeling of hopelessness and lack of self-confidence, leads to a fatalistic passivity, extreme conservatism, and a tendency to adapt bureaucratically to those parts of the environment that are most stable and least threatening. There is generally a leadership vacuum and a feeling of guilt and self-blame for whatever misfortunes the organization may experience.

5. The *schizoid* style, based on feelings that the world does not offer much in the way of satisfaction and that most interactions will eventually not work out, leads to detached aloofness and, in essence, a leadership vacuum. The leader neither leads nor delegates, but detaches himself, feels estranged from the organization, and lets the political struggles that result run their course. No concerted product market strategy can develop, and the firm muddles through in fits and starts.

These extreme neurotic or pathological types illustrate clearly how the emerging culture of a group will be shaped by the personality of the founder of that group (Schein, 1983). Inasmuch as founders do have personality biases, such biases provide a diagnostic basis for deciphering the organizational culture that eventually arises in a given organization. Further illustrations of how the assumptions of founders become embedded in their organization are provided in Chapters Nine and Ten.

Learning Theory

The final theoretical strand to weave into this complex tapestry is learning theory applied to group phenomena. What can we say about how groups learn cognitions, feelings, and behaviors? Underlying everything that has been said so far is the proposition that culture is *learned* and can be understood only in the context of an evolutionary, dynamic learning model. But the learning process is complex because it is groups rather than individuals that are doing the learning, and it is cognitions and emotions, not only overt behavior patterns, that are learned. Since group members are capable of experiencing many different forms of anxiety, learning and defensive behavior occur at many levels. And, as we will see, the paradox of cultural learning is that, while culture reduces one type of anxiety, it often increases other types.

Structurally, two types of learning mechanisms must be clearly distinguished because they have different consequences for the stability of what is learned: (1) *positive problem-solving situations,* which lead to positive reinforcement if the attempted solution works; and (2) *anxiety-avoidance situations,* which produce positive reinforcement if the anxiety is successfully reduced and if the painful consequences that produced the anxiety are prevented. In practice these two types of situations are intertwined, but they have different motivational bases, different underlying learning mechanisms, and different consequences (Solomon, Kamin, and Wynne, 1953; Solomon and Wynne, 1953; Mednick, 1964).

Positive Problem Solving. In the positive problem-solving situation, learning outcomes are "rewarding" in the sense that they reflect the achievement of a goal or the removal of a felt "lack," as in the case of finding food or water if one is hungry or thirsty. If a group is trying to develop a new and better product or to increase sales or market share, and it finds that something "works," then that something has been "positively reinforced" and will tend to be repeated the next time the same problem comes up. A "solution" can be overt behavior, a way of perceiving or thinking about a problem, a set of feelings, a set of beliefs, or new assumptions about some aspect of the world. Any or all of these categories of responses can be positively reinforced if they solve the problem.

For example, in a large chemical company the development of a new product required the complex coordination of marketing information, manufacturing skills, and R & D efforts. The traditional assumption in this organization was that these functions operated sequentially, but it had become clear after several product failures that such a process would no longer work because R & D was not familiar enough with what the market really needed. Yet the R & D department believed that its insight was sufficient and that it did not really have to pay attention to marketing data. In discussions with consultants, the "experimental" idea was proposed to construct a new product development "task force" that would include senior people from all of the functions. This group was defined as a "temporary system," which circumvented the threat to turf that a more permanent cross-functional organization would have represented. The task force was charged with developing several new products by considering simultaneously the marketing, manufacturing, and R & D implications. The group met for six months and was highly successful in launching several new products in a more coordinated fashion, which reinforced not only the task force as an overt behavioral solution but also the "concept" or assumption that functions could work productively together without threatening each other or wasting time. Furthermore, the success of this mechanism introduced a new organizational assumption: that "temporary systems" can solve permanent organizational problems.

Once a workable solution to a given problem has been found, it is likely to be repeated the next time the same problem comes up. Solutions that no longer work are given up quickly because their failure is highly visible to the group; but, paradoxically, solutions that may work only part of the time may be clung to longest (what Skinnerian learning theory calls partial or random reinforcement). In other words, if something has worked *some* of the time, but we cannot figure out exactly what causal factors determined any given instance of success or failure, it will continue to be tried after it ceases to work altogether for much longer than something that worked *all* the time. The past history suggests that it *might* work again, even though it is no longer working, and group members can remember other times when the solution had ceased to work for a time and then began to work again.

This learning mechanism is akin to what we experience when we learn a new physical skill or a sport—a gradual buildup of complex physical, emotional, and cognitive responses that become part of the group's actual repertory of "strengths" or "skills" and are incorporated into the group's ideology as positive elements of its self-image. Even though the solution initially may be discovered in a single trial through insight, the development of a *shared* insight requires repeated trials and successes. The culture, then, includes the learned group repertory of capacities to solve problems—the crafts, technologies, and arts that the group develops. Another part of this learned repertory will be the shared cognitions that the group develops about itself, its ideology, its rationalizations, its world views. Cultures come to include learned self-images based on past history: "We know how to engineer and produce good products." "We know how to sell, because we have learned to understand our customers." "We really know how to motivate people and get high-quality production." "We know how to raise capital and manage our financial resources." "Our marketing department really understands what products customers will need in the future." "Our research labs will come up with a stream of good products."

When such responses cease to work, when the environment no longer provides positive reinforcement either for the actual skills or for the ideology supporting them, the data are clearly visible to the group, even if the group chooses in a defensive way not to pay attention to the data. Such defensive denial of available information results from the other major learning mechanism—anxiety avoidance.

Pain and Anxiety Reduction. The other major learning mechanism is avoidance learning, where the reinforcement comes from the successful reduction of pain or the lessening of anxiety, which is the anticipatory response prior to pain. That is, we learn to perceive, think, feel, and behave in ways which prevent situations from recurring that have been painful in the past or which are intrinsically anxiety provoking because they produce uncertainty or cognitive overload.

Anxiety avoidance involves first of all a different motivational basis. Instead of positive goal-oriented tension and mobilization of effort, anxiety involves feelings of dread (of being threatened from known or unknown sources) and varying degrees of cognitive disorientation (of not knowing what is going on or what is ahead). Whereas problem-solving efforts mobilize attention on the problem, anxiety-based learning cannot be focused clearly if the source of the anxiety is not known. The individual or group is forced into a more random kind of trial-and-error learning, with less predictability of what will, in fact, reduce the anxiety.

Second, avoidance learning is often *one*-trial learning. Once something works, it will be repeated indefinitely, even if the source of pain is no longer active. Such a mechanism is the basis of most phobias, since the person may learn simply to avoid the situations that produce the anxiety and may never learn whether or not the actual danger persists. One can imagine a group counterpart, the development of a group phobia. For example, a unit of a large consumer-goods company introduced a new product that failed badly. The company not only lost a lot of money on this product introduction but experienced a great deal of emotional pain because the failure violated its self-image of competence. The managers identified with the decisions experienced *pain* at the time and experienced *anxiety* subsequently when a similar product was proposed. Such anxiety was itself painful, and the best way of reducing it was to refuse ever again to consider the introduction of that kind of product.

Once this cognitive response had been learned, it was

automatically reinforced by the absence of anxiety and pain in relation to that product area, which, of course, kept that group of managers from trying such products ever again. The problem is that if the organization does not try again, it cannot discover whether the original tacit assumption that "We are no good in that area" is correct. Other parts of the organization were, in fact, building up skill in that area, and the marketplace became more benign; but as long as the group that experienced the original trauma remained in control, it was not possible even to discuss the issue because that immediately brought up too much anxiety.

To give another example of how the two learning mechanisms differ, if a company has learned that an increase in its advertising budget always leads to an increase in sales (a positive problem-solving mechanism), it will discover immediately if and when such a relationship ceases to hold. The lack of increase in sales will be *visible*, whatever the cause may be. On the other hand, if a company has learned to increase its advertising budget because it once lost a major customer to a competitor through insufficient advertising (avoidance learning), it will get anxious whenever anyone proposes to reduce advertising expenditures and will "play it safe" by keeping such expenditures high. In avoidance learning the company has no way of testing whether or not it would lose customers with decreases in advertising, because such a test would be emotionally too painful. Thus, all rituals, patterns of thinking or feeling, beliefs, and tacit assumptions about oneself and the environment that were learned originally as ways of avoiding painful situations are going to be very stable, even if the causes of the original pain are, in fact, no longer present. Just as we can label such learned behavior as "defense mechanisms" in the individual personality, we can think of parts of a group's culture as being "social defense mechanisms" (Jaques, 1955; Menzies, 1960; DeBoard, 1978).

Young groups learn all kinds of things about themselves and their environment that may have been appropriate at one stage in their development but are not appropriate any longer. Some of that learning will be based on the assumptions of the founders and the interaction between the founder's unconscious playing out of his parental feelings and the group's unconscious playing out of its childhood feelings with respect to the founder as a symbolic parental figure. The realistic anxiety in the group situation is then enhanced by the further anxiety that is transferred by individual members from their own individual background.

Types of Anxiety

Primary Existential Anxiety. The ultimate source of anxiety for a human being is cognitive overload and/or an inability to decipher and categorize the multitude of stimuli impinging on the senses (Hebb, 1954). It is hard to imagine how traumatic it is if one truly cannot figure out at the basic perceptual level what is going on or if one is overloaded with stimuli to the point where one cannot react reliably to them. One level of primary existential anxiety, then, is related to the external survival task—what we might label *cognitive* anxiety.

Basic survival depends on the ability to categorize and predict environmental events—to sort out what is food, what is dangerous, and so on. How humans originally learned language and categories is not really known; but when they enter new situations where they do not know the language or the culture, deep levels of anxiety are easily aroused.

Humans also are more capable than other organisms of tolerating ambiguity, and they seek stimulation and novelty; but, as studies of infants make clear, attention shifts to the novel and unfamiliar only when "most of the objects, persons, and places encountered have become recognizable, and the infant has acquired an expectation that things 'should be recognizable' " (Hunt, 1979, p. 122). The human system appears not to tolerate either underload or overload. So one must always think of "optimal levels" of discrepancy for the functioning of the nervous system (Piaget, 1947). Paradoxically, what makes culture in all its complexity *possible* at all is the huge range of alternatives that the human mind can process. On the other hand, what makes culture as a stable system of cognitions, feelings, and behaviors absolutely *necessary* is the need to protect the human mind from overload, ambiguity, and uncertainty (Fox, 1979).

When a new organization is formed, the new members do not typically experience primary existential anxiety, because all of them bring to the group a common language and cultural categories based on the cultures in which they grew up. But as the organization begins to develop, one can see flare-ups of severe anxiety as different members discover that behind their common language lie vastly different assumptions about the world and how to operate in it. As people become frustrated over basic communication inabilities or breakdowns, they often lapse into regressive states, such as those described by Bion (1959), and these basic, deep levels of anxiety may be fueling the emotional responses we witness in the group.

As the members of a group learn new language categories reflecting their own experience, they can reduce anxiety. In fact, the new categories may manifest some of the existential anxieties but permit the group to distance itself from those anxieties by isolating the feeling from the symbolic content. As Hirsch and Andrews (1983) have shown, for example, the language of corporate mergers and takeovers reflects directly the underlying issues of aggression and love (marriages of two companies, matchmaking, battles for control, shootouts, and the like).

Basic existential anxiety occurs not only around external survival issues but also around the internal problems of social survival—whether or not one is included in the group and how one manages the balance between commitment to the group and to oneself. Such *social* anxiety is based ultimately on the feelings one brings from one's own childhood and family group, where one had to learn the rules of the game to be accepted, included, and loved. The conflict between self-seeking and loyalty to the group is intrinsic to the human condition, and we all have to learn how to be individualistic without being destructive of the group. Each group develops its own assumptions about the ultimately correct solution to this problem. But if and when such rules cease to solve the problem, the social anxiety that is unleashed is basic and primitive.

To illustrate to ourselves what this kind of anxiety feels like, we must reconstruct our feelings when we first entered a new school or a new organization, or when we entered a new culture where the rules of status were unknown to us (Schein, 1964, 1978; Louis, 1980). Until one has learned the basic cues of what is expected and how to handle different situations, there is an inevitable and deep source of tension and uncertainty. If there are no rules because the organization is in a formative stage, such tensions will be shared. The group's members then will make strong efforts to stabilize and routinize the situation by inventing rules of behavior and consensually committing themselves to these rules through both problem-solving and avoidance-learning mechanisms.

As psychoanalytical theories have shown, anxiety often is produced when our own instinctual impulses threaten to overwhelm us and make us do things that are dangerous to ourselves and others. The stability of the rules on how to handle one's impulses and feelings provides the opportunity to "borrow" the strength of the society via its shared rules. Culture, in this sense, also helps us defend ourselves against dangerous and powerful inner impulses. Evidence that cultural learning reduces anxiety can be found in the Hawthorne studies, where the worker norms of restriction of output were supported by a vague fear that if output increased "something bad would happen," even though no one could remember any specific historical events (Homans, 1950). Similarly, in the Tavistock studies of changing from short-wall to long-wall coal-mining technologies, the long-wall method was strongly resisted because it destroyed the close relationships between miners. Such relationships had become institutionalized because they reduced the basic anxiety to which miners were constantly exposed in their physically dangerous jobs (Trist and Bamforth, 1951).

Perhaps the most relevant evidence comes from Menzies' (1960) study of why hospital nurses tended to behave in a distant and bureaucratic fashion toward patients and why the nurses were rotated frequently. Neither patients nor nurses seemed to like the system, and there were many complaints that the quality of nursing care was undermined by the bureaucratic and rotational systems. Yet efforts to change the system consistently failed. Careful observation and interviewing suggested that the rules of impersonality grew up as a *defense* against the anxiety that would be unleashed if nurses developed close relationships with or feelings for patients who were severely and terminally ill. The apparently arbitrary, inhuman, and sometimes even ineffective nursing practices were, in fact, necessary for the hospital to function at all. The culture of this nursing service was functioning as a *social defense* against anxiety, performing for the group what individual defense mechanisms do for the individual (Jaques, 1955).

Secondary Role-Related Anxiety. Certain roles and tasks performed in societies and organizations entail risk and physical danger. These roles and tasks—such as flying, high steel construction, and deep-sea diving—can be thought of as sources of secondary or role-related anxiety. There are role-related sources of anxiety in most occupations, and some of the more ritualized aspects of occupational behavior are probably learned avoidance mechanisms. For example, in some organizations the compulsive tracking of certain financial data can be viewed as a defense against the anxiety of losing financial control. Such anxieties cannot always be clearly differentiated from the primary anxieties, since current known dangers can also trigger unconscious fears. However, members of an organization can more readily confront secondary anxieties and test the reality of how much risk or danger there is in trying a new response; the dangers are known, can be compensated for, and can be minimized. In contrast, primary anxiety cannot be reduced except by cultural solutions that serve as avoidance mechanisms.

Tertiary Anxiety. All living systems experience the unanticipated consequences of their own behavior and coping. Tertiary anxiety refers to the pain and consequent anxiety that derive from the very mechanisms designed to avoid primary and secondary anxiety. Thus, in Menzies' (1960) study of the nurses, the frequent rotation of nurses across wards ensured that no close relationships would form with patients, but such rotation also resulted in an inability on the part of the nurses to be effective. They were never on one ward long enough to get real feedback on their own performance, and they felt guilty about the impersonal treatment that they were giving to patients because it violated some of their professional ideals. But if proposals were made to spend more time with given patients, primary anxieties were stimulated, resulting in a paradoxical "Catch-22" situation, in which no matter what they did they would be anxious.

Organizations develop such seemingly contradictory and inconsistent practices because the cultural learning occurs at different stages of evolution, and later learning often contradicts earlier learning. If one is to understand such contradictions as a way of helping to reduce their dysfunctional effects, one must undertake the historical reconstruction that would expose the level and type of anxiety involved in the original learning. The earliest learning is the most likely to deal with primary anxiety, and thus is likely to be most stable. The coal miners studied by Trist and Bamforth (1951) accepted the long-wall technology only after they were able to rebuild social relationships to reduce their primary anxiety within the new technology, and the intervention of the change agents had to facilitate such learning.

Another reason for dysfunctional consequences is that groups may learn new solutions on the basis of "satisficing" (Simon, 1960). Chibnik (1981) points out that cultural innovation resulting from a period of turmoil often ends up being minimally adaptive, solving the short-run problem and not forcing too much change all at once. The partial solution then may be retained because it reduces the primary anxiety of uncertainty. For example, the typewriter keyboard in use today is apparently far from optimal, from either a technical or a human optimal ing point of view; yet attempts to introduce a more optimal keyboard have consistently failed. Tertiary anxiety is thus a source of motivation for cultural change but is constrained by the defensive resistance that is mobilized by primary anxiety.

Conclusion

Culture has been defined as the outcome of *group* learning. When a number of people simultaneously face a problematic situation and have to work out a solution together, we have the basic situation for culture formation. The process involves a *shared* problem definition and a *shared* recognition that something invented actually works *and continues to work.* The initial ability to share does involve prior cultural learning and understanding, but the *new* shared experience begins the formation of a new culture, which then becomes a characteristic of that particular group of people.

In this chapter I have tried to show that theories and findings about sociodynamics, leadership, and the learning process are essential to an understanding of culture formation. These theories are the basic building blocks for understanding how culture comes to be in the first place and, eventually, for understanding how culture evolves and changes.

I have been deliberately abstract in order to summarize a variety of relevant points of view and models. In the next several chapters, I will give more concrete illustrations from training-group situations and newly founded organizations to show how some of these mechanisms may work in practice.

8

Observing Culture Emerge in Small Groups

To examine how culture actually begins, how a group learns to deal with its external and internal environment and develops assumptions that then get passed on to new members, we need to analyze group situations where such events are actually observable. The bulk of this chapter will therefore deal with data from my own experience in running training groups for the National Training Laboratories and various companies, supplemented by observations made in small groups within organizations during my consulting activities (Bradford, Gibb, and Benne, 1964; Schein and Bennis, 1965; Schein, 1969). In the next chapter, I will extrapolate to the organization and report on observations made in the wider organizational context.

In making a detailed analysis of small groups, I am not implying that group phenomena can be automatically treated as models for organizational phenomena. Organizations, as we will see in the next chapter, bring in additional levels of complexity and new phenomena that are not visible in the small group. On the other hand, if we look at organizations in an evolutionary sense, we must realize that all organizations started as small groups and continue to function in part through various small groups within them. So the understanding of culture formation in small groups also is necessary to understanding how culture may evolve in the large organization through small-group sub-cultures and through the interplay of small groups within the organization.

Group Formation Through Originating Events

All groups start with some kind of "originating event": (1) an environmental accident (for instance, a sudden threat occurring in a random crowd and requiring a common response) or (2) a decision by an "originator" to bring a group of people together for some purpose or (3) an advertised event or common experience that has attracted a number of individuals. Human relations training groups start in the third mode: a number of people come together to participate in a one- or two-week workshop for the advertised purpose of learning more about themselves, groups, and leadership (Bradford, Gibb, and Benne, 1964; Schein and Bennis, 1965). The workshops are typically held in a geographically remote, isolated location and require full, round-the-clock participation.

The staff of the workshop, usually one trainer per ten to fifteen participants, have typically met for several days to plan the basic structure of lectures, group meetings, focused "exercises" designed to bring out certain points about leadership and group behavior, and free time. The staff members start out with their own assumptions, values, and behavior patterns in initiating the groups and therefore will bias the culture that is formed. But the culture is really built in the T (training) group, the key component of every workshop. The T group consists of ten to fifteen people who will meet for four to eight hours every day with one or two staff members. Because such groups typically develop distinct cultures within a matter of days, what goes on in these groups will be the focus of this chapter.

When the group first comes together, the most fundamental issue facing it as a whole is "What are we really here for? What is our task?" At the same time, each individual is facing the basic social survival issues identified in the previous chapters: "Will I be included in this group?" "Will I have a role to play?" "Will my needs to influence others be met?" "Will we reach a level of intimacy that meets my needs?" As the group gathers in its appointed space, various participants, coming to terms with the new situation, will display their own coping style. Some will silently await events; some will form immediate alliances with others; and some will begin to assert themselves by telling anyone who cares to listen that they know how to deal with this kind of situation.

Once the group has settled down to begin its first meeting, it faces the issue of its basic mission. Statements about the goal of "learning about itself" will have been spelled out in the training literature, the workshop brochure, the initial introductory lecture to the entire workshop, and again by the staff member who launches the group. Some people may even have had prior experiences with similar groups, but initially everyone is acutely aware of how ambiguous the words of the staff member are when he or she says: "This is the first meeting of our T group. Our goal is to provide for ourselves a climate in which we can all learn. There is no one correct way to do this. We will have to get to know each other, find out what our individual needs and goals are, and build our group to enable us to fulfill those goals and needs. My role as staff member will be to help this process along in any way that I can, but I will not be the formal leader of the group, and I have no answers as to the right way to proceed."

The ensuing silence, as each person experiences feelings of anxiety in the face of this ambiguous agenda and power vacuum, is usually a key marker event that almost everyone remembers vividly at a later time. Even though all the members come from the same host culture and share the same formal language, everyone is aware that this group is a unique combination of personalities and that those personalities are initially unknown. What makes the initial silence a marker event, even if it is only a few seconds long, is that every person is aware of his own emotional intensity level in response to the sudden silence. Whether or not the emotional tone is recognized as "anxiety" will vary from individual to individual; but once the silence is identified as something to be understood, all group members can easily recognize how much of their own response to the silence can best be characterized in tension or anxiety terms.

The formal agenda, leadership structure, and procedural rules or even suggestions are, of course, deliberately removed to heighten members' awareness of how much they typically depend on those external "crutches" to define the rules of the game. The group is deliberately thrown on its own resources to permit members to observe their own feelings and reactions as they cope with this initially "normless" and "ruleless" situation. Everyone suddenly realizes how dependent we are on culture and how uncomfortable it is to be deprived of procedures and rules. Physically locating the workshop in a remote area further deprives participants of cues, leading such places to be called "cultural islands."

Each member brings to this new situation a wealth of prior learning in the form of assumptions and expectations, but, as the group gets started by someone's making a suggestion or revealing a feeling, it immediately becomes apparent that there is little consensus within the group on how to proceed and that the group cannot become a copy of any other group. Thus, even though individual members bring prior cultural learning to the new situation, by definition this particular group starts out with no culture of its own. Goals, means, working procedures, measurements, and rules of interaction all have to be forged out of common experience, and a sense of mission, what the group is ultimately all about, develops only as members begin genuinely to understand each other's needs, goals, talents, and values and begin to integrate these into a shared mission.

How does group formation now proceed? Often the very first thing said by any person in the group will become the next marker event if it succeeds in reducing some of the tension. The silence is broken, there is a huge sigh of relief, and the group becomes aware through this *joint sensing of relief* that it is sharing something unique to it. No other group in the world will have this particular pattern of initial tension and manner of resolving the initial silence. Members also become aware of something that is easy to forget—that one cannot in an interpersonal situation "not" communicate. Everything that happens has potential meaning and consequences for the group.

If the suggestion or comment made gets the group started, not only will it have provided emotional relief and anxiety reduction, but the forward movement produced will also be positively reinforcing. This piece of behavior may then become more probable as a future means of starting meetings. For example, one of the more active members often will initiate with a suggestion of how to get started: "Why don't we go around the group and each introduce ourselves" or "Let's each of us tell what we are here for" or "I feel pretty tense right now. Does anyone else feel the same way?" or "Ed, can you give us some suggestion on how best to get started?" And so on. If that suggestion fits the mood of the group or at least of some other members who are ready to speak up, it will be picked up and may become the beginning of a pattern. If it does not fit the mood, it will elicit disagreement, countersuggestions, or some other response that will make members aware that they cannot easily agree. Whatever the response, however, the crucial event of group formation has taken place when the group, including the staff member, has participated in a *shared emotional reaction.* What makes the event *shared* is the fact that all members have been witnesses to the same behavior on the part of one of their members and have observed the responses together. After the meeting they can refer to the event and people will remember it. This initial sharing is what defines at an emotional level that "we are a group; we have been launched."

The most fundamental act of culture formation, the defining of crude group boundaries, has occurred with the shared emotional response. Everyone who has shared the response is, by definition, *in the group* at some level, and anyone who has not shared the experience is initially *not in the group.* And this fact of being in or out of the group is quite concrete in that the person who did not attend and witness the events cannot know what happened or how people reacted.

The nature of that initial shared response in various other kinds of groups will, of course, differ. Some theorists have speculated that early tribal formation may have resulted from a joint emotionally involving act, such as defeating an enemy or making a sacrifice. For our purposes the important thing to recognize is that the original intention to do something may have been *individually* motivated, but the result, if it leads to a shared emotional experience, may have important *group* consequences.

Thus, in any new group situation, whether we are talking about a new company, a task force, a committee, or a team, much of the initial behavior of founders, leaders, and other initiators is individually motivated and reflects their particular assumptions and intentions. But, as the individuals in the group begin to do things together and share experiences around such individually motivated acts, groupness arises.

Initially, this groupness is only an emotional substrate that permits the defining of who is in and who is not. For the group to begin to understand its sense of groupness, someone must articulate what the experience has been and what it means. Such articulation is again an individual act, motivated by individual intentions to lead or be a prophet, or whatever, but the consequences are group consequences if the articulation "works," if things are stated in a way that makes sense and helps group members understand what has happened and why they are feeling the way they are. Such articulation is, in fact, one of the most crucial components of what we call leadership and can be understood as an act of *culture creation* if the process imparts meaning to an important shared emotional experience. Some of the deepest and most potent shared experiences occur within the first few hours of group life, so the deepest levels of consensus on who we are, what our mission is, and how we will work are formed very early in the group's history.

The subsequent progress of group formation can best be understood as the confrontation of a sequence of shared underlying assumptions that are likely to arise in each of the major group stages, as outlined in Table 4. Culture formation takes

Table 4. Stages of Group Evolution.

Stage	Dominant Assumption	Socioemotional Focus
1. Group Formation	Dependence: "The leader knows what we should do."	Self-Orientation Emotional focus on issues of (1) inclusion, (2) power and influence, (3) acceptance and intimacy, (4) identity and role.
2. Group Building	Fusion: "We are a great group; we all like each other."	Group as Idealized Object Emotional focus on harmony, conformity, and search for intimacy. Member differences are not valued.
3. Group Work	Work: "We can perform effectively because we know and accept each other."	Group Mission and Tasks Emotional focus on accomplishment, teamwork, and maintaining the group in good working order. Member differences are valued.
4. Group Maturity	Maturity: "We know who we are, what we want, and how to get it. We have been successful, so we must be right."	Group Survival and Comfort Emotional focus on preserving the group and its culture. Creativity and member differences are seen as threat.

place around the efforts to deal with the anxieties characteristic of each of the basic assumptions.

Stages of Group Evolution

Stage 1: Group Formation

Initially, each member is struggling with the personal issues of inclusion, identity, authority, and intimacy, and the group is not really a group but a collection of individuals, each focused on how to make the situation safe and personally rewarding. In other words, at this stage people are much more preoccupied with their own feelings than with the problem of the group as a group and, most likely, are operating on the unconscious assumption of "dependency"—namely, that "the leader [staff member] knows what we are supposed to do." Therefore, the best way to achieve safety is to find out what we are supposed to do and do it. This group state, with its associated feelings and moods, is, in my experience, similar to what Bion (1959) described in his work as the dependence assumption.

The evidence for the operation of this assumption is the behavior one sees in the early minutes and hours of the group's life. First of all, much of the initial behavior of group members is, in fact, directed to the staff member in the form of questions, requests for explanations and for suggestions about how to proceed, and constant checking for approval. Even if the behavior is not directed to the staff member, one notes that members constantly look at him or her, pay extra attention if the staff member does speak, and in other nonverbal ways indicate their preoccupation with the staff member's reactions.

Members may share the common assumption of being dependent on the "leader" (staff member), yet react very differently. These differences can best be described in terms of the emotional styles described in Chapter Seven. Some members will have learned in their prior group experience, probably starting in the family, that the way to deal with authority is to suppress aggression, accept dependence, and seek guidance. If the staff member makes a suggestion, such members will automatically accept it and attempt to do what is asked of them. Others have learned that the way to deal with authority is to resist it. They also will seek to find out what the leader wants, but their motive is to find out in order to resist, not to comply (the "counterdependent" response). Still others will attempt to find people to share their feelings of dependence and set up, in effect, a subgroup within the larger group.

The mixture of tendencies in the personalities of group members is, of course, not initially predictable, nor is any given person inflexible. The range of possible variations in response to the initial leadership/authority vacuum is thus immense in a ten- to fifteen-person group. What one observes in watching the early interaction can best be described as a mutual testing out: testing of the staff member to see how much guidance will be offered, and testing by members of other members to see who can influence whom and who will control whom, a process not unlike the barnyard process of establishing a pecking order.

Several members will emerge as competitors for leadership and influence. If any one of these members suggests something or makes a point, one of the others will contradict it or try to go off in a different direction. This aggressive competition among the "sturdy battlers" keeps the group from achieving any real consensus early in its life, and one paradox of group formation is that there is no way to short-circuit this early power struggle. If it is swept under the rug by formal procedures, it surfaces around the task issues that the group is trying to address.

From the point of view of the staff member, confirmation that this process is indeed going on comes from the frequent experience of trying to give the group guidance and finding that some members leap at the help, while others almost blindly resist it. If frustration is high, one or the other extreme mood may build up in the group as a whole, what Bion labeled "fight or flight." The group may collectively attack the staff member, aggressively deny his suggestions, and punish him for his silence; or the group may suddenly go off on its own, led by a group member, with the implicit or explicit statement "We need to get away from the disappointing leader and do it on our own."

Building Behavioral Norms. The group in its early life cannot easily find consensus on what to do, so it bounces from one suggestion to another and becomes increasingly more frustrated and discouraged at its inability to act. And this frustration keeps the shared emotional assumption of dependency alive. The group continues to act as if the leader knew what to do. In the meantime members are, of course, beginning to be able to calibrate each other, the staff member, and the total situation. A common language slowly gets established; and, as shared experience accumulates, more of a sense of "groupness" arises at the emotional level, providing some reassurance to all of being included. Primary cognitive and social anxieties are slowly reduced.

This sense of groupness arises though successive dealing

with marker events, those that arouse strong feelings and then are dealt with definitively. The group is not consciously aware of this process of norm building, however, unless attention is drawn to it. For example, within the first few minutes, a member may speak up strongly for a given course of action. Joe suggests that the way to proceed is to take turns introducing ourselves and telling why we are in the group. This suggestion requires some behavioral response from other members; therefore, no matter what the group does, it will be setting some kind of precedent for how to deal with future suggestions that are "controlling," that require behavior from others.

What are the options at this point? One common response in groups is to act as if the suggestion had not been made at all. There is a moment of silence, followed by another member's comment irrelevant to the suggestion. In the "jargon" of group training, this is called a "plop," a group decision by nonaction. The member who made the suggestion may feel ignored. At the same time, a group norm has been established. The group has, in effect, said that members need not respond to every suggestion, that it is permissible to ignore someone. A second common response is for another person to agree or disagree overtly with the suggestion. This response begins to build another norm: that one should respond. It may also begin to build an alliance if there has been agreement, or it may begin a fight that will force others to take sides if there has been disagreement. A third possibility is for another person to make a "process" comment, such as "I wonder if we should collect some other suggestions before we decide what to do" or "How do the rest of you feel about Joe's suggestion?" Again a norm is being established: that one does not have to plunge into action but can consider alternatives. A fourth possibility is to plunge ahead into action. The suggestion is made to introduce ourselves, and the next person to speak launches into an introduction. This response not only gets the group moving but may set two precedents: that suggestions should be responded to and that Joe is the one that can get us moving. Finally, the group may ignore the suggestion yet come back to it later, demonstrating that what may have felt like a "plop" at the time was not forgotten.

Such a display of group memory may also set a norm that all suggestions should be dealt with in one manner or another.

Norms are thus formed when an individual takes a position and the rest of the group deals with that position by letting it stand (remaining silent), by actively approving it, by "processing" it, or by rejecting it. Three sets of consequences are always observed: (1) the personal consequences for the member who made the suggestion (he may gain or lose influence, disclose himself to others, develop a friend or enemy, and so on); (2) the interpersonal consequences for those members immediately involved in the interplay; and (3) the normative consequences for the group as a whole. So here again we have the situation where an *individual* has to act, but the subsequent shared reaction turns the event into a *group* product. It is the joint witnessing of the event and the reaction that makes it a group product.

The early life of the group is filled with thousands of such events and the responses to them. At the *cognitive* level, they deal with the effort to define working procedures to fulfill the primary task—to learn. Prior assumptions about how to learn will operate initially to bias the group's effort, and limits will be set by the staff member in the form of calling attention to the consequences of behavior considered clearly detrimental to learning: failure to attend meetings, frequent interruption, personally hostile attacks, and the like. At an *emotional* level, such events deal with the problem of authority and influence. The most critical of such events will be ones that overtly test or challenge the staff member's authority. Thus, one will note that the group pays special attention to the responses that occur immediately after someone has directed a comment, question, or challenge to the staff member.

One will also note anomalous behavior that can be explained only if one assumes that an authority issue is being worked out. For example, the group will actively seek leadership by requesting that some member should help the group to get moving, but then systematically ignore or punish anyone who attempts to lead. One can understand this behavior if one remembers that feelings toward authority are always ambivalent and that the anger felt toward the staff member for not leading the group cannot be expressed directly if one feels dependent on the staff member. The negative feelings are split off and projected onto a "bad leader," thus preserving the illusion that the staff member is the "good leader." Similarly, acts of insubordination or outbursts of anger at the staff member may be severely punished by other group members, even though those members have been critical of the staff member themselves.

How, then, does a group learn what is "reality," how does it develop workable and accurate assumptions about how to learn and how to deal with influence and authority—assumptions that will ultimately be a part of that group's culture?

Reality Test and Catharsis. Though members begin to feel they know each other better, the group continues to be frustrated by its inability to act in a consensual manner, because the unconscious dependence assumption is still operating and members are still working out their influence relationships with each other. The event that moves the group forward at such times, often many hours into the group's life, is an insightful comment by a member who is less conflicted about the authority issue and, therefore, able to perceive and articulate what is really going on. In other words, while those members who are most conflicted about authority are struggling in the dependent and counterdependent mode, some members find that they care less about this issue, are able psychologically to detach themselves from it, and come to recognize the reality that *the leader does not, in fact, know what to do.*

The less conflicted members may intervene in any of a number of ways that expose this reality: (1) by offering a direct *interpretation* ("Maybe we are hung up in this group because we expect the staff member to be able to tell us what to do"); (2) by offering a direct *challenge* ("I think the staff member doesn't know what to do; we better figure it out ourselves"); (3) by offering a direct *suggestion* for an alternative agenda ("I think we should focus on how we feel about this group right now, instead of trying to figure out what to do"); or (4) by making a *process* suggestion or observation ("I notice that we ask the leader for suggestions but then don't do what he suggests" or "I wonder why we are fighting so much among ourselves in this group").

If the timing is right, in the sense that many members are "ready" to hear what may be going on because they have all observed the process for a period of time, there will be a strong cathartic reaction when the assumption-lifting intervention is made. The group members will suddenly realize that they have been focusing heavily on the staff member and that, indeed, the person is not all-knowing and all-seeing and, therefore, probably does not, in fact, know what the group should do. With this insight comes the feeling of responsibility: "We are all in this together, and we each have to contribute to the group's agenda." The magical leader has been killed, and realistic leadership begins to be sought from whoever can provide it.

Leadership comes to be seen as a shared set of activities rather than a single person's trait, and a sense of ownership of group outcomes arises. Some work groups never achieve this state, remaining dependent on whatever formal authority is available and projecting magically onto it; but in the training situation, the emphasis on process analysis makes it very likely that the issue will be surfaced and dealt with.

A comparable process occurs in formally constituted groups, but it is less visible. The group founder or chairperson does have real intentions and plans, but the group initially tends to attribute far more complete and detailed knowledge to the leader than is warranted by reality. Thus, early in the life of a company, the entrepreneur is viewed much more magically as the source of all wisdom, and only gradually is it discovered that he or she is only human and that the organization can function only if other members begin to feel responsible for group outcomes. But all this may occur implicitly and without very visible marker events. If such events occur, they will most likely be in the form of challenges of the leader or outright insubordination. How the group and the leader then handle the emotionally threatening event will determine to a large extent the norms around authority that will become operative in the future.

I have described the "insight" that the leader is not omniscient or omnipotent as a cathartic reaction. Members feel a sense of relief not to be struggling any longer with the staff members, and they are likely to develop a feeling of euphoria that they have been able to deal with the tough issue of authority and leadership. There is a sense of joy in recognizing that everyone in the group has a role and can make a leadership contribution, and that, in turn, strengthens the group's sense of itself.

At this point the group often takes some joint action, as if to prove to itself that it can do something, and gets a further sense of euphoria from being successful at it. Such action is often externally directed—winning a competition with another group or tackling a difficult task under time pressure and completing it. Whatever the task, the end result is a feeling of "We are a great group" and possibly at a deeper level even the feeling of "We are a better group than any of the others." It is this state of affairs that leads to the unconscious assumption of fusion.

Stage 2: Group Building

At stage 2 the primary assumption that is operating is the fusion assumption. The essence of this assumption is "We all like each other," which, in turn, is buttressed by the assumption "We are a great group," based on the euphoria of having "solved" the problem of dependence and put the formal authority in its proper place. Turquet (1973) used the same label ("fusion") to reflect a strong emotional need to feel merged with the group and to deny internal differences. How do we know when this assumption is operating? What one observes at the overt behavior level is a marked absence of interpersonal conflict, a tendency to lean over backward to be nice to each other, emotional expressions of affection, a mood of euphoria, and a group solidarity in the face of any challenge. Symptoms of conflict or lack of harmony are ignored or actively denied. Hostility is suppressed or punished severely if it occurs. An image of solidarity must be presented at all costs.

Different members of the group will vary in their need to attain and maintain a high level of intimacy, and those who care most will become the most active guardians of the group harmony image. In particular, the group that Schutz (1958) called the "overpersonal" will resolve conflicts about intimacy by seeking it and by attempting to maintain harmony. But other group members, those who resolve their conflict about intimacy by avoiding it, the group that Schutz called the "counterpersonal," will rock the boat and challenge the harmony image because the harmony makes them anxious. They will complain that the group is wasting time, is being too "cozy," and is ignoring conflicts that are visible. But their complaints will be ignored or actively put down if the need to prove group harmony is strong.

The staff member suddenly notices that he is now "one of the regulars" and is labeled as "no different from the rest of us," which is, of course, just as unrealistic as the assumption that the staff member is omniscient and omnipotent. At this stage interventions that may be disturbing to the group are simply ignored or laughed off.

The strength of the fusion assumption will be a function of the individual needs of group members and the actual experience of the group. The more the group feels itself to be in a hostile environment or vulnerable to destruction, the more it may cling to the assumption as a way of claiming strength. Or, to put it the other way, only when the group feels reasonably secure can it give up the false solidarity that the fusion assumption claims. Such security comes gradually from increasing experience, success with tasks, and tests of strength against other groups.

The group moods of fight or flight are likely to arise around the fusion assumption, because both fight and flight involve solidarity and joint action. Thus, if the authority issue arises again, the group may at this point turn collectively against the staff member or may deliberately run away from its real task of learning about itself by rationalizing that it has overcome all of its problems already, that there is nothing more to learn. Or the group may project its negative feelings onto someone outside the group, the administration of the workshop or some other group, and fight or flee from that outside enemy.

What Bion (1959) called "pairing" will also be common in this stage, since the need for love and intimacy that is operating can easily be projected onto those members who display such feelings overtly. By projecting the fate of the group into the "pair," by hoping for a magic solution through what the pair will produce, the group can maintain its sense of solidarity. All these responses preserve the assumption that the group is "great" and "can do things together."

Many organizations get stuck at this level of group evolution, developing an adequate authority system and a capacity to defend themselves against external threat but never growing internally to a point of differentiation of roles and clarification of personal relationships.

Reality Test and Catharsis. The fusion assumption will not be given up until some marker event brings its falsity into consciousness. The group events that have the potential for revealing the assumption are (1) the subtle disagreements and conflicts that will occur in the attempts to take joint action, (2) the noticeable avoidance of confrontation, (3) the overt denial that some members may not like each other, and (4) the occasional eruptions of negative feelings toward other members. The actual marker event that tests the reality of the fusion assumption is most likely to come from those group members who are least conflicted about intimacy issues and who, therefore, are most likely to have insight into what is happening. For example, on one of the many occasions when a counterpersonal member challenges the solidarity of the group, one of the less conflicted members may support the challenge by providing incontrovertible examples indicating that group members actually do not seem to get along all that well. This introduction of data that cannot be denied will pierce the illusion and thus force the recognition of the assumption.

A vivid example occurred in a group that had been undergoing a number of experiential learning exercises. The group had built up a strong illusion of its solidarity and superiority. At one meeting an exercise elicited the following chain of events. Two group members volunteered to play the "nickels auction," an exercise that permits either player to be cooperative or competitive, but the only way to beat the game is for *both* to cooperate. The game is played in front of the rest of the group, and the audience typically catches on very fast to the need to cooperate. In this instance one person cooperated, but the other did not catch on and continued to compete. As the two returned to their seats, the one who had cooperated yelled in a loud but playful voice: "You asshole." There was an immediate tension in the air, but group members and the staff member remained silent, thereby tacitly denying that anything had happened. The discussion then shifted to an unrelated topic as if the incident had not taken place. A few minutes later, the person to whom the remark had been addressed volunteered in a highly emotional way that he did not like being called an asshole in front of an entire group even if it was meant playfully, that he was hurt and embarrassed, and that he thought he should make his feelings known. Several members of the group applauded the statement, and shortly thereafter the name caller sincerely apologized, a response that was greeted with relief and a marked lessening of tension in the room. The apology was not applauded.

My interpretation of what had happened was as follows. First, if the group had still been basically insecure and unable to handle strong differences, the incident would have been glossed over, and the climate would not have permitted the offended party to speak up about his feelings. The marker event of playful name calling would have been ignored, therefore implying that it did not count, and the group could have gone on with its assumption of harmony. A norm might have begun to be built that "In this group we shrug off conflict or brush it under the rug." In other words, the attacked person had to feel a certain amount of security to be able to share his hurt. His speaking up was a second marker event, which again permitted the group a variety of response options. The group could have remained silent, indicated disapproval, or turned on the attacker. The group's response of applause had a cathartic effect, since it legitimized expression of personal feelings even if they were directed at another member, thus shattering the assumption of "We all like each other." At the same time, by applauding the confession of hurt, the group left room for the attacker to reenter the group through his apology. The apology reinforced the feeling that the group was strong enough to tolerate expressions of hostility. But by not applauding the apology, the group was also able to express some disapproval of the outburst.

The release of tension showed that the group had survived a strongly disruptive event, but the event itself clearly demonstrated that not everyone liked everyone else and that hostility could erupt. Thus, norms of openness about the expression of feelings began to be built. It was demonstrated that hostility as well as weakness and tender feelings could be expressed in this group. The net result was a group climate that was much more open to the exploration of diverse feelings and styles in the group. Though it was noticed only in retrospect, the group had given up the fusion assumption.

I have frequently observed counterpart events in more formally constituted groups. A work group in a growing company erupts into a hostile confrontation between two members. The manner in which the ensuing tense silence is handled by the group builds a norm for future expressions of feeling. If the group or the leader punishes either or both combatants, norms get built that feelings should be kept in check; if the group or leader encourages resolution, norms get built that hostility is "OK" and that feelings can be expressed. The moments when these norm-building activities occur are often very brief and easy to miss if one is not alert to them. But it is at those moments that culture begins to form, and the eventual assumptions about what is appropriate and right will reflect a long series of such incidents and the reactions to them.

Role of Learning: Which Norms Survive? How are norms reinforced and built up into the *assumptions* that eventually come to be taken for granted? The two basic mechanisms of learning involved are *positive problem solving,* to cope with *external survival* issues, and *anxiety avoidance,* to cope with *internal integration* issues. For example, if a group challenges its formal leader and begins to build norms that support more widely shared leadership and higher levels of member involvement, it is an empirical matter whether or not this way of working is effective in solving real-world problems. In the T group, it is an empirical matter whether or not the group feels that such norms are enabling it to fulfill its primary task of *learning*. In formal work groups, it is a matter of actual experience whether or not the work gets done better with a given set of norms that have evolved.

If the group fails repeatedly, sooner or later someone will propose that a new leadership process be found or that the original leader be reinstated in a more powerful role, and the group will find itself experimenting with new norms of how to work with authority. It then again must test against reality how successful it is. The norms that produce the greatest success will be the ones that survive. As they continue to work, they gradually turn into assumptions about how things really are. At the same time, as new norms form, there is always an immediate test of whether the members of the group are more or less comfortable as a result of the new way of working; that is, do the new norms enable them to avoid the anxiety inherent in the initially unstable or uncertain situation? If the leader is challenged, gives up some authority, and shares power with the group, some group members, depending on their own pattern of needs and prior experiences, may feel less comfortable than before. In some groups a greater comfort level might be achieved by norms that, in effect, reassert the authority of the leader and make members more dependent on the leader. The needs of the leader will also play a role in this process, so the ultimate resolution, what makes everyone most comfortable, will be a set of norms that meet the many internal needs as well as external experiences. Because so many variables are involved, the resultant group culture will usually be a unique and distinctive one.

If a group successfully deals with the fusion assumption, it usually achieves an emotional state that could best be characterized as *mutual acceptance*. The group will have had enough experience so that members not only know what to expect of each other but also will have had the chance to learn that they can coexist and work together even if they do not all like each other. The emotional shift from maintaining the illusion of mutual liking to a state of mutual acceptance is important in that it frees up emotional energy for work. Being dominated by either the dependence or the fusion assumption ties up emotional energy because of the denial and defensiveness required to avoid confronting the disconfirming realities. Therefore, if a group is to work effectively, it must reach a level of emotional maturity at which reality-testing norms prevail. At this stage a new implicit assumption arises, the work assumption.

Stage 3: Group Work

As the group begins to give up its assumption that it is perfect, that everyone likes everyone else, and that feelings of hostility are always destructive, it is able to move to a new assumption, which can best be stated as "We know each other well enough, both in a positive and negative light, that we can work well together and accomplish our external goals." As pointed out above, underlying this assumption is the substitution of "We all *accept* each other" for the prior assumption that "We all *like* each other."

When the fusion assumption is operating, the group often exerts strong conformity pressures on any individual members who deviate in their actions, perceptions, or feelings, because individual differences are seen as a threat to group integrity. As the group evolves and the need for perfect harmony diminishes, members recognize differences as "real" and potentially valuable. At this stage the group exerts less pressure to conform and builds norms that encourage some measure of individuality and personal growth, on the assumption that the group ultimately will benefit if all members grow and become stronger. However, because many groups never get to this stage, some observers judge groups as inherently demanding of conformity. In my own experience, high conformity pressures are symptomatic of unresolved issues in the group, and the best way to get past them is to help the group to a more mature stage.

As Bion (1959) pointed out, groups always have some kind of task, even if that task is to provide learning or therapy to its members; so the need to "work," to fulfill the task, is always psychologically present. But the ability to focus on the task is a function of the degree to which group members can reduce and avoid their own anxieties. Such anxieties are intrinsically highest when the group is very young and has not yet had a chance to build up cultural assumptions to control the anxiety. Therefore, the energy available for work is lowest in the early stages of group formation, though a focus on work is often a convenient way to work out underlying group issues. The important point to note is that a focus on work does not necessarily produce good results if members' energy and attention are bound up in personal issues.

A way of thinking about group evolution, then, is to recognize that the work of the group gradually attracts more and more of the members' attention, with the periods of regression into dependence, fusion, fight-flight, or pairing becoming less frequent as the group evolves a culture, stabilizes its ways of working, and thus releases energy for the task at hand. At the same time, if this model is correct, it warns us that the quickest way for the group to lose its ability to work productively is to question some of its cultural assumptions, because such a threat rearouses the primary anxieties that the cultural solutions dealt with in the first place.

As the group works on its tasks, a new issue arises. Do members seek solutions that "satisfice" and institutionalize them because they reduce anxiety? Or do they seek optimal solutions and create a climate for perpetual creativity in order to remain externally adaptive even though internally more anxious? It is a paradox of evolution or development that the more we learn how to do things and to stabilize what we have learned, the more unwilling or unable we become to adapt, change, and grow into new patterns, even when our changing environment demands such new patterns.

Stage 4: Group Maturity

Only a few remarks will be made about this final group stage because much more focus will be given to it in later chapters. If a group works successfully, it will inevitably reinforce its assumptions about itself and its environment, thus strengthening what culture it has developed. Since culture is a learned set of responses, culture will be as strong as the group's learning history has made it. The more the group has experienced, the stronger the culture of that group will be. The more intense the experiences members have shared, the more intense the learning outcomes and the stronger the learned responses.

Given these forces, a group or organization inevitably will begin to develop the assumption that it knows who it is, what its role in the world is, how to accomplish its mission, and how to conduct its affairs. If the culture that develops *works,* it will ultimately be taken for granted as the only correct way for group members to see the world.

The inevitable dilemma for the group, then, is how to avoid becoming so stable in its approach to its environment that it loses its ability to adapt, innovate, and grow. At the individual level, this translates into whether the socialization tactics used will ultimately produce conformity or will enable new members to continue to innovate and grow as individuals, thus helping the group remain innovative (Van Maanen and Schein, 1979). And if the present culture presents a barrier to group survival, what are the issues raised by the prospect of "changing the culture," if indeed that is even possible?

Do Training Groups Develop Cultures?

I have described a process of group evolution, but can we say after a group has passed through these stages that it now has a culture? Two lines of evidence have to be assessed, based on our prior definition of organizational culture. Does the group develop assumptions about itself and its environment, and are these assumptions passed on to new group members as the "correct" way to perceive, think about, and feel about itself and the environment?

In the workshop setting, different groups develop clearly different assumptions about how to learn, even though they start with the same conditions. Typically, one or two groups will develop strong norms of intimacy, reflecting the assumption that the only way to learn in the workshop is to open up to each other, give strong personal feedback, and take good care of each other. At the same time, one or more groups will develop strong norms that only group events are fair game for personal analysis and that one should be careful not to get into the private sphere of any one member. The assumption seems to be that it is neither necessary nor appropriate to "invade personal privacy" for learning to occur.

If we look at specific issues with respect to the external environment, we find that groups develop different assumptions about each of the following areas:

1. Regarding the ultimate *mission* or *primary task* of the group, some groups will focus strictly on cognitive events, while others will emphasize the emotional responses of individual members.

2. Regarding the group's specific *goals,* some groups will define learning success by whether or not every member of the group has had a "turn in the barrel" and received personal feedback, while other groups seek to compete and win in various tasks.

3. Regarding the *process* by which learning takes place, some groups will carefully analyze any and all group events that members wish to review, while others prefer to focus on external tasks and leave all process learning implicit.

4. Regarding the manner in which learning *progress is measured,* some groups will settle for a "mood" of satisfaction, while other groups decide always to fill in a postmeeting reaction form to assess quantitatively how each person responded to each session.

5. Regarding the *mechanisms for correction,* some groups will assume that, if any one member is dissatisfied, the group must continue to work with that person, while other groups will assume that issues need to be reviewed only if a majority or critical mass wants to conduct such a review.

On the internal side, the differences are easily apparent in the different jargon, authority systems, peer norms, role differentiation, and public ideologies projected by groups. One of the best ways of illustrating these differences is to have each group present itself through some artistic production and to note the wide variation among those productions. Some groups present themselves as complex collages, reflecting the assumption that members have established rich and complex relationships with each other. Other groups present themselves in the form of organization charts, reflecting the assumption that roles have been clearly defined. Still others paint word pictures, sing songs, or in various complex expressive ways depict their assumptions about themselves.

Do training groups have a long and complex enough shared history to develop deeper consensus on assumptions about the environment, reality, time, space, human nature, activity, and relationships? In my experience, some groups, especially if they have members from different ethnic groups, have been able to confront these deeper issues and begin to form their own consensus on how to view their world.

The clearest test of culture formation, perhaps, comes when a member arrives late for the workshop and has to be incorporated into the group. It suddenly becomes very clear to everyone, including the new member, that missing even a few meetings is very critical because so much has already come to be taken for granted. The new member must learn a great deal to feel comfortable in the new group, and many of the norms may be articulated explicitly in order to speed up the process. It is when the norms are articulated that one realizes most clearly how groups differ even after just a few meetings. Though the process is largely outside awareness, culture formation often occurs very rapidly, giving groups the distinctiveness that newcomers notice immediately.

9

How Organization
Founders
Shape Culture

Organizations evolve from small groups. But organizations develop dynamics that go beyond those of the small group. In order to understand organizational cultures, therefore, we have to extrapolate from what one can observe in small groups to the situation of organizational growth and development. In the next several chapters, we will draw on the insights that can be gained from the detailed analysis of small-group dynamics and culture formation, but the focus will shift to founders, leaders, and managers who are creating larger systems.

Role of the Founder

Organizations do not form accidentally or spontaneously. Instead, they are goal oriented and have a specific purpose. Organizations are "created" because one or more individuals perceive that the coordinated and concerted action of a number of people can accomplish something that individual action cannot.

Social movements or new religions begin with prophets, mes-
siahs, or other kinds of charismatic leaders. Political groups are
begun by leaders who sell new visions and new solutions to
problems. Firms are created by entrepreneurs who have a vision
of how the concerted effort of the right group of people can
create a new product or service in the marketplace. The process
of culture formation is, in each case, first a process of creating a
small group.

In the business organization, this process will usually involve some version of the following steps:

1.   A single person (founder) has an idea for a new enterprise.
2.   The founder brings in one or more other people and creates
     a core group that shares a common vision with the founder.
     That is, they all believe that the idea is a good one, is work-
     able, is worth running some risks for, and is worth the in-
     vestment of time, money, and energy that will be required.
3.   The founding group begins to act in concert to create an or-
     ganization by raising funds, obtaining patents, incorporat-
     ing, locating space, and so on.
4.   Others are brought into the organization, and a common
     history begins to be built.

Founders usually have a major impact on how the group
defines and solves its external adaptation and internal integration problems. Because they had the original idea, they will
typically have their own notion, based on their own cultural history and personality, of how to get the idea fulfilled. Founders
not only have a high level of self-confidence and determination,
but they typically have strong assumptions about the nature of
the world, the role that organizations play in that world, the nature of human nature and relationships, how truth is arrived at,
and how to manage time and space (Schein, 1978, 1983).

Three Case Examples

Jones Company. Founder Jones was an immigrant whose
parents had started a corner grocery store in a large urban area.
His parents, particularly his mother, taught him some basic atti-

tudes toward customers and helped him form the vision that he could succeed in building a successful enterprise. He assumed from the beginning that if he did things right he would succeed and could build a major organization that would bring him and his family a fortune. Ultimately, he built a large chain of supermarkets, department stores, and related businesses that became the dominant force in its market area. Jones was the major ideological force in his company throughout its history and continued to impose his assumptions on the company until his death in his late seventies.

Jones assumed that his primary mission was to supply a high-quality, reliable product to customers in clean, attractive surroundings and that his customers' needs were the primary consideration in all major decisions. There are many stories about how Jones, as a young man operating the corner grocery store with his wife, gave customers credit and thus displayed trust in them, always took products back if there was the slightest complaint, and kept his store absolutely spotless to inspire customer confidence in his products. Each of these attitudes later became a major policy in his chain of stores and was taught and reinforced by close personal supervision. Jones believed that only personal example and close supervision would ensure adequate performance by subordinates; so he would show up at his stores unexpectedly, inspect even minor details, and then—by personal example, by stories of how other stores were solving the problems identified, by articulating rules, and by exhortation—"teach" the staff what they should be doing. He often lost his temper and berated subordinates who did not follow the rules or principles laid down.

Jones expected his store managers to be highly visible, to be very much on top of their own jobs, and to supervise closely in the same way he did. These assumptions became a major theme in later years in his concept of "visible management," the assumption that a "good" manager always had to be around to set a good example and to teach subordinates the right way to do things.

Most of the founding group in this company consisted of brothers of the founder, but one "lieutenant" who was not a family member was recruited early and became, in addition to the founder, the main culture creator and carrier. He shared the founder's basic assumptions about how to run a business and set up formal systems to ensure that those assumptions became the basis for operating realities. After Jones's death this man continued to articulate the theory of "visible management" and tried to set a personal example of how to do it by continuing the same close supervision policies that Jones had had.

Jones assumed that one could "win" in the marketplace only by being highly innovative and technically on the forefront. He encouraged his managers to try new approaches, brought in a variety of consultants who advocated new approaches to human resource management, started selection and development programs through assessment centers long before other companies tried this approach, traveled to conventions and other businesses where new technological innovations were displayed, and generally was willing to experiment in order to improve the business. His view of truth and reality was that one had to find it wherever one could, and, therefore, one had to be open to one's environment and never take it for granted that one had all the answers. If things worked, Jones encouraged their adoption; if they did not, he ordered them to be dropped.

Measuring results and solving problems were, for Jones, intensely personal matters, deriving from his theory of "visible management." In addition to using a variety of traditional business measures, he always made it a point to visit all his stores personally and, if he saw things not to his liking, to correct them immediately and decisively even if that meant going around his own authority chain. He trusted only those managers who operated by assumptions similar to his own, and clearly had favorites to whom he delegated more authority.

Power and authority in this organization remained very centralized, and the ultimate source of power, the voting shares of stock, were kept entirely by Jones and his wife, so that after his death his wife was in total control of the company. Jones was interested in developing good managers throughout the organization, but he never assumed that sharing ownership through granting stock options would contribute to that process. He paid his lieutenants very well but clearly did not share ownership even with those who had been with the company throughout its history.

Jones introduced several members of his own family into the firm in key managerial positions and gave them favored treatment in the form of good developmental jobs that would test them early for ultimate management potential. As the firm diversified, family members were made heads of divisions, often with relatively little management experience. If a family member performed poorly, he would be bolstered by having a good manager introduced under him; and if the operation then improved, he would likely be given the credit. If things continued badly, the family member would be moved out, but with various face-saving excuses.

Peer relationships among nonfamily members inevitably became highly politicized. They were officially defined as competitive, and Jones believed firmly in the value of interpersonal competition. Winners would be rewarded and losers discarded. However, since family members were in positions of power, one had to know how to stay on the good side of those family members without losing the trust of one's peers, on whom one was dependent.

Jones wanted open communication and high trust levels among all members of the organization, but his own assumptions about the role of the family and the correct way to manage were, to a large degree, in conflict with each other. Therefore, many of the members of the organization banded together in a kind of mutual protection society that developed a culture of its own. They were more loyal to each other than to the company and had a high rate of interaction with each other, which bred assumptions, values, and norms that became to some degree countercultural to the founder's.

Several points should be noted about the description given thus far. By definition, something can become part of the culture only if it works. Jones's assumptions about how things should be done were congruent with the kind of environment in which he operated, so he and the founding group received strong reinforcement for those assumptions. As the company grew and prospered, Jones felt more and more confirmation of his assumptions and thus more and more confidence that they were correct. Throughout his lifetime he steadfastly adhered to those assumptions and did everything in his power to get others to accept them.

At the same time, however, Jones had to share concepts and assumptions with a great many other people. So, as his company grew and learned from its own experience, his assumptions gradually had to be modified in some areas or he had to withdraw from those areas as an active manager. For example, in its diversification efforts, the company bought several production units that would enable it to integrate vertically in certain food and clothing areas where that was economically advantageous. But, because Jones learned that he knew relatively little about production, he brought in strong managers and gave them a great deal of autonomy. Some of those production divisions never acquired the culture of the main organization, and the heads of those divisions never enjoyed the status and security that "insiders" had.

Jones had to learn somewhat painfully that he did not send as clear and consistent signals as he thought he did. He did not perceive his own conflicts and inconsistencies, and hence could not understand why some of his best young managers failed to respond to his competitive incentives and even left the company. He thought he was adequately motivating them and could not see that for some of them the political climate, the absence of stock options, and the arbitrary rewarding of family members made their own career progress too uncertain. Jones was perplexed and angry about much of this, blaming the young managers, while holding on to his own assumptions and conflicts.

Following his death the company experienced a long period of cultural turmoil because of the vacuum created by Jones's absence and the retirement of several other key culture carriers, but the basic philosophies of how to run stores were thoroughly embedded and remained. Various family members continued to run the company though none of them had the business skills that Jones had. With the retirement of Jones's chief lieutenant, a period of instability set in, marked by the discovery that some of the managers who had been developed under Jones were not as strong and capable as had been assumed. None of Jones's children or their spouses were able to take over the business decisively, so an outside person was brought in to run the company. This person predictably failed because he could not adapt to the culture and to the family. At this point the family turned to a manager who had originally been with the company and had subsequently made a fortune outside the company in various real estate enterprises. It remains to be seen whether this person, by virtue of his prior membership in the culture, can adapt to the family, gain control, and put the company back on track.

Smithfield Enterprises. Smithfield built a chain of financial service organizations, using sophisticated financial analysis techniques in an area of the country where insurance companies, mutual funds, and banks were only beginning to use such techniques. He was the conceptualizer and salesman, but once he had the idea for a new kind of service organization, he got others to invest in, build, and manage them.

Smithfield believed that he should put only a very small amount of his own money into each enterprise because if he could not convince others to put up money, maybe there was something wrong with the idea. He made the initial assumption that he did not know enough about the market to gamble with his own money, and he reinforced this assumption publicly by telling a story about the one enterprise in which he failed. He had opened a retail store in a midwestern city to sell ocean fish because he loved it, assumed others felt as he did, trusted his own judgment about what the marketplace would want, and failed. Had he tried to get many others to invest in the enterprise, he would have learned that his own tastes were not necessarily a good predictor of what others would want.

Smithfield saw himself as a creative conceptualizer but not as a manager, so he not only kept his financial investment minimal, but he also did not get personally very involved with his enterprises. Once he put together the package, he found people whom he could trust to manage the new organization. These were usually people like himself who were fairly open in their approach to business and not too concerned with imposing their own assumptions about how things should be done.

One can infer that Smithfield's assumptions about concrete goals, the best means to achieve them, how to measure results, and how to repair things when they were going wrong were essentially pragmatic. Whereas Jones had a strong need to be involved in everything, Smithfield seemed to lose interest once the new organization was on its feet and functioning. His theory seemed to be to have a clear concept of the basic mission, test it by selling it to investors, bring in good people who understood what the mission was, and then leave them alone to implement and run the organization, using only financial criteria as ultimate performance measures.

If Smithfield had assumptions about how an organization should be run internally, he kept them to himself. The cultures that each of his enterprises developed therefore had more to do with the assumptions of the people he brought in to manage them, and, as it turned out, those varied a good deal.

This brief case illustrates that there is nothing automatic about founders imposing themselves on their organizations. It depends on their personal needs to externalize their various assumptions. For Smithfield the ultimate personal validation lay in having each of his enterprises become financially successful and in his ability to continue to form creative new ones. His creative needs were such that, after a decade or so of founding financial service organizations, he turned his attention to real estate ventures, then became a lobbyist on behalf of an environmental organization, and ultimately went into politics.

Action Company. The third example is the Action Company, which has already been used to illustrate various aspects of organizational culture. Action's founder, Murphy, was a very dominant personality who had a clear theory of how things should be. He and four others founded the company because they believed they could build a product for which there would be a large market. They were able to convince investors because of their own credibility and the unanimity of their basic vision of the company's core mission. However, after some years they found that they did not share a vision of how to build an organization, and all except Murphy left the organization.

Murphy's assumptions about the nature of the world and how one discovers truth and solves problems were very strong and were reflected in his management style. He believed that good ideas could come from anyone, regardless of rank or background, but that neither he nor any other individual was smart enough to determine whether a given idea was correct. Murphy felt that open discussion in a group was the only way to test ideas and that one should not take action until the idea had survived the crucible of an active debate. One might have intuitions, but one should not act on them until they had been tested in the intellectual marketplace. Hence, Murphy set up a number of committees and groups and insisted that all ideas be discussed and debated before they were acted on. If asked why he did not make more decisions, he said that he was not smart enough to evaluate an idea if he was alone in thinking about it; but if he heard a group debating it and examining it from all angles, he thought he could judge how sound it was. Thus, Murphy set up groups as a kind of extension of his own intelligence and often used them to think out loud and get his own ideas straight in his head.

Murphy also believed that one could not get good implementation of ideas if people did not fully support them and that the best way to get support was to let people debate. Therefore, on any important decision, Murphy insisted on a wide debate, with many group meetings to test the idea and sell it down the organization and laterally; and only when it appeared that everyone wanted to do it and fully understood it would he "ratify" it. He even delayed important decisions when he was personally already convinced of the course of action to take. He said that he did not want to be out there leading all by himself and run the risk that the troops were not committed and might disown the decision if it did not work out. Past experiences of this kind had taught him to ensure commitment before going ahead on anything even if the procedure was time consuming and frustrating.

While Murphy's assumptions about decision making and implementation led to a very group-oriented organization, his theory about how to organize and manage work led to a strong individuation process, which reinforced his assumption that individuals are ultimately the source of creativity. His theory was that one must give clear and simple individual responsibility and then measure the person strictly on that area of responsibility. Groups could help to make decisions and obtain commitment, but they could not under any circumstances be responsible or accountable.

Murphy believed completely in a proactive model of human nature and in people's capacity to master nature, a set of assumptions that appeared to be correlated closely with his engineering background. Hence, he always expected people to be on top of their jobs and was very critical of them, both in public and in private, if he felt that they were not completely in control. Recognizing that circumstances might change the outcome of even the best-laid plans, Murphy expected his managers to renegotiate those plans as soon as they observed a deviation. Thus, for example, if an annual budget had been set at a certain level and the responsible manager noticed after six months that he would overrun it or else miss the schedule, he was expected to get the situation under control, according to the original assumptions, or to come back to Murphy and senior management to *renegotiate*. It was absolutely unacceptable either not to know what was happening or to let it happen without informing senior management and renegotiating.

Murphy believed completely in open communications and the ability of people to reach reasonable decisions and make appropriate compromises if they openly confronted the problems and issues, figured out what they wanted to do, and were willing to argue for their solution and honor any commitments they made. He assumed that people have "constructive intent," a rational loyalty to organizational goals and shared commitments. Withholding information, playing power games, competitively trying to win out over another member of the organization on a personal level, blaming others for one's failures, undermining or sabotaging decisions one had agreed to, and going off on one's own without getting others' agreements—all were defined as sins and brought public censure.

As previously noted, the architecture and office layout of Action reflected Murphy's assumptions about creativity and decision making. He insisted on open office landscaping; preferred cubicles for engineers instead of offices with doors; encouraged individualism in dress and behavior; and minimized the use of status symbols, such as private offices, special dining rooms for executives, and personal parking spaces. Instead, there were many conference rooms and attached kitchens to encourage people to interact comfortably.

This "model" of how to run an organization to maximize individual creativity and decision quality worked very successfully in that the company experienced dramatic growth and had exceptionally high morale. However, as the company grew larger, people found that they had less time to negotiate with each other and did not know each other as well personally, making these processes more frustrating. Some of the paradoxes and inconsistencies among the various assumptions came to the surface. For example, to encourage individuals to think for themselves and do what they believed to be the best course of action, even if it meant insubordination, clearly ran counter to the dictum that one must honor one's commitments and support decisions that have been made. In practice the rule of honoring commitments was superseded by the rule of doing only what one believes is right.

When the company was small and everyone knew everyone else, there was always time to renegotiate, and basic consensus was high enough to ensure that, if time pressure forced people to make their own decisions and to be "insubordinate," others would, after the fact, mostly agree with the decisions that had been made locally. In other words, initial decisions made at higher levels often did not "stick," but this did not bother anyone until the organization became larger and more complex. What was initially a highly adaptive system began to be regarded by more and more members of the organization as disorganization and chaos.

Murphy believed in the necessity of organization and hierarchy, but he did not trust the authority of position nearly as much as the authority of reason. Hence, managers were de facto granted authority only to the extent that they could sell their decisions, and, as indicated above, insubordination was not only tolerated but positively rewarded if it made sense and led to better outcomes. Managers often complained that they could not control any of the things they were responsible for; yet, at the same time, they believed in the system and shared Murphy's assumptions because of the kinds of people they were and the degree to which they had been socialized into the system.

Murphy also believed that the intellectual testing of ideas, which he encouraged among individuals in group settings, could be profitably extended to organizational units if it was not clear what products or markets to go after. He was willing to create overlapping product/market units and to let them compete with each other for success, not realizing, however, that such internal competition undermined openness of communication and made it more difficult for groups to negotiate decisions. Yet this way of doing things had enough success in the marketplace that Action managers came to believe in it as a way of operating in a rapidly shifting market environment.

The company thrived on intelligent, assertive, individualistic people who were willing and able to argue for and sell their ideas. The hiring practices of the company reflected this bias clearly in that each new hire had to undergo a large number of interviews and be convincing in each one of them to be viewed as a positive candidate. So, over the course of its first decade, the organization tended to hire and keep only those kinds of people who fitted the assumptions and were willing to live in the system even though it might at times be frustrating.

The people who were comfortable in this environment and enjoyed the excitement of building a successful organization found themselves increasingly feeling like members of a family and were emotionally treated as such. Strong bonds of mutual support grew up at an interpersonal level, and Murphy functioned symbolically as a brilliant, demanding, but supportive father figure. These familial feelings were implicit but important, because they provided subordinates with a feeling of security that made it possible for them to challenge each other's ideas when a proposed course of action did not make sense. A person might be severely challenged and even accused of having dumb ideas, but he could not lose his membership in the family. Frustration and insecurity grew, however, as the size of the company made it more difficult to maintain the level of personal acquaintance that would make familial feelings possible.

Murphy represents an entrepreneur with a clear set of assumptions about how things should be, both at the level of how to relate externally to the environment and how to arrange things internally in the organization. His willingness to be open about his theory and his rewarding and punishing behavior in support of it led both to the selection of others who shared the theory and to strong socialization practices that reinforced and perpetuated it. Consequently, the founder's assumptions are reflected in how the organization operates today. However, as noted above, Action also illustrates how a set of assumptions that works under one set of circumstances may become dysfunctional under other sets of circumstances. The growing frustration that resulted from trying to maintain such assumptions on a large scale in a more competitive environment has led to a number of efforts to reassess the organizational model and to figure out how to continue to be adaptive with the kind of culture that Action has developed.

Summary and Analysis

The above three cases illustrate how organizations begin to create cultures through the actions of founders. Culture is learned and taught through a variety of explicit and implicit mechanisms. The things that solve a group's problems repeatedly and that reduce anxiety will survive and become a part of the culture. But only those solutions that are proposed or invented can become candidates for cultural elements. Cultures do not start from scratch. Founders and group members always have prior experience to start with. Powerful members will try to impose their assumptions as the proposed solutions to problems, and the group selects something to try before the process of learning whether or not it works can operate. The creation and embedding process, therefore, has to be viewed simultaneously as a learning and a teaching process. At every stage the role of the leader and the group must be understood if one is to make sense of how the culture evolves.

At the most basic level, learning occurs through the reduction of anxiety that is present in any group situation. As the founder's prescriptions for how to do things are adopted, they help to stabilize cognitively how to deal with the new world, and they help to structure the initially unstructured relationships among the new group members. Whereas in the training group the members forge their consensus out of shared trial-and-error efforts, in new organizations the proposed ways of doing things typically reflect the assumptions of the founder. If the responses work, in the sense that the young organization is successful in accomplishing its goals, those responses will be doubly reinforced in that they will both reduce anxiety and produce goal accomplishment.

If the founder is surrounded by strong members who are not willing to accept his initial assumptions, the process of forging initial responses will involve conflict, negotiation, compromise, or, in some cases, a fractionation of the group (since some members will leave). Conflict also may result if the founder's proposed actions do not produce consistently good outcomes. In either case, in the early history of an organization the founder has to fight for and explicitly embed his assumptions to ensure that they will be tried out. This situation is not unlike what often happens in mature organizations where a new leader comes in with new assumptions and tries to embed these new assumptions in a group that has reached consensus on different assumptions. Both situations require one to be able to analyze how this process of "embedding" occurs and what mechanisms founders or later leaders use to ensure that their ways are tried out. In the next chapter we will examine these "mechanisms" systematically.

10

How Leaders Embed and Transmit Culture

How do founders and other powerful figures in a group get their proposed solutions implemented? How do they get the assumptions underlying those solutions communicated and embedded in the thinking, feeling, and behavior of the group? One element of that mysterious quality called "charisma" is undoubtedly a leader's ability to get across major assumptions and values in a vivid and clear manner. When leadership theorists talk about the importance of the leader's "articulating a vision" for the group, they are talking of this same set of issues (Bennis, 1983).

Some of the mechanisms that leaders use to communicate their assumptions are conscious, deliberate actions; others are unconscious and may be unintended. The same person may be conflicted and may be sending mutually contradictory messages. Among the leaders described in the preceding chapter, Jones officially stated a philosophy of delegation and decentralization but retained tight centralized control, intervened frequently on very detailed issues, and felt free to go around the

223

hierarchy. Murphy sent inconsistent signals concerning simplicity and complexity. He always advocated simple structures in which accountability was clearly visible; yet his decision-making style forced high degrees of complexity as various managers worked their proposed solutions through various committees. Managers who grew up in the company understood that one could simultaneously advocate both, but newcomers often had difficulty with what seemed to be obvious inconsistencies. On the one hand, Murphy wanted simpleness, clarity, and high levels of cooperation, but, on the other hand, he often supported overlaps, ambiguity, and competitiveness.

Subordinates will tolerate and accommodate to contradictory messages because, in a sense, founders, owners, and "higher" levels are always granted the "right" to be inconsistent or, in any case, are too powerful to be confronted. The emerging culture will then reflect not only the leader's assumptions but the complex internal accommodations created by subordinates to run the organization "in spite of" or "around" the leader. The group, acting on the assumption that the leader is a "creative genius" who has idiosyncrasies, may develop compensatory mechanisms, such as buffering layers of managers, to protect the organization from the dysfunctional aspects of the leader's behavior. In the extreme, subordinates or the board of directors may have to find ways to move the founder out altogether, as has happened in a number of first-generation companies.

But the initiative tends to be with the founder, so we will examine the process of embedding from the point of view of how the power of the founder can be used to inculcate assumptions. The mechanisms to be described vary along several dimensions: (1) how powerful their effects are, (2) how implicit or explicit the messages conveyed are, and (3) how intentional they are.

Primary Embedding Mechanisms

The most powerful primary mechanisms for culture embedding and reinforcement are (1) what leaders pay attention to, measure, and control; (2) leader reactions to critical incidents and organizational crises; (3) deliberate role modeling, teaching, and coaching by leaders; (4) criteria for allocation of rewards and status; (5) criteria for recruitment, selection, promotion, retirement, and excommunication.

What Leaders Pay Attention to, Measure, and Control. One of the best mechanisms that founders, leaders, managers, or even colleagues have available for communicating what they believe in or care about is what they systematically pay attention to. By "paying attention to," I mean anything from what is noticed and commented on, to what is measured, controlled, rewarded, and in other ways *systematically dealt with.* Even casual remarks and questions that are *consistently* geared to a certain area can be as potent as formal control mechanisms and measurements.

If leaders are aware of this process, then being systematic in paying attention to certain things becomes a powerful way of communicating a message, especially if the leaders are totally consistent in their own behavior. On the other hand, if leaders are not aware of the power of this process, or they are inconsistent in what they pay attention to, subordinates and colleagues will spend inordinate time and energy trying to decipher what the leader's behavior really reflects and even project motives where none may exist.

As a consultant I have learned that my own consistency in what I ask questions about sends clear signals to my audience about my priorities, values, and beliefs. It is the consistency that is important, not the intensity of the attention.

To illustrate, McGregor (1960) told of a company that wanted him to help install a management development program. The president hoped that McGregor would propose exactly what to do and how to do it. Instead, McGregor asked the president if he really cared about identifying and developing managers. On being assured that he did, McGregor proposed to him that he should build his concern into the reward system and set up a consistent way of monitoring progress. The president decided that he should communicate his concern by paying attention to what was being done and by reinforcing it through the reward system. He announced that henceforth 50 percent of each senior manager's annual bonus would be contingent on what he had done to develop his own immediate subordinates during the past year. He added that he himself had no specific program in mind but that each quarter he would ask each senior manager what had been done. As it turned out, the subordinates launched a series of different activities, many of them pulled together from work that was already going on piecemeal in the organization; a coherent program was forged over a two-year period and has continued to serve this company well. The president continued his quarterly questions and evaluated once a year how much each of his subordinates had done for development. He never imposed any program; but, by giving consistent attention to management development, he clearly signaled to the organization that he considered management development important.

Some of the most important signals of what the founders/leaders pay attention to are sent during meetings and other activities devoted to "planning," which is one reason why planning is such an important managerial process. In forcing subordinates to focus on certain issues in a certain way, leaders can get across their own view of how to look at problems. The ultimate content of the plan may not be as important as the learning that goes on during the planning process. For example, in his manner of planning, Smithfield (one of the leaders described in the preceding chapter) made it clear to all his subordinates that he wanted them to be autonomous, completely responsible for their own operation, but financially accountable. He got this message across by focusing only on financial results. In contrast, both Jones and Murphy would ask detailed questions about virtually everything during planning processes. Jones's obsession with store cleanliness was clearly signaled by the fact that he always commented on it, always noticed deviations from his standards, and always asked what was being done to ensure it in the future. Murphy's assumption that a good manager would always be in control of his own situation surfaced clearly in his questions about future plans and his anger when plans did not reveal detailed knowledge of product/market issues.

Focused questioning of the sort that goes on in planning and monitoring processes is, of course, reinforced by *emotional outbursts,* reactions of founders/leaders when they feel that an important assumption is being violated. Subordinates find such outbursts painful and try to avoid them. In the process they gradually come to adopt the assumptions of the leader.

For example, Murphy's concern that line managers stay on top of their jobs was originally signaled most clearly in an incident at an executive committee meeting when the company was still very young. A newly hired treasurer was asked to make his report on the state of the business. The treasurer had analyzed the three major product lines and brought his analysis to the meeting. He distributed the information and then pointed out that one product line in particular was in financial difficulty because of falling sales, excessive inventories, and rapidly rising manufacturing costs. It became evident in the meeting that the vice-president in charge of the product line had not seen the treasurer's figures and was somewhat embarrassed by what was being revealed. As the report progressed, the tension in the room rose because everyone sensed that a real confrontation was about to develop between the treasurer and the vice-president. The treasurer finished and all eyes turned toward the VP. The VP said that he had not seen the figures and wished he had had a chance to look at them; since he had not seen them, however, he had no immediate answers to give. At this point Murphy blew up at the VP, to the surprise of the whole group. Several members of the group later revealed that they had expected the president to blow up *at the treasurer* for his obvious grandstanding in bringing in figures that were new to everyone. However, no one had expected Murphy to turn his wrath on the *product line VP* for not being prepared to deal with the treasurer's arguments and information. Protests that he had not seen the data fell on deaf ears. He was told that if he were running his business properly he should have known everything the treasurer knew, and he certainly should have had answers for what would now be done.

Suddenly everyone realized that there was a powerful message in Murphy's behavior. He clearly expected and assumed that a product line VP would always be totally on top of his own business and would *never* put himself into a position of being embarrassed by financial data. The fact that he did not have his own numbers was a worse sin than being in trouble. The fact that he could not answer the troublesome figures was also a worse sin than being in trouble. The blowup at the line manager was a far clearer message than any amount of rhetoric about delegation and the like would have been.

If a manager continued to display ignorance or lack of control of his own situation, Murphy would continue to get angry at him and accuse him of incompetence. If the manager attempted to defend himself by noting that his situation was the result of actions on the part of others over whom he had no control, or resulted from prior agreements made by Murphy himself, he would be told emotionally that he should have brought the issue up right away to force a rethinking of the situation and a renegotiation of the prior decision. In other words, Murphy made it very clear, by the kinds of things that he emotionally reacted to, that poor ultimate performance could be excused, but not being on top of one's own situation and not informing others of what was going on could never be excused.

Murphy's deep assumption about the importance of always telling the truth was signaled most clearly on the occasion of the executive committee's discovery that the company had excess inventory because each product line, in the process of protecting itself, had exaggerated its orders by a small percentage. The accumulation of these small percentages across all the product lines produced a massive excess inventory, which the manufacturing department disclaimed because it had only produced what the product lines had ordered. At a meeting where this situation was reviewed, Murphy indicated that he had rarely been as angry as he was then because the product lines had "lied." He stated flatly that if he ever caught a manager exaggerating orders again it would be grounds for instant dismissal no matter what the reasons. The suggestion that manufacturing could compensate for the sales exaggerations was dismissed out of hand because that would compound the problem. The prospect of one function "lying" while the other function tried to figure out how to compensate for it totally violated Murphy's assumptions about how an effective business should be run.

Both Jones and Murphy shared the assumption that meeting the customer's needs is one of the most important ways of ensuring business success, and their most emotional reactions consistently occurred whenever they learned that a customer had not been well treated. In this area the official messages, as embodied in company creeds and the formal reward system, were totally consistent with the implicit messages that could be inferred from founder reactions. In Jones's case, the needs of the customer were even put ahead of the needs of the family, and one way that a family member could "mess up" and get into trouble was by mistreating a customer.

Other powerful signals that subordinates interpret for evidence of the leader's assumptions are what they observe *does not get reacted to*. For example, in the Action Company, managers were frequently in actual trouble with cost overruns, delayed schedules, and imperfect products, but such troubles rarely caused comment if the manager had displayed that he or she was in control of the situation. Trouble could be expected and was assumed to be a normal condition of doing business, but failure to cope and regain control was unacceptable. In Action's product design departments, one frequently found excess personnel, very high budgets, and lax management with regard to cost controls, none of which occasioned much comment. Subordinates correctly interpreted this to mean that it was far more important to come up with a good product than to control costs.

The combinations of what founders/leaders do and do not pay attention to can create problems of deciphering, because they reveal the areas where unconscious conflicts may exist. For example, in Action the clear concern for customers was signaled by outbursts if customers complained. But this attitude coexisted with an implicit arrogance toward customers, since the engineers often assumed that they knew what the customer would like in the way of product design and Murphy implicitly reinforced this attitude by *not* reacting in a corrective way when such attitudes were displayed. Murphy's own attitudes on this issue were not clear, but his silent condoning of his engineers' behavior made it possible for others to project that Murphy also believed deep down that he knew better what the customer really wanted.

The company's own history reinforced this set of assump-

tions, since the original product designs were based on the principle that in this new technology the engineers were, in fact, a
good surrogate of the ultimate customers: "If we like it, our
customers will like it." As the market matured and the products
became much more differentiated, however, managers began to
notice that the original assumption no longer held and that a
marketing orientation involving market research might be
needed. As the conflicts between engineering and marketing increased, Murphy's own behavior became less consistent, leading
subordinates to assume that he too was unsure of which assumption was correct.

*Leader Reactions to Critical Incidents and Organizational
Crises.* When an organization faces a crisis, the manner in which
leaders and others deal with it creates new norms, values, and
working procedures and reveals important underlying assumptions. Crises also are significant in culture creation and transmission partly because the heightened emotional involvement
during such periods increases the intensity of learning. If people
share intense emotional experiences and collectively learn how
to deal with very emotionally involving situations, they are
more likely to remember what they have learned.

What is defined as a crisis is, of course, partly a matter of
perception. There may or may not be actual dangers in the external environment, and what is considered to be dangerous is
itself often a reflection of the culture. For purposes of this
analysis, a crisis is what is *perceived* to be a crisis.

Not all crises are equally important in revealing cultural
assumptions. Crises that arise around the major external survival
and internal integration issues discussed in Chapter Three are
the most important. On the external side, innumerable organizations have faced the crisis of shrinking sales, excess inventories, technological obsolescence, and the subsequent necessity
of laying off employees in order to cut costs. How the organization deals with such a crisis reveals some of its assumptions
about the importance of people and its view of human nature.
Ouchi (1981) cites several dramatic examples where United
States companies faced with layoffs decided instead to go to
short work weeks or to have all employees and managers take

cuts in pay to manage the cost reduction without people reduction. In one such company, which survived the financial crisis
without laying anyone off, a series of organizational stories are
told and retold to show what kinds of values were operating in
the organization at the time.

The assumption in Action that "We are a family who will
take care of each other" comes out most clearly during periods
of crisis. When the company was doing well, Murphy often had
emotional outbursts reflecting his concern that people were getting complacent; but when the company was in difficulty,
Murphy never punished anyone or displayed anger. Instead, he
became the strong and supportive father figure, pointing out
to both the external world and the employees that things were
not as bad as they seemed, that the company had great strengths
that would ensure future success, and that people should not
worry about layoffs. Instead, things would be controlled by
slowing down hiring.

On the internal side, issues of language and communication, how to determine what is true or false, how to deal with
authority and with peers, how to handle conflict, and how to
allocate property are probably most important. I have found
that a good time to observe an organization very closely is when
acts of *insubordination* take place. So much of an organization's
culture is tied up with hierarchy, authority, power, and influence that the mechanisms of conflict resolution have to be
worked out and consensually validated. No better opportunity
exists for leaders to send signals about their own assumptions
about human nature and relationships than when they themselves are challenged. For example, Murphy clearly and repeatedly revealed his assumption that he did *not* feel that he knew
best. Through his tolerant and even encouraging behavior when
subordinates argued with him or disobeyed him, he signaled
that he was truly depending on his subordinates to know what
was best and that they should be insubordinate if they felt they
were right. In contrast, a bank president insisted that he wanted
his subordinates to think for themselves, but his behavior belied
his overt claim. During an important meeting of the whole staff,
one of these subordinates, in attempting to assert himself, made

some silly errors in a presentation. The president laughed at him and ridiculed him. Though the president later apologized and said he did not mean it, the damage had been done. All the subordinates who witnessed the incident interpreted the outburst to mean that the president was not really serious about delegating to them and having them be more assertive. He was still sitting in judgment on them and was still operating on the assumption that he knew best.

Deliberate Role Modeling, Teaching, and Coaching. Founders and new leaders of organizations generally seem to know that their own visible behavior has great value for communicating assumptions and values to other members, especially newcomers. I know of one organization where the president has made a number of videotapes that outline his explicit philosophy, and these tapes are shown to new members of the organization as part of their initial training. However, there is a difference between the messages delivered from staged settings, such as when a president gives a welcoming speech to newcomers, and the messages received when a president is observed "informally." The informal messages are the more powerful teaching and coaching mechanism.

Jones, for example, demonstrated his need to be involved in everything at a detailed level by his frequent visits to stores and minute inspections once he got there. When he went on vacation, he called the office every day at a set time and asked detailed questions about all aspects of the business. This behavior persisted into his semiretirement, when he would call every day from his retirement home thousands of miles away. Through his questions, his lectures, and his demonstration of personal concern for details, he hoped to show other managers what it meant to be highly visible and on top of one's job.

By his unwavering loyalty to family members, Jones also "trained" people in how to think about family members and the rights of owners. As previously noted, he often ignored bad business results if family members were involved, tolerated insubordination from them, and publicly excused their behavior. Family members shared completely in the financial rewards of the business even if they had contributed very little or had actually done damage. If his behavior was questioned, Jones explained that the family had special rights by virtue of its ownership position.

In the Action Company, Murphy made an explicit attempt to downplay status and hierarchy because of his assumption that good ideas can come from anyone. He communicated this assumption in many ways. For example, he drove a small car, had an unpretentious office, dressed informally, and spent many hours wandering among the employees at all levels getting to know them informally. Stories developed around this informality, and such stories institutionalized the president's behavior.

An example of more explicit coaching occurred in a floundering company that brought back a former executive who had had a decade or more of experience in other more dynamic organizations. One of the first things he did as the new president was to display at a large meeting his own particular method of analyzing the performance of the company and planning its future. He said explicitly to the group: "Now that's an example of the kind of good planning and management I want in this organization." He then ordered his key executives to prepare a long-range planning process in the format in which he had just lectured and gave them a target time to be ready to present their own plans in the *new* format. At the meeting he coached their presentations, commented on each one, corrected the approach where he felt it had missed the point, and gave them new deadlines for accomplishing their goals as spelled out in the plans. Privately he told an observer of this meeting that the organization had done virtually no planning for decades and that he hoped to institute formal strategy planning as a way of reducing the massive deficits which the organization had been experiencing. From his point of view, he had to change the entire "mentality" of his subordinates, which, he felt, required him to instruct, model, correct, and coach.

Criteria for Allocation of Rewards and Status. Members of any organization learn from their own experience with promotions, performance appraisals, and discussions with the boss what the organization values and what the organization punishes. Both the nature of the behavior rewarded and punished and the nature of the rewards and punishments themselves carry the messages. An organization's leaders can quickly get across their own priorities, values, and assumptions by consistently linking rewards and punishments to the behavior they are concerned with.

What is being referred to here is the actual system, what really happens, not what is espoused, published, or preached. For example, the product managers in a large food company were expected to develop a successful marketing program for a specific product and then were rewarded by being moved to a "better" product after about eighteen months. Since the results of a marketing program could not possibly be known in eighteen months, what was *really* rewarded was not the ultimate performance of the product in the marketplace but the performance of the product manager in creating a "good" marketing program, as measured by the ability to sell it to colleagues and senior managers.

The implicit assumption was that only senior managers could be trusted to evaluate a marketing program; therefore, even if a product manager was "accountable" for his product, it was, in fact, senior management that took the real responsibility for launching expensive marketing programs. What junior managers learned from this was how to develop programs that had the right characteristics and style from senior management's point of view. If a junior-level manager developed the illusion that he really had independence in making marketing decisions, he had only to look at the actual rewards given to successful managers: they received a better product to manage, they might get a slightly better office (which was graded according to a company manual specifying size, type of furniture, allowable wall decorations, and carpeting), and they received a good raise. But they still had to present their marketing programs to senior management for review, and the preparations for and dry runs of such presentations took four to five months of every year.

To reiterate the point, if the founders or leaders are trying to ensure that their values and assumptions will be learned, they must create a reward, promotion, and status system that is consistent with those assumptions. Whereas the message initially gets across in the daily behavior of the leader, it is judged in the long run by whether the important rewards are allocated consistently with that daily behavior. If these levels of message transmission are inconsistent, one would find a highly conflicted culture or no culture at all at a total organizational level.

Criteria for Recruitment, Selection, Promotion, Retirement, and Excommunication. One of the most subtle yet most potent ways in which culture gets embedded and perpetuated is in the initial selection of new members. If a founder holds the assumption that the best way to build an organization is to hire very tough, independent people and then leave them alone, and is successful in continuing to hire tough and independent people, he will create the kind of culture that he assumes will work best. He may never realize that the success of the culture lies in the success of the recruitment effort and that his beliefs about how to organize might become disconfirmed if he no longer could hire the right kinds of people to fit his assumptions.

Since culture perpetuates itself through the recruitment of people who fit into it, an ongoing culture can be hard to change. One is then asking a large number of people to adopt assumptions that do not fit their own cultural background and that therefore might be totally unpalatable. On the other hand, culture change can be accelerated if one recruits and selects new members according to criteria that fit new cultural assumptions. That strategy will produce a period of interim turmoil, but the new members will not be personally uncomfortable with the new culture if they have been initially hired to fit into it.

This cultural embedding mechanism is subtle because it operates unconsciously in most organizations. Organizations tend to find attractive those candidates who resemble present members in style, assumptions, values, and beliefs. They are perceived to be the "best" people to hire and have attributed to them characteristics that will justify their being hired. Unless someone outside the organization is explicitly involved in the hiring, there is no way of knowing how much the current implicit assumptions are dominating recruiters' perceptions of the candidates. It would be interesting to study search firms from this perspective. Since they operate outside the cultural context of the employing organization, do they become implicitly culture reproducers or changers, and are they aware of their power in this regard? Do organizations that employ outside search firms do so in part to get away from their own biases in hiring?

In any case, it is clear that initial selection decisions for new members, followed by the criteria applied in the promotion system, are powerful mechanisms for embedding and perpetuating the culture, especially when combined with socialization tactics designed to teach cultural assumptions. In the Action Company, this mechanism was very clear from an outsider's point of view, since the only candidates who passed the interviewing screen were very bright, articulate, self-reliant, assertive people. In the interviews they would be told exactly what kind of place Action was and would be advised not to come to work there unless they thought they could really survive in the environment with relatively little support. Subsequent socialization practices reinforced these criteria by giving a great deal of freedom, relatively little nurturance, more criticism than positive feedback, and a maximum of opportunity to get involved. Managers talked of an "Action type," and, even though they could not exactly describe one, they all believed that they could recognize one. Multi tended to hire primarily scientific people right out of college or university and then to look for managerial potential some years after the person had been hired. Attempts to speed up the process of locating future general managers by hiring MBAs were unsuccessful because the MBAs were not considered the "right type" and were not given the necessary opportunity to develop. Interestingly, in both companies the marketing and/or general management type was held in low esteem, so that both companies found it difficult to launch good marketing programs or to develop general managers more quickly.

Basic assumptions are further reinforced through criteria of who does or does not get promoted, who is retired early, and who is, in effect, excommunicated. In the Action Company, an employee who was not bright enough or articulate enough to play the idea-debating game and to stand up for his own ideas, soon became walled off and eventually was "forced out" through a process of benign but consistent neglect. In Multi a similar kind of isolation occurred if an employee was not concerned about the company, the products, and senior management. Neither company fired people except for dishonesty or immoral behavior, but in both companies such isolation became the equivalent of excommunication.

Because the messages transmitted by these mechanisms are to a large extent implicit, conflicting messages can be sent. Sometimes such messages result from unconscious conflicts in the message senders, and sometimes they result from conflicts among key leaders in what they believe, assume, and value. In either case, the messages are implicit, and it is therefore possible for conflicting assumptions to coexist in a group and for the group to accommodate to such inconsistencies and conflicts.

Secondary Articulation and Reinforcement Mechanisms

The most important secondary articulation and reinforcement mechanisms are (1) the organization's design and structure; (2) organizational systems and procedures; (3) design of physical space, facades, and buildings; (4) stories, legends, myths, and parables about important events and people; (5) formal statements of organizational philosophy, creeds, and charters.

I have labeled these mechanisms "secondary" because they work only if they are consistent with the primary mechanisms discussed previously. When they are consistent, they begin to build organizational ideologies and thus to formalize much of what is informally learned at the outset. If they are inconsistent, they either will be ignored or will be a source of internal conflict. But the operating cultural assumptions will always be manifested first in what the leaders demonstrate, not in what is written down or inferred from designs and procedures.

For example, with respect to Murphy's decision-making theory, he formally states that he wants broad consensus across a wide range of committees and managers. That is the official formal position. Yet many of his subordinates will say that he usually does know what he wants and is only manipulating the situation to have the answer come out of the group, so that he does not have to take sole responsibility. Observing him in action reveals that both patterns occur. Sometimes he appears to manipulate toward predetermined solutions that he believes in; sometimes he genuinely discovers new solutions in the group decision processes. The only conclusion one can draw is that he is himself conflicted on this issue and that the Action Company's culture reflects the conflict.

Organization Design and Structure. As I have observed executive groups in action, particularly first-generation groups led by their founder, I have noticed that the design of the organization—how to divide up product lines, market areas, functional responsibilities, and so on—elicits high degrees of passion, but not too much clear logic. The requirements of the primary task—how to organize in order to survive in the external environment—seem to get mixed up with powerful assumptions about internal relationships and with theories of how to get things done that derive more from the founder's background than from current analysis. If it is a family business, the structure must make room for key family members, or trusted colleagues, cofounders, and friends. Even in the first-generation publicly held company, the organization's design is often built around the talents of the individual managers rather than the external task requirements.

Founders often have strong theories about how to organize for maximum effectiveness. Some assume that only they can ultimately determine what is correct; therefore, they build a tight hierarchy and highly centralized controls. Others assume that the strength of their organization is in their people and therefore build an organization that pushes authority down as low as possible. Still others believe that their strength is in negotiated solutions; therefore, they hire strong people but then create a structure that forces such people to negotiate their solutions with each other. Some leaders believe in minimizing interdependence in order to free each unit of the organization; others believe in creating checks and balances, so that no one unit can ever function autonomously.

The design of the organization initially and the periodic reorganizations that companies go through thus provide ample opportunities for the founders/leaders to embed their deeply held assumptions about the task, the means to accomplish it, the nature of people, and the right kinds of relationships to foster among people. Some leaders are able to articulate why they have designed their organization the way they have; others appear to be rationalizing and are not really consciously aware of the assumptions they are making, even though such assumptions can easily be inferred from the results.

Organizational Systems and Procedures. The most visible part of life in any organization is the daily, weekly, monthly, quarterly, and annual cycle of routines, procedures, reports, forms, and other recurrent tasks that have to be performed. The origin of such routines is often not known to participants, or sometimes even to senior management, but their existence lends structure, predictability, and concreteness to an otherwise vague and ambiguous organizational world. The systems and procedures thus serve a function quite similar to the formal structure: they make life predictable and, thereby, reduce ambiguity and anxiety.

Given that group members seek this kind of stability and anxiety reduction, founders and leaders have the opportunity to reinforce their assumptions by building systems and routines around them. For example, Murphy reinforced his belief in groups processing ideas by creating and attending many different kinds of committees. If he either discouraged committee formation or failed to attend meetings, subordinates might assume that he did not really mean to have ideas processed in groups. But by strongly embedding meetings in daily, weekly, and monthly routines, Murphy gets his message reinforced.

Systems and procedures can formalize the process of "paying attention" and thus reinforce the message that the leader really cares about certain things. Thus, the president who wanted management development programs helped his cause immensely by formalizing his quarterly reviews of what each subordinate had done. Formal budgeting or planning routines are often adhered to less to produce plans and budgets and more to provide a vehicle to remind subordinates what the leader considers to be important things to pay attention to.

If founders or leaders do not design systems and procedures as reinforcement mechanisms, they open the door to historically evolved inconsistencies in the culture, or weaken their own message from the outset. Thus, a strong president who believes, as Murphy did, that line managers should be in full control of their own operation must ensure that the organization's financial control procedures are consistent with that belief. If he allows a strong centralized corporate financial organization to evolve, and if he pays attention to the data generated by this organization, he is sending a signal inconsistent with the assumption that managers should control their own finances. The organization may then evolve one subculture in the line organization and a different subculture in the corporate finance organization. If those groups end up fighting each other, it will be the direct result of the initial inconsistency in design logic.

Design of Physical Space, Facades, Buildings. This category is intended to encompass all the visible features of the organization that clients, customers, vendors, new employees, and visitors would encounter. The messages that can be inferred from the physical environment are, as in the case of structure and procedures, potentially reinforcing of the leader's messages, but only if they are managed to be so (Steele, 1973). If they are not explicitly managed, they may reflect the assumptions of architects, the planning and facilities managers in the organization, local norms in the community, or other subcultural assumptions.

Leaders who have a clear philosophy and style often choose to embody that style in the visible manifestations of their organization. For example, Action, with its assumptions about truth through conflict and the importance of open communications, has chosen an open office layout with partitions only high enough to permit a sense of privacy when one is sitting down. Private offices are given to only a few people who need them, and then typically have glass doors so that one can always see who is in. Kitchens and eating facilities are provided in every work area to facilitate luncheon get-togethers, and most conference rooms have round or oval tables to symbolize the unimportance of formal status and to facilitate communication. The office layout clearly articulates the emphasis on equal-ity, ease of communication, and importance of relationships. What the visitor experiences visually in this organization is an accurate reflection of deeply held values and assumptions, and one indicator of this depth is that the effects are reproduced in the offices of this organization all over the world.

Multi also strongly values individual expertise and autonomy; but, because of its assumption that an occupant of a given job becomes the ultimate expert on the area covered by that job, it physically symbolizes turf by giving people privacy. Managers at Multi spend much more time thinking things out alone, having individual conferences with others who are centrally involved, and protecting the privacy of individuals so that they can get their work done. What the visitor encounters in this organization is a lobby manned by a guard and closed doors on all sides. As the visitor is led by the host to the appointment, he passes only closed doors. Even the secretaries have closed doors, so that one might encounter no one in moving from one office to another. There are no conference rooms, but each executive office has an attractive conference area within it. The building is massive, the doors are heavy and thick, and there is a silence in the corridor.

In Multi, as in Action, these are not incidental or accidental physical artifacts. They reflect the basic assumptions of how work gets done, how relationships should be managed, how one arrives at truth. So one can learn a great deal from such artifacts, if one knows how to interpret them, and leaders can communicate a great deal if they know how to structure and create such settings.

Stories About Important Events and People. As a group develops and accumulates a history, some of this history becomes embodied in stories about events and leadership behavior (Martin and Powers, 1983; Wilkins, 1983). Thus, the story— whether it is in the form of a parable, legend, or even myth— reinforces assumptions and teaches assumptions to newcomers. However, since the message to be found in the story is often highly distilled or even ambiguous, this form of communication is somewhat unreliable. Leaders cannot always control what will be said about them in stories, though they can certainly reinforce stories that they feel good about and perhaps can even launch stories that carry desired messages. Leaders can make themselves highly visible to increase the likelihood that stories will be told about them, but sometimes attempts to manage the message in this manner backfire in that the story may focus more on the inconsistencies and conflicts which observers detect in the leader.

Formal Statements of Organizational Philosophy, Creeds, Charters. The final mechanism of articulation and reinforcement to be mentioned is the formal statement, the attempt by the founders or leaders to state explicitly what their values or assumptions are. These statements will highlight only a small portion of the assumption set that operates in the group and, most likely, will highlight those aspects of the leader's philosophy or ideology that lend themselves to public articulation. Such public statements may have a value for the leader as a way of emphasizing special things to be attended to in the organization, as values around which to "rally the troops," and as reminders of fundamental assumptions not to be forgotten; but formal statements cannot be seen as a way of defining the culture of the organization. At best they cover a small, publicly relevant segment of the culture, those aspects that leaders find useful to publish as an ideology for the organization.

Conclusion

Five of the mechanisms discussed in this chapter are powerful primary ways by which founders or leaders are able to embed their own assumptions in the ongoing daily life of their organizations. Through what they pay attention to and reward, through the role modeling they do, through the manner in which they deal with critical incidents, and through the criteria they use for recruitment, selection, promotion, and excommunication, they communicate both explicitly and implicitly the assumptions they really hold. If they are conflicted, the conflicts and inconsistencies also get communicated and become a part of the culture.

Less powerful, more ambiguous, and more difficult to

control are the messages embedded in the organization's structure, its procedures and routines, its physical layout, its stories and legends, and its formal statements about itself. Yet these secondary mechanisms can be a powerful reinforcement of the primary messages if the leader is able to control them. The important point to grasp is that all these mechanisms do communicate culture content to newcomers. Leaders do not have a choice about whether to communicate. They have a choice only about how much to manage what they communicate. Organizations differ in the degree to which the cultural messages are consistent and clear; and this variation in cultural clarity is probably a reflection of the clarity and consistency of the assumptions of the leaders. But it is not their public statements which must be assessed to measure clarity; it is the entire range of messages discussed in this chapter that must be assessed.

11

Understanding
Culture Change
in the Context of
Organizational Change

The concept of organizational culture is structurally complex. By definition it consists of a large set of taken-for-granted implicit assumptions that cover how group members view both their external relationships with their various environments and their internal relationships with each other. If the group has a shared history of any length, these assumptions will have become aligned with one another and will have generated a pattern that reflects higher-order assumptions about the nature of reality, time, space, people, and relationships. This patterning of basic assumptions, or the cultural paradigm, becomes the deepest and most strongly held level of the culture because of the human need for consistency and order.

If culture has developed in this sense, it will affect most of the aspects of an organization—its strategy, its structure, its processes, its reward and control systems, and its daily routines. If the organization is unfrozen by external or internal events, if it perceives some form of crisis that motivates a need

244

to change, the change process will typically start at the strategy, structure, and procedures level. How does culture affect such a change process, and does culture itself change in the process? And what, in fact, is meant by "culture change"? For example, when we talk of culture change, do we mean behavioral changes, value changes, or changes in assumptions? Do we mean changes in the whole paradigm or merely in one set of assumptions? How much has to change at what level before we consider it a "real" change in culture? Under what conditions is such change desirable and/or possible? If a change process reinforces some elements of the culture, is that culture change?

A Case of Organizational (Cultural?) Change

As an approach to answering these questions, I will present data from Multi—along with contrasting observations of Action—to illustrate through concrete events how the change process unfolds as I have observed it. As we will see, I became involved in a major change program at Multi, which changed some of the directions of this organization. My purpose in giving a detailed account is twofold. On the one hand, I cannot get across the complexity of the change process without giving a detailed review of situations in which I have been personally involved as a consultant. On the other hand, such detail is necessary to show how even the diagnosis of what is cultural can be problematic. No matter how clear the definition of culture is conceptually, the culture of any given organization is, in fact, very difficult to decipher.

The cultures of Action and Multi did not reveal themselves easily or automatically. Rather, I had to reconstruct, with the help of members of the organization, why certain events that struck me as incongruent made sense if viewed from a cultural point of view. I will therefore interweave into the account below how I made some of the cultural inferences that have been reported in this book.

The information I will present here is, of course, not complete, either historically or ethnographically. It is limited by the clinical perspective I am taking and is therefore biased by what the client's purpose was in talking with me. I am trying to give a picture of the change processes that I observed during my consulting work with these organizations. My goal was not to study change but to help with ongoing organizational problems. My reconstruction of events is therefore selective, focusing on the particular issues that bear on the process of cultural change and the role of culture in organizational change.

Initial Involvement in Multi: First Annual Meeting. My involvement with Multi began over five years ago with a major "educational intervention" for the top-management group at its annual worldwide meeting. The manager of management development had heard me speak at an open seminar and suggested to his boss, Ted Richards, the chairman of the executive committee (the group accountable for the company's performance), that my material on career dynamics might be worth sharing with Multi's senior management (Schein, 1978). Richards wanted to combine work on company problems with some stimulating input for the group, broadly in the area of leadership and creativity. He saw that the company was moving into a more turbulent economic, political, and technological environment that would require new kinds of responses.

The company had apparently seen the need to stimulate creativity for some years and had conducted a variety of seminars on the creative process. At the annual meetings, outsiders had been invited to speak, but in previous years they had concentrated more on marketing and technical issues. My two days of lecturing were to be focused on leadership and creativity in the context of individual career development.

Both the topic of *creativity* and the approach of *lecturing* to the group are completely congruent with Multi's assumptions that (1) creativity is important in science and (2) knowledge is acquired through a scientific process and then communicated through experts in a didactic way. In the pragmatic environment of Action, in contrast, it would have been inconceivable to devote two whole days of senior management time to a seminar involving primarily outside lecturers, and the topic of creativity would not have interested the senior managers. It would have been viewed as too abstract.

In fact, my initial involvement with Action came about because its senior managers were having problems in communication and interpersonal relationships. They wanted a consultant at their meetings to observe and to help *on line*. If I did attempt to lecture the group, even for fifteen minutes, I was interrupted and forced either to make my comments immediately relevant or to let the group get back to work.

Whereas in Action much took place without preplanning, in Multi everything was planned to the smallest level of detail. The seminar administrator, a former line manager who had moved into executive training, met with me for many hours some months prior to the seminar to plan for the materials to be used, the exercise to be designed to involve the participants, the schedule, and so on. In this process I observed how carefully Multi managers planned for every detail of an activity that they were responsible for. I had to provide a plan that showed virtually minute by minute what would happen during the two days, and the company was clearly willing to commit all the time and energy it might take to design as nearly "perfect" a meeting as possible.

Not only was Multi's high degree of commitment to structure revealed in this process, but, in retrospect, it also revealed how basic the assumption was about managerial turf. The seminar administrator had clear responsibility for the conduct of the meeting, though he was two levels below the participants. He had formed a review committee for purposes of checking the seminar plan and obtaining prior involvement. This committee included Richards, the chairman of the executive committee, but the group gave considerable freedom to the administrator to make final decisions on seminar format. Thus, both in Action and in Multi, the culture was displaying itself in the manner in which I encountered the organization, but I did not know this at the time.

The participants at the Multi annual meeting were the chairman of the board, Richards' boss, several board members who showed up as visitors, the nine-person executive committee, all the senior functional and divisional managers, and the most important country managers, totaling forty-five in number. This group met annually for five days or less, depending on specific agenda to be covered.

Though I did not know it at the time, the meeting served a major integrative and communication function in that it legitimized during the meeting what culturally did not happen in day-to-day operations—a high level of open and lateral communication. It also reflected the hierarchical emphasis, however, in that this sharing across units took place in public under the scrutiny of the executive committee and board members. Moreover, there was still a strong tendency to be deferent toward others and to share ideas only when information was specifically asked for. The meeting also provided an opportunity for senior management to get a major message across quickly to the entire organization and, as we will see, to involve the entire organization in crisis management when that was needed.

Impact of First Annual Meeting. The major effects of the two days as I now reconstruct these events were as follows:

1. The group obtained new insights and information about creativity and innovation, especially the insight that innovation occurs within a variety of careers and organizational settings and should not be confused with the pure creative process that scientists are engaged in (Schein, 1978). The assumption had crept in that only scientists are creative, so those managers who had left their technical identities behind long ago were reassured by my message that managerial role innovations in all the functions of the business were much needed in a healthy organization. This legitimized a great many activities as "creative" that had previously not been perceived as such and liberated some problem-solving energy by linking innovation to day-to-day problem solving. This insight would not have been dramatic but for the fact that the group was so embedded in assumptions about science and the creative process within science.

2. The group obtained new insights from the discussion of career anchors, which emphasized the variety of careers and the different things people are looking for in their careers (Schein, 1978). The effect was to unfreeze some of the monolithic notions about careers and the role of scientific back-

grounds in careers. In an informal dinner, the chairman of the board gave a humorous talk about his own career, which further legitimized the notion of individual differences in careers.

3. The group got to know me and my style as a responsive process consultant through several spontaneous interventions that I made during the two days. For example, after I had observed the group's limited view of the creative process, based on a science model, I decided to highlight the difference between "creativity" and "role innovation" (Van Maanen and Schein, 1979). (Incidentally, I still had to clear my proposed deviations from the original format with the seminar administrator and the review committee.)

During the informal times at meals and in the evening, my spontaneous responses were geared to getting out of the expert role. I had observed that group members put me into an expert authority role, reflected in the frequent use of my title, "Professor," and in the kinds of general questions posed to me about what was known in my "field" and what I thought of certain approaches to management. I found myself evading answers to these questions, turning the topics back to what was going on in Multi, and reacting to specific inquiries with examples of alternatives rather than broad generalizations. For example, if I was asked what companies were doing today in the field of participative management, I would give examples and highlight the diversity of what I observed rather than generalizing as I was expected to do. I had the sense in this process that I was disappointing some of the managers with whom I was speaking, because I did not fit the stereotype of the scientist who is willing to summarize the state of knowledge in a field. On the other hand, my willingness to delve into the problems of Multi appealed to some managers, and they accepted my self-definition as a process rather than an expert consultant (Schein, 1969).

My participation in the meeting ended when my two days were finished, but plans were made to institute in broader segments of the company two of the activities that had been illustrated in the seminar and were described in detail in my book *Career Dynamics,* which had been given to all participants

(Schein, 1978). Specifically, Richards and the executive committee decided to ask all senior managers to do the "job/role-plan-
ning exercise," which involves rethinking one's own job in the
context of how it has changed and will continue to change as
one projects ahead five years and analyzes the environment
around the job. Richards also encouraged more managers to do
the "career anchor interview exercise" as an input to the annual
management development process and authorized the development of an adaptation of the original questionnaire for use specifically in the company. This exercise involves the reconstruction of all the major career steps in order to identify the pattern
of reasons for each step. The purpose is to locate the "anchor"
—those things that the person would not give up if forced to
make a choice. I was asked to work with the headquarters management development group to help to implement these two
activities by spending roughly ten to fifteen days during the subsequent year as a consultant. My clients were to be the management development manager and Richards, and the broad mission was to increase the ability of the company to innovate in
all areas.

First Year's Work: Getting Acquainted. I visited the
company several times during the year, each time for two to
three days. During these visits I learned more about the management development system, met some of the members of the
executive committee, and gradually got involved in what *I* considered my most important activity, the planning of the next
annual meeting. From my point of view, if innovation was to
take hold, the relatively more open climate of the annual meeting was the most important thing to take advantage of. My goal
was to be accepted as a *process* consultant to the entire meeting, not as an educator coming in with wisdom for one or two
days.

I found that the notion that I could help "on line" was
quite foreign to most of the managers, though in Action I had
learned the opposite lesson: that unless I worked "on line with
real problems," the group considered me more or less useless.
Initially I thought that the reactions of Multi's managers were
simply based on misunderstanding. It was only with repeated

experiences of not being invited to working meetings in Multi, of always being put into an expert role, and of always having to plan my visits in great detail that I realized I was up against something which could be genuinely defined as "cultural."

The perception of Multi managers of what consultants do and how they work reflected their more general assumptions about what managers do and how they work. For example, on several occasions I noticed that managers whom I had met on previous visits looked past me and ignored me when I encountered them in the public lobby or the executive dining room. As I later learned, to be seen with a consultant meant that one had problems and needed help—a position that managers in Multi strongly avoided. Why, then, could I be accepted at all in the system? Because I could be seen as an academic expert telling management development managers how to improve the total function, or I could lecture to management and thereby bring new concepts to them. This formulation of my role fitted Multi's cultural model.

The point is important because my request to attend the next annual meeting in a process consultant role was, unbeknownst to me, strongly countercultural. But Richards was intrigued, and his own innovativeness swayed other members of the planning committee. We compromised on the notion that I would give some lectures on relevant topics based on the events I observed at the meeting, thus legitimizing my attendance. My role as a consultant was further legitimized by my being cast as a scientist who had to be given an opportunity to get to know top management better, so that I could be more helpful in the future. Richards and other senior managers had a specific view of what the total group needed and were prepared to introduce an outsider in the consultant role to facilitate this process. I believe that they wanted to unfreeze the group to get it more receptive to the crisis message they were preparing to deliver. An outsider with new ideas was seen as helpful both as a source of feedback to the group and as an expert on the change process that was about to be launched. Another "outsider," a professor of policy and strategy who also occupied a position on the board of Multi, was invited as well. Our attendance at the meeting was related to a decision made by Richards and the executive committee: that at the annual meeting a major review of company performance, division by division, would be undertaken. Such a review, they believed, would bring out the need for change and innovation and thereby reverse a slide into unprofitability that had been going on but was not clearly recognized or accepted. They also planned to introduce a program of change called the Redirection Project. This business problem had been developing over several years but had not yet been identified as a crisis to be collectively shared with senior management worldwide.

The major divisions of the company, whose headquarters were in the same city as the corporate headquarters, were the primary profit centers. These divisions knew what their individual situations were but seemed unaware of the impact of dropping profit levels in many areas on the company as a whole. Only the executive committee had the total picture. This situation could easily arise because of the low amount of lateral communication, permitting the manager of a division that was losing money to rationalize that his loss was easily compensated for by other divisions and that "things would soon improve." The culture encouraged each manager to worry only about his own piece of the organization, not to take a broad corporate view. Although communications that had gone out to the divisions over the year had suggested a total company problem, no one seemed to take it very seriously. Therefore, much of the annual meeting was to be devoted to "selling" the idea that there was a total company problem, and helping managers in small-group meetings to accept and deal with those problems. Given these goals, the planning committee saw the point of having me help in the design of the meeting and to plan lectures as needed on how to initiate and manage various change projects. In other words, the economic and market environment was creating a financial crisis, top management decided it was time to deal with it, and the consultation process became one piece of management's more general process of launching the Redirection Project.

Unfreezing at Second Annual Meeting. The first segment of the meeting was devoted to presenting financial data, division by division, followed by small-group meetings to digest and analyze the situation and formulate proposals for reversing the business decline. What made the situation complicated was that some of the divisions, those operating in mature markets, were losing money and needed major restructuring, while other divisions were growing and making good contributions to overall profit levels.

The division managers from the problem divisions were embarrassed, apologetic, and overconfident that they could reverse the situation, while others said privately that the losing divisions could not possibly accomplish their goals, were not really committed to change, and would make only cosmetic alterations. The division managers from the profitable divisions bragged, felt complacent, and wondered when top management would do something about the "losers" who were dragging others down with them. But many people from the losing divisions said privately that even the profitable divisions—although they might look good relative to others *inside* the company—were not performing as well as they should if compared to *outside* competitors in their own industrial market segment.

During the divisional reviews and presentations, another important cultural assumption surfaced. The company had been diversifying for a number of years and was attempting to get into consumer goods via a line of toiletries and cleaning products. I was sitting next to a chemist, a member of the executive committee, when some of the consumer-oriented advertisements were shown on the screen as part of the division review. He was clearly upset by the "low" level of the message and whispered to me in an agitated tone, "Those things aren't even *products*; they don't do anything." The assumption seemed to be that a "product" had to be something useful, such as a cure for disease or a successful pesticide that reduces starvation. Managers took pride in the important and useful products that were a current source of success. Selling something only because it made money did not fit into some of their cultural assumptions about the nature of their business; and, as we will see, the fate of the consumer products division is still very much a matter of internal debate.

The *country managers,* representing subsidiary companies in the major countries of the world, who were measured on their total cross-divisional performance, acknowledged the cross-divisional issues but were actually more upset because the headquarters organization—representing such functions as research and development, finance and control, personnel, and manufacturing—had become overgrown both in corporate headquarters and in the divisional headquarters. These managers insisted that the headquarters functional staffs should be reduced, because they were an unnecessary overhead and, in many cases, an active interference in running the businesses in the countries. A high degree of centralization of research and development, manufacturing, and financial control had made sense when the company was young and small; but as it expanded and became a worldwide multinational, the small regional sales offices had gradually become large autonomous companies that managed all the functions. Country heads needed their own staffs; but these staffs then came into conflict with the corporate staffs and the division staffs, who felt that they could communicate directly with their division people in each country.

Because of the hierarchical nature of the organization, the headquarters groups asked for enormous amounts of information from the regions and frequently visited the regions. If they had worldwide responsibility for something, their way of staying in control was to be fully informed about everything at all times. Because of the lack of lateral communication, the functional staffs did not realize that their various inquiries and visits often paralyzed local operations because of the amount of time it took to answer questions, entertain visitors, get permission to act, and so on.

As the cost structure of the company came under increasing scrutiny, the country organizations were asked to reduce costs, while the headquarters organizations remained complacent, fat, and happy. The question that most worried the country managers was whether top management considered the crisis serious enough to warrant reductions in the headquarters functional staffs. If not, it must mean that this was only a fire-fighting drill, not a real crisis.

By the end of the first day of the second annual meeting, the financial data had been presented and groups had met to consider what should be done, but the feedback from the groups indicated neither a complete understanding nor a real acceptance of the problem. The planning committee met to consider what to do and decided that the other consultant could help the group recognize the seriousness of the problem if he "interrogated" the group members in the style of a Harvard case discussion and led them to the inevitable conclusion that a crisis really existed. He did this very effectively on the second day of the meeting in a two-hour session that proved conclusively to all present that the group could not sustain any profitability in the long run unless major changes were made. The result was a real sense of panic and depression. For the first time, the message had really been accepted collectively, laying the stage for the introduction of the Redirection Project.

Why did this work? I had the sense that, in a culture where senior managers function symbolically as parent figures, it is difficult for the parents to tell the children that the family may fail if they don't shape up. The children find it too easy to blame each other and the parents and to collectively avoid feeling responsible. There was too much of a tradition that senior managers (the parents) will take care of things as they always have. The anxiety of facing up to the "family problem" was too overwhelming, so a great deal of denial had been operating. The outside consultant could, in this case, take the same information but present it as a problem that the family as a whole owned and had to confront and handle as a total unit. He could be much more direct and confrontive than insiders could be with each other, and, at, the same time, he could remind the total group that everyone was in this together—the executive committee as the symbolic parents along with all the children. This recognition did not reduce the resultant panic; however, it forced it out into the open, since denial was no longer possible. The group had been genuinely unfrozen.

The next problem, then, was how to deal with the panic and discouragement that were now present in the group. How could we provide some psychological safety that would permit the group to redefine the situation, to begin to feel capable of doing something constructive? The other consultant and I took a long walk to think this out and came up with the idea that now would be a good time to give some lectures on the nature of resistance to change and how to overcome it. He had been confrontive, so I should now come on as supportive and facilitative.

I hurriedly pulled together notes, made transparencies, and on the following morning gave lectures on (1) why healthy organizations need to be able to change; (2) why individuals and groups resist change; (3) how to analyze forces toward and forces resisting change; and (4) how to develop valid change targets for the coming year, in the context of the Redirection Project, with timetables, measurements of outcomes, and accountabilities. I emphasized a point that is central to change projects: that the period of change has itself to be defined as a stage to be managed, with transition managers specifically assigned (Beckhard and Harris, 1977).

These lectures had the desired effect of giving the group members a way of thinking positively, so that when they were sent back into small groups to develop priority issues for making the Redirection Project a success, they were able to go off to these meetings with a sense of realism and optimism. The general results of the small-group meetings were quite clear. They saw the need for the unprofitable divisions to shrink and restructure themselves and the need for profitable divisions to become more effective relative to the competition, but they stated clearly that neither of these could happen if the headquarters organization did not confront the excess people in the headquarters and the style of management that was emanating from the functional groups. The ideas were not new, but they were now shared and with some conviction.

Creating a Structure for the Redirection Project: The Use of Groups. The Multi managers were skillful at working in groups. Richards and the executive committee used this skill by creating a project team to organize the Redirection Project into thirty or so separate manageable tasks; they also created steering committees for each of these tasks and assigned one of the members of the executive committee to be accountable for the performance of that task group. Some of the tasks were to shrink and restructure the less profitable divisions, something that would be inherently difficult for the executive committee member who had previously been responsible for that division to confront. Too many prior loyalties and commitments would get in the way of seeing clearly what had to be done and then ensuring that it was done. To avoid putting executive committee members into such conflicts, the group reshuffled formal responsibilities and ensured that each redirection task would fall to someone who could be objective about it. This structural change in job responsibilities was a major innovation invented by the project team itself, but everyone agreed that it was a major facilitator of later project success.

The skillful use of groups both at the annual meeting and in the design of the projects struck me as paradoxical. How could a company that was so hierarchical and so concerned about individual turf be so effective in inventing groups and in operating within a group context? I do not know the facts historically, but, because the top management of the company is itself a group, and because as scientists most of the members of the company recognize the value of input from others, they not only respect group effort but have acquired skills in managing group meetings. This point was reinforced recently in a meeting where I was advising two young managers of executive training programs on the design of a one-week middle-management course. I suggested the use of one of the group survival exercises that illustrates clearly how groups can solve some objective problems better than individuals. I was told that they used to do the exercise but that participants routinely asked why their time was being wasted, since they were already committed to the use of groups and therefore felt that the training should go straight to the skill level, where much needed to be done.

The overall steering committee for the Redirection Project created the individual component projects, the teams that would run them, the managers who would be accountable, the timetables, and the broad targets; they also invented some subtle devices to ensure action. For example, each project group was assigned one or two outside "challengers," managers not involved in the project, who were to examine critically what the group had done and was proposing to do. This provided an opportunity to test diagnoses and remedies before presenting them to top management. Each team was also given the services of an internal organizational consultant to help with the organization of the team itself, and several of the teams asked for and obtained my help on how to structure their work.

All this was communicated clearly by top management in written form, through meetings, and through trips to various parts of the company. Not only the process but the necessity for it and top management's commitment to it were highlighted in the communications. Great emphasis was given to the particular project that would reexamine the headquarters structure, functioning, and head counts and attempt to reduce the overhead by at least one third.

One might speculate that group work had such importance in Multi because it was virtually the only form of lateral communication available in the company. The sensitivities that might be operating if managers from one division offered or asked for help from another division could be overcome, with faces saved, if a task force consisting of members of both divisions adopted a process of taking turns reporting to each other on the progress of effective and ineffective interventions. The listener could then learn and get new ideas without either identifying himself as a problem or having others identify him as a target of their input. Group meetings thus preserved "face" all the way around.

It was also recognized that groups helped to build commitment to projects even though the implementation system was essentially hierarchical. If groups had discussed the issue, the hierarchy worked more smoothly—as in the Japanese system, where consensus is sought before a decision is announced. In various ways the Redirection Project was using the cultural strengths of the company and was redefining its formal procedures in order to deal with the business problem without changing the culture overtly.

Second Year: Consolidation of the Redirection Project.
During my several visits following the second annual meeting, I
worked on two important areas. First, I made myself available
to any project group or group members who wished to discuss
any aspect of how to proceed, the appointment to be made at
their initiative. If I learned something that would help other
projects, I would summarize it and write it up for circulation
to others. I was consulted by several managers on how best to
think about early retirement, how to ease people out in their
home community, how to get managers to think about innovative restructuring, and so on. As mentioned, I soon discovered
that my memos pulling good ideas together died on the desks of
the people to whom I gave those memos. That was my first encounter with the cultural norm that at Multi information does
not circulate laterally.

I also spent a good deal of time with the executive committee member who was responsible for this project, helping
him keep his role and his leadership behavior in his project
group clear and effective. Several project managers wanted help
in thinking through their roles as project chairmen and solicited
my reactions to proposals prior to running them by the challengers.

Second, I became more familiar with the management development inventory and planning system and began a series of
meetings with the manager of this function by way of seeing
how it could be improved. Bringing in and developing better
and more innovative managers was seen as a high-priority longer-
range implication of the Redirection Project. It was also known
that the present manager of the function would retire within a
year and his successor might need a consultant who had learned
something about the company to help him think out his program.

Planning for Third Annual Meeting. I had made it clear
that one should think of change as a stage to be managed, with
targets and assigned change managers. From this point of view,
the third annual meeting provided a natural opportunity to review progress, check out what problems had been encountered,
share successes and good innovations, replan some projects if

necessary, and, most important, announce newly defined role relationships between executive committee members, division heads, and country heads.

Experience with the Redirection Project had revealed that the headquarters organization was too involved in the day-to-day operation of the local businesses. As the functions were shrunk and restructured, it also appeared desirable to redefine the corporate headquarters role as more "strategic," while the operating units would do more of the day-to-day management. This was possible because country managers were now willing and able to assume more responsibilities and because the executive committee increasingly recognized the importance of its strategic role. The whole economic crisis forced some strategic rethinking, which highlighted the role of the executive committee in formulating a new direction for Multi's future.

Third Annual Meeting: Consolidating Gains and Remotivating for Future Efforts. At the opening session of the third annual meeting, I was asked to review the progress of the Redirection Project. My review was based on interviews with a series of managers about their experiences with the project. This lecture was designed to remind the participants of change theory, to legitimize their individual experiences and frustrations by giving a wide range of examples, to illustrate how restraining forces had been dealt with by innovative managers, and to introduce to the group the concept of corporate culture as a force to be analyzed.

I had spent some time during the second year working with members of the management development group to try to decipher the assumptions that were operating, to develop a "concept" of the company culture that could be shared with managers in order to assess how it aided or hindered the Redirection Project. I learned two powerful lessons from this process and from my lecture.

First, it was very difficult for insiders to decipher their own culture without my active intervention, probing, stating hypotheses, mentioning incidents that had happened to me, citing puzzling anomalies, and so on. Together we could reach some clarity, at least enough clarity to present a picture of the culture for discussion following the lecture.

The reaction to the lecture produced the second important insight. Many participants said that I had stated things more or less accurately, but they clearly were not pleased that I, as an outsider, had made their culture public. Some of them insisted that I had made errors of misinterpretation, and one or two executive committee members subsequently decided that I was not a useful consultant. Once I had revealed my "misunderstanding" or unwittingly revealed some feelings about aspects of their culture, I created a polarized situation. Some managers moved closer to me, while others moved further away. I concluded that, if one did not want that kind of polarization, one should help the group decipher its own culture rather than presenting one's own view of that culture in a didactic manner.

Both consultants were present throughout the meeting to serve as audience, reinforcers, and sources of new ideas. Following the general presentation on change, each of the projects was asked to give a brief review of its status, and small groups met to consider implications and make suggestions. The last part of the meeting, and from the point of view of the planning group the most difficult, concerned the problem of how to inform everyone about the new roles of the executive committee, the division heads, and the country heads.

The executive committee members planned a major change in their own role, pushing toward strategic management and toward more individualized accountability for divisions and functions, but they were not sure that the message would get across just by saying it. We therefore planned a three-step process: (1) a formal announcement of the new roles; (2) a brief lecture by me on the implications of role realignment, emphasizing the systemic character of role networks and the need for each manager to renegotiate his role downward, upward, and laterally if the new system was to work; and (3) a powerful emotional speech by the vice-chairman of the executive committee on the effect of this new alignment in streamlining the company for the future.

The third annual meeting ended on a high note, based on a sense of what had already been accomplished in one year, what accomplishments were in the works, and what improvements could be expected from the new role that the executive committee had taken for itself. The fact that the headquarters organization had begun to shrink through early retirements and had reduced some of its more bothersome control activities sent the clear message that top management was serious about its role in the Redirection Project even though the early retirement of headquarters people was an extremely painful process. The fact that people were being retired destroyed the taken-for-granted assumption that people had a guaranteed career in the company, but the highly individualized and financially generous manner in which retirements were handled reinforced another basic assumption: that the company cared very much for its people and would not hurt them if there was any way to avoid it.

Assessment During Third Year. Most of my regular visits subsequent to the third annual meeting were devoted to working with the new manager of management development. Though I continued to meet with members of the executive committee on Redirection matters, the priority shifted to helping the new head of the management development function think through his own role and reexamine how the entire process could be improved. The former manager of this function wanted to continue some project involvement following his retirement. Therefore, he and I jointly proposed a project in which his insights could be used to study the careers of the top two hundred senior managers in the company, with the purpose of identifying critical success factors or problems in those careers. The project was approved by the executive committee with the condition that I was to act as "technical supervisor" of the project, to ensure that any findings would be scientifically valid. I was reminded once again that my credibility as a consultant rested heavily on my scientific reputation and that scientific validity was the ultimate decision criterion for the company.

The study involved a detailed reconstruction of the careers and revealed surprisingly little geographical, cross-functional, and cross-divisional movement as those careers progressed. A presentation of these and other results was given to the executive committee by the former manager of management development, which led to a major discussion of how future general managers should be developed. A consensus was

reached that there should be more early career rotation geographically and into and out of headquarters, but cross-functional
and cross-divisional movement remained a controversial issue.

The executive committee members also realized that rotational moves, if they were to be useful, had to occur early in the
career. They decided that such early movement would occur
only if a very clear message went out to the entire organization.
This decision led to the design of a half-day segment on management development, to be inserted into the management
seminars that are periodically given to the top five hundred
managers of the company.

A new policy on early rotation was mandated, and the
data from the project were used to justify the new policy. Once
senior management accepted a conclusion as valid, it was able to
move decisively and to impose a proposed solution on the entire
company. The message was communicated by having executive
committee members at each seminar, but implementation was
left to local management.

During this year Richards relinquished the job of chairman of the executive committee for reasons of health, providing
a potential succession problem. However, the executive committee had anticipated the problem and had a new chairman and
vice-chairman ready. The persons chosen for these new positions allowed the company to reaffirm its strategic posture,
which, not surprisingly, reemphasized its scientific values. The
succession also provided a test of the executive committee's
commitment to the Redirection Project, since its launching was
associated with Richards' leadership. The new chairman and
vice-chairman strongly reaffirmed that commitment and thereby sent a further clear signal to the organization that the crisis
was real and needed to be addressed.

By the end of the third year, the financial results were
much better, and the restructuring process in the unprofitable
divisions was proceeding rapidly. Each unit learned how to
manage early retirements, and a measure of interdivisional cooperation was achieved in the process of placing people who
were redundant in one division into other divisions. Initial attitudes were negative, and I heard many complaints from man-

agers that even their best people were not acceptable to other
divisions; but this attitude was gradually eroded because the assumption that "We don't throw people out without maximum
effort to find jobs for them" eventually overrode the provincial-
ism of the divisions. Managers who were too committed to the
old strategy of running those divisions were gradually replaced
with managers who were deemed to be more innovative in their
approach.

Because it had fulfilled its functions, the Redirection
Project was officially terminated. Relevant change projects
would now be handled by the executive committee, and I was
asked to be "on call" to line managers needing help. The new
head of one of the previously unprofitable divisions, for example, wanted help in restoring the morale of those managers who
remained after many of their colleagues were retired or farmed
out to other divisions. He sensed a level of fear and apathy that
made it difficult to move forward positively. In true Multi fashion, he had tried to solve this problem on his own by bringing in
an *outside* training program, but it had been unsuccessful. He
then requested a meeting with me to seek alternative solutions.
Given the Multi culture and his own commitment, it was obvious that he should build his program internally and enlist the
aid of the corporate training people, who would know how to
design a program that would be culturally congruent. He had
never considered using the corporate training group to help him,
though he knew of it and liked some of the people in it. I found
myself being the broker between two parts of the organization
that could have been talking to each other directly. He did follow up, and in the subsequent year a successful in-house program was developed.

Looking Ahead. On the original issue that Richards had
asked me to get involved with, the stimulation of innovation,
very little change has taken place from my point of view. But
the culture of Multi "works," so one cannot readily assume that
some other way would be better. Rather, my job as a consultant is to help the company be more innovative within the constraints of its culture. I meet with several cross-departmental
groups who are at a low level of the organization and want to

share the kind of information that does not circulate freely at senior levels. As a result of these meetings, some lateral communication links are being built.

By continuing to work on management development issues, I can raise questions (as indeed many in the company are) about what kind of manager should be recruited in the future, and what kinds of job assignments and rotation system should be used to produce the manager of the future, leading to a gradual reevaluation of what is effective management in Multi.

Summary and Assessment: What Changed?

Based on what I have observed and heard, the company feels that it has successfully weathered a major crisis and reassessment. Let us look at some specifics.

1. The financial trend toward nonprofitability was decisively reversed, though the future is viewed with some caution.
2. Two previously unprofitable divisions restructured themselves by drastic cutting of products, facilities, and people, and by reorganizing their production and marketing activities to fit the current market and economic realities. One of these divisions was considered a "loser," but, because of its successful restructuring under a dynamic manager, it is now considered the "hero" in the company.
3. The functions in the corporate headquarters were reduced by 30 to 40 percent, and more line responsibility was delegated to the countries and divisions.
4. The functions in the divisions were also reassessed, and their role was changed in line with headquarters becoming more strategic.
5. The profitable divisions thoroughly reassessed themselves and began programs to be more competitive in their particular industries.
6. Executive committee members restructured their own accountabilities so that each division, country, and function would have a clear line boss but one whose focus was stra-

tegic. In the previous system, these groups had felt accountable to the entire committee.
7. A major management succession occurred and was nego-
    tiated successfully in that the new chairman and vice-
    chairman of the executive committee were perceived by
    senior management as good choices.
8. In this whole three-year change process, many managers
    who were considered less effective were weeded out
    through early retirement, permitting key jobs to be filled
    by managers considered more dynamic and effective.
9. Senior managers acquired insight into the ways in which
    their culture both constrains and helps them.
10. A major cultural assumption about career stability, par-
    ticularly in headquarters, was reassessed and violated. In
    that process another major assumption—about dealing
    with people on an individualized and humane basis—was
    reaffirmed.

Most managers in Multi undoubtedly would say that they
had undergone some great changes and that many of their assumptions about the world and the company had changed.
However, the *cultural paradigm* of the company has not essentially changed. There is the same bias toward scientific authority; the hierarchy functions as strongly as ever, but with redefined roles; the assumption that managers do their best job
when left alone to learn for themselves is still very strong; lateral communication is still considered mostly irrelevant (for
example, there is no regular meeting of division heads except
at the annual meeting, where they meet with everyone else; and
there are no functional meetings across countries or divisions).
Various projects—for example, to bring in MBAs on a
trial basis and to hold worldwide meetings of functional people,
such as the management development coordinators from divisions and key countries—are being pushed; but one senses that
they are tolerated in the culture, not encouraged. On one of my
visits, the head of management development arranged for me to
meet five of the MBAs to see how they were reacting to their
various company situations. We had a productive and construc-

tive meeting. A week later this manager was criticized by several of the bosses of the MBAs for organizing the meeting because he was stepping into the turf of these other managers, who would not have given permission for such a cross-departmental group to meet.

I mention all this because, when the Redirection Project began, we all talked of "culture change." To label a change as culture change enhances the drama of what is happening, so it may have some motivational value even if inaccurate; at the same time, it focuses people on the culture, so that they can identify both the constraints and the enhancing features of the culture. But the important thing to note is that considerable change can take place in an organization's operations *without the cultural paradigm's changing at all.* In fact, some of the assumptions could not have changed but for the even stronger action of deeper assumptions. Thus, some parts of the culture helped many of the changes to happen in other parts of the culture.

This insight leads to a further point. Many assumptions around mission, goals, means, measurement systems, roles, and relationships can be "superficial" within the total structure of the cultural paradigm yet be very important for the organization's functioning on a day-to-day basis. The assumption that the headquarters functional groups had worldwide responsibility for tracking everything was not a very "deep" assumption within the whole Multi culture, but it was having a major impact on business performance and managerial morale in the country companies. Changing some of these superficial assumptions may be crucial to effective adaptation. The deeper assumptions may drive the whole process but may not have to change.

What, then, really happened in the Redirection Project and why? Many in the company are also asking this question in order to understand the reasons for the success of the change effort. My own observation is that the effort was successful because the executive committee sent a clear message that a change was needed, involved itself fully in the change process, tackled the impossible job of reducing headquarters staff as well as the power of the functional groups, and, thereby, not only created involvement and ownership down the line in the country groups but made it clear that operational problems would increasingly be delegated down. Even though communication laterally is minimal, the vertical channels were more opened up. Financial information was shared more than before, suggestions coming up through the project structure were listened to, and proposals that were accepted were effectively implemented through the existing hierarchy as a result of clear top-down signals. In this sense Multi used its cultural strength to redirect itself more rapidly than might have been possible in a less structured organization.

Contrasts in Action Company

Multi was a mature, multidivisional, diverse organization, over one hundred years old, and managed by professional managers. Real change was needed to get control of what could have become a serious survival situation. The culture had to be reexamined, even though it did not change fundamentally. But the culture, as a variable to be examined, surfaced only after the project was well under way.

In contrast, Action is a younger company, still in its first generation, highly conscious of itself and its culture. In fact, one might hypothesize that the culture of Action is one of its major managerial "tools," in the sense that the common understanding of how to get things done has given Action some of its competitive advantages. Action considers its culture to be unique, a resource to be exploited, a source of pride. Whereas culture can be thought of as simply present in Multi, in Action culture is an active and conscious force to be enhanced and used. For example, several functional groups, particularly manufacturing, were worried that with rapid growth their new managers would not acquire the culture, so they started a series of socialization workshops designed to "teach" the culture. Similarly, in the human resource function, several projects have sprung up to examine the value system of Action by way of publishing charters, philosophies, doctrines, and ideologies that capture what managers and employees are most proud of in the company. As the company has grown, I have heard increasing concerns that the culture is being eroded, that things are no longer done the way they used to be, with the clear implication that the loss of some of those ways is considered highly undesirable. Meetings are devoted to discussions about how to preserve and enhance the culture.

Given the various forces described in this chapter, the culture issue in Action is completely different from the culture issue in Multi. Culture change in Action is viewed as an undesirable product of evolutionary forces. Management would prefer to preserve and enhance the culture. Culture change in Multi is viewed as something to be examined rationally and to be promoted if necessary. In my own consulting, I found that some parts of the Multi culture stood in the way of my mission of increasing innovation. In contrast, parts of the Action culture are positive and constructive, but other parts cause frustration and paralysis as the company grows. The dilemma in Action is whether the desirable parts of the culture can be preserved as the company grows and becomes more differentiated. A further unknown in Action is what will happen when the founder is replaced by a next-generation manager, possibly someone who is much more professionally oriented, possibly someone who does not value the founding culture as much as the first generation clearly does.

Whether or not one can or should change parts of cultures or whole cultures appears to depend very much on the age of the organization, the situation it finds itself in in its environment, its size and complexity, and its present managers' view of the situation. In the next chapters, I will review in a more formal way some of the issues that managers should think about and the mechanisms available to them if culture change appears to be desirable.

12

Organizational Growth Stages and Culture Change Mechanisms

The function of culture in the life of the group changes as a group matures. When a group first forms, its evolving culture creates a stable, predictable environment and provides meaning, identity, and a communication system. That same group many generations later may find that its culture has become so well embedded, so traditional, that it serves only to reinforce the assumptions and values of the older, more conservative elements in the group. It may continue to provide stability, but it may no longer provide meaning and identity to those segments of the group who are more responsive to external changes. Under these conditions a rebellious "counterculture" often is created by the younger, more externally oriented elements in the

A number of the ideas discussed in this chapter have been explored in a seminar on organizational culture at the Management Analysis Center, Cambridge, Mass. Stanley Davis was especially helpful in developing the idea that the cultural issues are different in different business situations and at different stages (Davis, 1982).

group, and the total group culture begins to suffer from loss of integrity (Martin and Siehl, 1983). In an even more extreme condition, revolution, restructuring, and massive replacement of people may occur, and possibly a genuinely new cultural paradigm may be created—although the cultures of France, the United States, the Soviet Union, and China actually changed very little in spite of major revolutions.

The kind of change that is possible depends not only on the developmental stage of the organization but on the degree to which the organization is unfrozen and ready to change, either because of an externally induced crisis or because of internal forces toward change (Schein, 1980). The forces that can unfreeze a given culture are also likely to be different at different stages of organizational development, and certain mechanisms of change will have particular relevance at certain stages of development.

Table 5 shows three major developmental periods in or-

Table 5. Growth Stages, Functions of Culture, and Mechanisms of Change.

Growth Stage	Function of Culture/Issue
I. *Birth and Early Growth* Founder domination, possible family domination	1. Culture is a distinctive competence and source of identity. 2. Culture is the "glue" that holds organization together. 3. Organization strives toward more integration and clarity. 4. Heavy emphasis on socialization as evidence of commitment.
Succession Phase	1. Culture becomes battleground between conservatives and liberals. 2. Potential successors are judged on whether they will preserve or change cultural elements.

Change Mechanisms
1. Natural Evolution
2. Self-Guided Evolution Through Organizational Therapy
3. Managed Evolution Through Hybrids
4. Managed "Revolution" Through Outsiders

(continued on next page)

Table 5. Growth Stages, Functions of Culture, and Mechanisms of Change,
Cont'd.

Growth Stage	Function of Culture/Issue
II. *Organizational Midlife* 　1. Expansion of products/ 　　markets 　2. Vertical integration 　3. Geographical expansion 　4. Acquisitions, mergers	1. Cultural integration declines as 　new subcultures are spawned. 2. Loss of key goals, values, and 　assumptions creates crisis of 　identity. 3. Opportunity to manage direc- 　tion of cultural change is pro- 　vided.

Change Mechanisms
　5. Planned Change and Organization Development
　6. Technological Seduction
　7. Change Through Scandal, Explosion of Myths
　8. Incrementalism

III. *Organizational Maturity* 　1. Maturity or decline of mar- 　　kets 　2. Increasing internal stability 　　and/or stagnation 　3. Lack of motivation to change	1. Culture becomes a constraint on 　innovation. 2. Culture preserves the glories of 　the past, hence is valued as a 　source of self-esteem, defense.
Transformation Option	1. Culture change is necessary and 　inevitable, but not all elements 　of culture can or must change. 2. Essential elements of culture 　must be identified, preserved. 3. Culture change can be managed 　or simply allowed to evolve.
Destruction Option 　1. Bankruptcy and reorganiza- 　　tion 　2. Takeover and reorganization 　3. Merger and assimilation	1. Culture changes at fundamental 　paradigm levels. 2. Culture changes through massive 　replacement of key people.

Change Mechanisms
　9. Coercive Persuasion
　10. Turnaround
　11. Reorganization, Destruction, Rebirth

ganizations and, for each period, the major culture issues and
most relevant change mechanisms. Implicit in this delineation of
stages is a theory of development that emphasizes generational
age, size, and complexity. By generational age I mean whether

the company is still managed by the founder (first generation), by a family who controls the company (second or third generation), or by professional managers who have no substantial ownership or control. A first- or second-generation company can become very large and complex, and a fully professionalized company can remain small and simple. From a cultural point of view, the most important variable is generational age. In companies of equivalent age, their size and complexity become secondarily important, as we will see, but it is age that is crucial.

Birth and Early Growth

In Stage 1, the birth and early growth of a new group or organization, the main cultural thrust comes from the founders and their assumptions. The cultural paradigm that becomes embedded, if the organization succeeds in fulfilling its primary task and survives, can then be viewed as that organization's distinctive competence, the basis for member identity, and the psychosocial "glue" that holds the group together. The emphasis in this early stage will be on differentiating oneself from the environment and from other groups. The group will make its culture explicit, integrate it as much as possible, and teach it firmly to newcomers (or select them for initial compatibility).

This process can be clearly seen in rapidly growing young companies. Their self-image of how they do things is strongly articulated, explained in detail to newcomers, and rearticulated frequently in ambiguous or critical situations. When the Action Company was young, two assumptions—(1) that "Creativity can come from anyone" and (2) that "One must always screen decisions through groups"—virtually became "sacred cows."

Around the concept of distinctive competence, one can see in young companies biases toward certain business functions. In Action the bias was clearly toward engineering and manufacturing. Not only was it difficult for the other functions to acquire status and prestige, but professionals in those functions—that is, professional marketers—often were told by managers who had been with the company from its origin that marketers never knew what they were talking about. In Multi a similar bias is still present toward science and research, even though the company is much older. Since R & D was historically the basis of the company's success, science is still defined as the distinctive competence, even though overtly more and more managers are admitting that the future hinges more on marketing, tight financial controls, and efficient operations.

Distinctive competences are usually defined in accordance with the assumptions about how to deal with the external environment; but in some instances the distinctive competence may involve assumptions about how members should relate to one another, as in the lawn care business that has chosen its employees—not its customers or stockholders—as its primary stakeholders. All its truck drivers, secretaries, and maintenance people fully understand the economics of the business, on the theory that employees who feel totally committed and professional will be able to find customers and make sure that they are well treated. The continued success of the business hinges on its ability to maintain its employees' identification with the core mission.

The implications for change at this stage are clear. The culture in young and successfully growing companies is likely to be very strong because (1) the primary culture creators are still present, (2) the culture helps the group define itself and make its way into a potentially hostile environment, and (3) many elements of the culture have been learned as defenses against anxiety as the group struggled to build and maintain itself. Proposals to deliberately change the culture from either inside or outside are therefore likely to be totally ignored or resisted. Instead, dominant members or coalitions will attempt to preserve and enchance the culture by changing the structure or some other manipulable element in the situation. The only force that might unfreeze such a situation is an external crisis of survival in the form of a sharp drop in growth rate, loss of sales or profit, a major product failure, or some other event that cannot be ignored. If such a crisis occurs, the next stage may automatically be launched in that a new senior manager may come into the picture. If the founding group itself stays intact, so will the culture, though it may evolve from within through a process of selection of hybrids, which will be described later.

Succession Phase. The succession phase involves a very large variety of subphases and processes. How companies actually move from being under the domination of a founder or a founding family to a state of being managed by second-, third-, and fourth-generation managers has so many variants that one can only identify some prototypical processes and events.

The first and often most critical of these processes is the shift from founder to a second-generation chief executive officer. Even if that person is the founder's son or another trusted family member, it is in the nature of founders/entrepreneurs to have difficulty giving up what they have created (Schein, 1978). In Chapter Nine I cited the extreme example of Jones, an entrepreneur who was unconsciously willing to destroy his organization to prove to the world how indispensable he was. On the other hand, I also described Smithfield, an entrepreneur whose passion was to keep creating new ventures, which made it easy for him to turn successful ones over to friends and colleagues.

During this phase conflicts over what elements of the culture employees like or do not like become surrogates for what they do or do not like about the founder, since most of the culture is likely to be a reflection of the founder's personality. Battles thus develop between "conservatives" who like the founding culture and "liberals" or "radicals" who want to change the culture, partly because they want to enhance their own power position. The danger in this situation is that feelings about the founder are projected onto the culture, and, in the effort to displace the founder, much of the culture comes under challenge. If members of the organization forget that the culture is a set of learned solutions that have produced success, comfort, and identity, they may try to change the very things they value and need.

In the Jones Company, several efforts were made to bring in chief executives who would embody different assumptions, based on "professional" managerial principles; but the assumptions about the rights and privileges of the family asserted themselves in every case, leading to the firing of the new chief executive officer after six to eighteen months, on the grounds that "he did not really understand our business." In the Action Company, there have been repeated efforts to bring in outsiders with new approaches to the conduct of the business; but if they are too different, the candidates never survive even the initial interview process. There has also been a high turnover of such people during their first year of employment, much of which can be seen as being de facto "forcing out."

Often missing in this phase is an understanding of what the organizational culture is and what it is doing for the group, regardless of how it came to be. Succession processes must therefore be designed to enhance those parts of the culture that provide identity, distinctive competence, and protection from anxiety. Such a process can probably be managed only from within, because an outsider could not possibly understand the subtleties of the cultural issues and the emotional relationships between founders and employees.

The first actual succession often serves to unfreeze the organization. In this growth step, the organization typically moves from a few hundred to a few thousand people, and from a small team to a multilayered management. The founder is still in control, but he now develops a team with whom responsibility is increasingly shared. The critical variables at this stage are the kinds of people whom the founder selects for future powerful roles (family members, insiders but not of the family, or outsiders) and the amount of development and grooming they are given.

The preparation for succession is usually psychologically difficult both for the founder and for potential successors because entrepreneurs typically like to maintain high levels of control. They may officially be grooming successors, but unconsciously they may be preventing powerful and competent people from functioning in those roles. Or they may designate successors but prevent them from having enough responsibility to learn how to do the job, what we might call the "Prince Albert" syndrome, remembering that Queen Victoria did not permit her son many opportunities to practice being king. This pattern is particularly likely to operate with a father-to-son transition.

When senior management or the founder confronts the *criteria* for a successor, cultural issues are forced into the open. It is now clear that much of the culture has become a property of the organization even though it may have started out as the property of the founder. In either case, if the founder or the founder's family is still dominant in the organization, one may expect little culture change but a great deal of effort to clarify, integrate, maintain, and evolve the culture, primarily because it is identified with the founder.

Change Mechanism 1: Natural Evolution. If the organization is not under too much external stress and if the founder or founding family is around for a long time, the culture simply evolves by assimilating what works best over the years. Such evolution involves two basic processes (Sahlins and Service, 1960; Steward, 1977; McKelvey, 1982): general evolution and specific evolution.

General evolution toward the next historical stage of development involves diversification, complexity, higher levels of differentiation and integration, and creative syntheses into new and higher-level forms. Implicit in this concept is the assumption that social systems do have an evolutionary dynamic, as was described for the small group in earlier chapters. Just as groups go through logical stages, so organizations go through logical stages, though it has not been unequivocally demonstrated what those stages are or what the internal dynamic is that creates the evolutionary thrust. The elements of the culture that operate as defenses are likely to be retained and strengthened over the years, but they may be refined and developed into an integrated and more complex structure. Basic assumptions may be retained, but the form in which they surface may change, creating new behavior patterns that ultimately feed back into the basic assumptions. Not all systems would have the capacity to evolve to greater levels of complexity, but the evidence that human systems are capable of such evolution is overwhelming.

Specific evolution involves the adaptation of specific parts of the organization to their particular environments. Thus, a high-technology company will develop highly refined R & D skills, while a consumer products company in foods or cosmetics will develop highly refined marketing skills. In each case such differences will reflect important underlying assumptions about the nature of the world and the actual growth experience of the organization. In addition, if the different parts of the organization exist in different environments, each of those parts will evolve to adapt to its particular environment (Lawrence and Lorsch, 1967).

General evolution can be clearly seen in Multi as it grew and developed from regional sales offices in many countries to fully integrated companies in each of a number of major countries. These country companies learned to adapt to their own technological, economic, social, and market environments and, in the process, became less and less aligned with the functional units in headquarters. For the company to maintain its integrity as a total system, it had to change its structure by shrinking headquarters and changing the role of senior management to more of a strategic one. Had the company decided to give up its divisional structure and delegate profit and loss to the countries, that would have been more of a general evolutionary cultural change because it would have meant changing a core assumption about company mission deriving from the product structure embodied in the divisions. The reaffirmation of the division structure, the rejection of full-scale entry into new businesses through acquisition, and the reaffirmation that the company was scientific/technically based represented a clear choice to maintain basic cultural integrity. But evolution had to be managed; hence, adaptive structural and procedural changes were made, as described in the preceding chapter.

Change Mechanism 2: Self-Guided Evolution Through Organizational Therapy. If one thinks of culture as in part a defense mechanism to avoid uncertainty and anxiety, then one should be able to help the organization assess for itself the strengths and weaknesses of its culture, and modify it if that is necessary for survival and effective functioning. Therapy that operates through creating self-insight permits cognitive redefinition to occur and thereby can produce dramatic changes. Outsiders probably will be needed to (1) unfreeze the organization, (2) provide psychological safety, (3) help to analyze the present defensive nature of the culture, (4) reflect back to key people in the organization how the culture seems to be operating, and (5) help the process of cognitive redefinition (Schein and Bennis, 1965; Schein, 1969, 1980).

When this process works, usually because the client is highly motivated to change, dramatic shifts in assumptions can take place. One company, for instance, could not make a crucial transition because it had traditionally defined marketing in very limited merchandising terms and hence saw little value in the function. Only when key executives had real personal insight into how they viewed marketing, and cognitively redefined the function in their own minds, were they able to adopt the assumption that marketing can help, change their hiring policy, and give marketing-oriented managers more real power.

Many of the interventions that have occurred over the years in the Action Company can be seen as therapeutic in that the goal was insight. For example, at an annual meeting where the company's poor performance was being discussed, a depressive mood overtook senior management and was articulated as "We could do better if only our president or one of his key lieutenants would decide on a direction and tell us which way to go." A number of us familiar with the culture heard this not as a realistic request but as a wish for a magic solution. I was scheduled on the regular program to give a short presentation on the company's culture and used the opportunity to raise the following question: "Given the history of this company and the kinds of managers and people that you are, if there really were marching orders coming down from on high, do you think you would follow?" There was a long silence and then gradually a few knowing smiles, followed by a more realistic discussion of how *together* the whole group could work on defining its sense of direction.

Defenses do not always have to be given up. Sometimes it is enough to recognize how they operate so that their consequences can be realistically assessed; if they are considered too costly, one can engage in compensatory behavior. For example, Action's commitment to checking all decisions laterally before moving ahead may be a defense against the anxiety of not knowing whether a given decision is correct. As the company has grown, the costs of such a defense have mounted, since it not only takes longer and longer to make a decision but also checking with others who have not grown up in the company and whose opinions one cannot calibrate may not resolve issues.

The options are then to (1) give up the mechanism, which is difficult to do unless some way is found to contain the anxiety that would be unleashed in the short run (for example, find a strong leader who will absorb the anxiety); or (2) design compensatory mechanisms (for example, have less frequent but longer meetings, or classify decisions and seek consensus only on certain ones, or find ways to speed up meetings); or (3) break the company down into smaller units where the consensual process can work because people can know each other and build efficient consensual processes.

Much of the field of planned change and organization development operates on the therapeutic and self-insight model (Schein, 1969). The assumption has to be made that the system is motivated to change and ready for self-insight, however much pain that might entail. Organizations sometimes have to get into real trouble, however, before they recognize their need for help, and then they often do not seek the right kind of help. Sadly, organizations are no different in this regard from individuals.

Change Mechanism 3: Managed Evolution Through Hybrids. The above two processes highlight development in the sense of keeping and enhancing the culture as it exists. If the unfreezing pressures are more disconfirming, implying that the present culture must change in some way if survival is to be ensured, how can a young organization manage such change without losing its identity? One process is to selectively fill key positions with "hybrids"—that is, "insiders" who have grown up in the culture and are accepted but whose personal assumptions are somewhat different from the mainstream in the direction in which the company needs to move. When such managers are put in key positions, they often elicit the feeling from others: "We don't like what he is doing in the way of changing the place, but at least he is one of us."

For this mechanism to work, some of the most senior leaders of the company must have insight into what is missing, which implies that they first must get somewhat outside their own culture through a therapeutic process. They may obtain such insight through the questions of board members or from consultants or through educational programs where they meet other leaders. If the leaders then recognize the need for change, but do not know how to achieve it, they can begin to select for key jobs those members of the old culture who best represent the new assumptions that they want to enhance. For example, a highly decentralized company that grew on the assumption of extreme autonomy and delegation down to the lowest possible level found itself with rapid growth going "out of control" in the sense of losing the ability to coordinate and formulate a coherent strategy. The senior managers knew that bringing an outsider into a key position would be rejected, so they gradually filled several of the division management positions with managers who had grown up in manufacturing, where more discipline and centralization had been the norm. These managers operated within the culture but gradually imposed more centralization and discipline.

Formal management succession when the founder or founding family finally relinquishes control provides an opportunity to change the direction of the culture if the successor is the right kind of hybrid, representing what is needed for the organization to survive, yet being seen as acceptable "because he is one of us" and therefore also a conserver of the old culture. An interesting special case is to *create* a hybrid by having an outsider who is intended to be the successor to the founder serve for a number of years on the board of directors. If he accepts the culture and is accepted by the company, he can then succeed in the job.

Change Mechanism 4: Managed "Revolution" Through Outsiders. A young and growing company may select outsiders to fill key positions, on the grounds that the organization needs to be more "professionally" managed—that is, needs to bring in modern management tools that the founder did not have. Turning to outsiders is also the most likely course if the company is in economic difficulty due to perceived inefficiencies associated with the founder culture. Dyer (1984) has examined this change mechanism in several organizations. Apparently, the following scenario is prototypical: (1) The organization develops a sense of crisis, because of declining performance or some kind of failure in the marketplace, and concludes it needs new leadership. (2) Simultaneously there is a weakening of "pattern maintenance" in the sense that procedures, beliefs, and symbols that support the old culture break down. (3) A new leader with new assumptions is brought in to deal with the crisis. (4) Conflict develops between the proponents of the old assumptions and the new leadership. (5) The crisis is eased, the company feels itself getting back on track, and the new leader is given credit. (6) The new assumptions are now embedded and reinforced by a new set of pattern maintenance activities. People may feel "We don't like the new approach, but we can't argue with the fact that it made us profitable once again, so maybe we have to try the new ways." If improvement does not occur, or the new leader is not given credit for the improvement that does occur, he will be forced out—a fairly common situation in first-generation companies.

To understand fully the dynamics of the process described by Dyer, one would, of course, need to know more about why and how the pattern maintenance mechanisms have become weakened. One source of such weakening is a change in ownership. For example, when founders give up ownership of the company, this structural change substantially reduces their ability to continue to impose their own assumptions on the organization and opens the door to power struggles among diverse elements, which, in turn, weakens whatever cultural assumptions were in place (Schein, 1983; Dyer, 1984). But cultural assumptions typically are bolstered by (1) the organization's structure, its recurring processes and physical architecture; (2) organizational stories and symbols; and (3) well-articulated statements of philosophy and charters. Thus, there is a lot to "weaken" before the new leader can get his own assumptions in place. It is no wonder that outsiders have difficulty changing cultures.

Organizational "Midlife"

When the founding family is no longer in an ownership or dominant position by virtue of occupying key jobs, or after a number of generations the organization has grown in size to the point where the sheer number of nonfamily managers over-weighs the family members, we are talking about "midlife." From a cultural perspective, the organization is now facing a very different situation. It is established and must maintain it-self through some kind of continued growth and renewal pro-cess. It now must decide whether to pursue such growth through further geographical expansion, development of new products, opening up of new markets, vertical integration to improve its cost and resource position, mergers and acquisitions, division-alization, or spinoffs. The past history of the organization's growth and development is not necessarily a good guide to what will succeed in the future because the environment may have changed and, more important, internal changes may have altered its unique strengths and weaknesses.

Whereas culture was a necessary glue in the growth peri-od, the most important elements of the culture have now be-come institutionalized or embedded in the structure and major processes of the organization; hence, consciousness of the cul-ture and the deliberate attempt to build, integrate, or conserve the culture have become less important. The culture that the organization has acquired during its early years now comes to be taken for granted. The only elements that are likely to be conscious are the credos, dominant values, company slogans, written charters, and other public pronouncements of what the company wants to be and claims to stand for, its espoused values and theories (Argyris and Schön, 1978; Deal and Ken-nedy, 1982; Ouchi, 1981). At this stage it is difficult to de-cipher the culture and make people aware of it because it is so embedded in routines. It may even be counterproductive to make people aware of the culture unless there is some crisis or problem to be solved. Managers view culture discussions as bor-ing and irrelevant, especially if the company is large and well established. On the other hand, geographical expansions, mergers and acquisitions, and introductions of new technologies require a careful self-assessment to determine whether the cultures to be integrated or merged are, in fact, compatible.

Also at this stage, there may be strong forces toward cul-tural diffusion, toward loss of integration, because powerful subcultures will have developed and because a highly integrated culture is difficult to maintain in a large, differentiated, geographically dispersed organization. Furthermore, it is not clear that all the cultural units of an organization must be uniform and integrated. Several conglomerates I have worked with have spent a good deal of time wrestling with the question of whether to attempt to preserve or, in some cases, build a common culture. Are the costs associated with such an effort worth it? Is there even a danger that one will impose assumptions on a subunit that might not fit its situation at all? On the other hand, if subunits are all allowed to develop their own cultures, what is the competitive advantage of being a single organization? At this stage it is less clear what functions are served by the total culture, and the problem of managing cultural change is therefore more complex and diverse.

Unfreezing forces at this stage can come either from the outside or from the inside, as in the first stage: (1) The entire organization or parts of it may experience economic difficulty or in some other way fail to achieve key goals because the environment has changed in a significant manner. (2) The organization may develop destructive internal power struggles among subcultures. Both kinds of forces could be seen in Multi prior to its launching of the Redirection Project described in Chapter Eleven. Some of the divisions were consistently declining, to the point where the total economic health of Multi was called into question, so that a major reassessment and change program had to be undertaken. At the same time, the functional groups in the country companies were increasingly fighting the headquarters organization and were complaining that profits were undermined by the heavy overhead burdens imposed on them by the "fat" headquarters. In functionally organized companies, one often sees real intergroup struggles between functions such as sales, manufacturing, engineering, marketing, and research and development because each of these groups develops a strong subculture based on its occupational background and adaptation to a specific environment (Lawrence and Lorsch, 1967).

In the first stage, integration per se and clear identity were crucial; hence, power struggles among individuals and even groups would be unacceptable until a clear cultural identity was forged. In organizational midlife the culture may be able to accommodate, even expect, individual clashes, because it may be built on assumptions of individual competitiveness. Only when the integrity of the total culture is called into question by competing subcultures is there a potential cultural problem.

Managing the change process once the organization is unfrozen is more complicated at this stage, because the organization is not likely to be conscious of its culture, as it was in the first stage. It only knows its own slogans and myths. Key managers now need a deeper level of insight into the content of their culture and into the cultural process that is probably going on, possibly requiring some therapeutic interventions as a precursor to other kinds of change.

Change Mechanism 5: Planned Change and Organization Development. Much of the work of organization development practitioners deals with the knitting together of diverse and warring subcultures, helping the dominant coalition or the managerial client system figure out how to integrate constructively the multiple agendas of different groups (Beckhard and Harris, 1977). The various conflicts that develop require the creation of interventions that permit mutual insight and the development of commitment to superordinate company goals. Such commitment always seems to involve insight into one's own assumptions and into the assumptions of other groups with whom one feels in conflict. Organizational development efforts therefore almost always start with therapeutic interventions designed to increase self-insight but then continue into various kinds of managed change programs where the outside consultant may play various roles to facilitate the process. Culture change is not usually a goal per se, but culture change is usually inevitable if the source of the difficulty is conflict among subcultures within the organization. Since there is now an entire literature on this form of change, I will not review it further here (see Bennis, 1969; Beckhard, 1969; Beckhard and Harris, 1977; Bennis and others, 1976; French and Bell, 1978; Beer, 1980).

Change Mechanism 6: Technological Seduction. At one extreme this category includes the diffusion of technological innovation and various forms of acculturation where new technologies have subtly changed entire cultures. At the other extreme, it includes the deliberate, managed introduction of specific technologies for the sake of seducing organization members into new behavior, which will, in turn, require them to reexamine their present culture and possibly adopt new values, beliefs, and assumptions. The diffusion and acculturation processes will not be discussed in detail because here again there is a large literature both in organization theory and in anthropology. My focus will be on situations where senior management's goal is to reduce what it perceives as too much cultural diversity, and therefore it deliberately introduces a seemingly "neutral" or "progressive" technology that has the effect of getting people to think and behave in common terms.

Many companies have introduced programs of leadership training built around models such as the Blake Managerial Grid (Blake and Mouton, 1964), in order to provide all layers of management with a common vocabulary and common concepts. The assumption underlying this strategy is that a new common language in a given cultural area, such as "how one relates to subordinates," will gradually force organization members to adopt a common frame of reference that will eventually lead to common assumptions. It is doubtful that such a strategy is sufficient to produce real culture change. But the program does reduce initial diversity by creating a common vocabulary and conceptual scheme for addressing the problems of how to deal with people. As the organization builds up a further history and resolves crises, it can then gradually develop new underlying assumptions.

The current practice of introducing personal computers to several layers of management and the mandatory attendance at training courses may be intended to serve a similar unifying function. Senior management sees too much diversity in the assumptions governing management decisions and brings this issue into the open by introducing a technology that forces decision-making premises and styles into consciousness. Some managers also see in the technology the opportunity to impose the assumptions that underlie the new technology itself, such as the importance of precision, measurement, quantification, model building, and so on, in which case we may be talking more about coercive persuasion following the seduction process, but in many cases the seduction is designed simply to *surface* the cultural diversity so that it can be addressed.

Another example of technological seduction was provided by a manager who noted that the volume of written memos in his organization had become unmanageable and had led to the assumption that one did not really have to deal with *any* memos. Because managers learned to ignore the memos, additional mechanisms for communication were established and the system became overloaded, with devastating effects on the exchange of information. The manager convinced the company to install an electronic mail system as an experiment, without in any way tying the experiment to his diagnosis of the information overload. Once it was installed, it provided managers with a ready alternative to the overloaded phone and memo system. Managers began to use it initially as a way of ensuring that their messages got through, so only important messages were entered into the system. Because there were fewer messages, they were responded to, so that the use of the system was reinforced. The written memo system and the use of phones to communicate gradually atrophied, so the total information load was in the end sharply reduced and new assumptions around what one can and should communicate began to be learned and embedded. This manager is convinced that if he had attacked the information overload problem directly, merely cosmetic changes would have been made, and the underlying assumption that no one really cared what was in the memos would not have been addressed.

Technological seduction can be coercive as well. A manager took over a transportation company that had grown up with a royal charter one hundred years earlier and had developed strong traditions around its blue trucks with the royal coat of arms painted on their sides.* The company was losing money because it was not aggressively seeking new concepts of how to

*This example was provided by Geoffrey Lewis of the University of Melbourne.

sell transportation. After observing the company for a few months, the new chief executive officer abruptly and without giving reasons ordered that the entire fleet of trucks be painted solid white. Needless to say, there was consternation: delegations urging the president to reconsider, protestations about loss of identity, predictions of total economic disaster, and other forms of resistance. All of these were patiently listened to, but the president simply reiterated that he wanted it done, and soon. He eroded the resistance by making the request nonnegotiable. After the trucks were painted white, the drivers suddenly noticed that people were curious about what they had done and inquired what they would now put on the trucks in the way of new logos. This got the employees at all levels thinking about what business they were in and initiated the market-oriented focus that the president had been trying to establish. Rightly or wrongly he assumed that he could not get this focus just by requesting it. He had to seduce the employees into a situation where they had no choice.

We should, of course, recognize that many people resist new technologies because they correctly sense that their cultural assumptions are being challenged and threatened. Technological changes not only disrupt behavioral patterns but force one to look at and possibly change underlying assumptions.

Change Mechanism 7: Change Through Scandal, Explosion of Myths. As a company matures, it develops a positive ideology and a set of myths about how it operates, what Argyris and Schön (1974, 1978) have labeled "espoused theories"; at the same time, it continues to operate by other assumptions, which they label "theories-in-use" and which more accurately reflect what actually goes on. For example, an organization's espoused theory may be that it takes individual needs into consideration in making geographical moves; yet its theory-in-use— that anyone who refuses an assignment is taken off the promotional track—virtually negates the espoused theory. An organization's espoused theory that it uses rational decision-making techniques based on market research in introducing new products may be superseded by its actual indulgence of the biases and pet projects of a certain key manager.

It is where such incongruities exist between espoused and in-use theories that this change mechanism applies most clearly. Nothing changes until the consequences of the *theory-in-use* create a public and visible scandal that cannot be hidden, avoided, or denied. For example, in the company that prided itself on taking individual feelings into account in overseas moves, a senior executive who had been posted to a position he did not want committed suicide. He left a note that was revealed to the newspapers, and the note made clear that he felt the company had forced him to take the undesirable assignment. This event suddenly exposed an element of the culture in such a way that it could not be denied or rationalized away. The company immediately instituted a new set of procedures built on the espoused theory and was able to abandon the theory-in-use because its negative consequences were now visible. In the case of the domination of the decision-making process by a key manager, what eventually happened is that one of the products he had insisted on failed in such a dramatic way that a reconstruction of why it had been introduced had to be made public. The manager's role in the process was revealed by unhappy subordinates and was labeled as scandalous, he was moved out of his job, and a more formal process of product introduction was immediately mandated.

In these cases external events precipitated the change, but one can imagine situations where insiders "engineer" scandals in order to induce some of the changes they want by leaking information to the right place at the right time. Such leaks are often defined as "whistle blowing," in the sense of exposing internal inconsistencies. Since whistle blowing has the potential for precipitating a crisis that may force some cultural assumptions to be reexamined, one can see why people are cautious about it and why the organization often punishes it.

Change Mechanism 8: Incrementalism. Certain kinds of changes can be produced best if one patiently but consistently uses every opportunity to influence the organization in a certain direction. Incrementalism means that in every decision area under the discretion of a manager, the decision is consistently biased toward a new set of assumptions, but individually each decision is a small change. One version of this concept was introduced by Quinn (1978) to describe what he saw as the *actual* process by which strategy is implemented in organizations. Leaders do not create massive changes even though they have a clear concept of where they eventually want to end up. Instead, they look for opportunities to make small changes, constantly test how these changes worked out, and concentrate on using fortuitous events to move the system in a desired direction.

Such a process changes parts of the culture slowly over a long period of time, especially if one set of such incremental decisions is the replacement of people in key positions by people with different assumptions. Executive selection and staffing processes are, in this sense, powerful processes of cultural change, but they are also very slow. But even without controlling staffing and selection, one can gradually produce change by coercing behavior changes that create dissonance and, over a period of time, put people into the position of realizing that they are no longer acting according to their prior assumptions. If the new behavior has been successful and become embedded, it may be easier to change the assumptions to fit the behavior than to undo the behavior to fit one's original assumptions, as dissonance research has shown (Festinger, 1957; Cooper and Croyle, 1984). This process may happen silently and without conscious awareness, so that one day the organization's members find that things are really different but they don't quite know when it all happened.

Tichy (1983) has noted that organizations can get into great difficulty if they do not notice small but consistent changes in the environment. He likens this process to the "boiled frog phenomenon," in which the frog who is sitting in the cooking pot does not notice his own demise if the increases in water temperature are small enough. It is well known in the psychology of perception that one can change someone's "level of adaptation" by increasing or decreasing stimuli at below the "JND" or "just noticeable difference" level. Thus, if we want someone to adapt to a very brightly lit room, one way of doing it is to increase the brightness so gradually that the person does not notice the increments. In the same way, a culture can change so slowly that one does not notice the changes for a long time.

Another metaphor, "turning the ship around," implies something different about incrementalism. It implies that even when the leadership knows where it wants to go and is open about it, it takes time and energy to get large numbers of people to hold different basic assumptions about something fundamental. There is a massiveness about large organizations because of the sheer numbers of people involved. There is an inertia that must be overcome to change direction. Similarly, the metaphor "Rome wasn't built in a day" reminds us that, even when there is consensus on a sense of direction, it takes a lot of effort to turn concepts into behavioral realities and to embed them into all the daily routines. Thus, experienced change managers talk in terms of five to ten years for any substantial change projects. The Redirection Project in Multi was relatively rapid in what it accomplished in three years, but it did not involve major culture change. Managers in Multi also realize that the project is not finished merely because they have announced a formal end to the task force work.

In summary, organizational midlife is the period when managers have the most choice of whether and how to manage cultural issues, and therefore need to be most aware of how to diagnose where the organization is and where it is going. If organizations face increasingly turbulent environments, one might well advocate not *strong* cultures, but *flexible* cultures, where flexibility hinges on cultural diversity rather than uniformity and on looseness in the application of cultural assumptions.

Organizational Maturity and/or Stagnation and Decline

The next and last stage to be considered is perhaps the most important from the point of view of culture change, because some organizations find that over a longer period of time significant segments of their culture become dysfunctional in a dynamic competitive environment. This stage is reached when the organization is no longer able to grow because it has saturated its markets or become obsolete in its products. It is not necessarily correlated with age, size, or number of managerial generations, but rather reflects the interaction between the organization's outputs and the environmental opportunities and constraints.

Age does matter, however, if culture change is required. If a company has had a long history of success with certain assumptions about itself and the environment, it is unlikely to want to challenge or reexamine those assumptions. Even if the assumptions are brought to consciousness, the members of the company want to hold on to them because they justify the past and are the source of their pride and self-esteem (Sofer, 1961).

Such assumptions now operate as filters that make it difficult for key managers to understand alternative strategies for survival and renewal (Donaldson and Lorsch, 1983). Outside consultants can be brought in and clear alternatives can be identified; but no matter how clear and persuasive the consultant tries to be, some alternatives will not even be understood if they do not fit the old culture, and some alternatives will be resisted even if understood. They could not be implemented down the line in the organization because people simply would not comprehend or accept what the new strategy might require (Davis, 1984).

Several parts of Multi had to confront the unpleasant realities that patents on some of their better products had run out; younger, more flexible, and more aggressive competitors were threatening; and it was not clear whether there was enough "left to be invented" to warrant the continued emphasis on research. The company needed to become more innovative in marketing, but the culture was built around research and the creative marketers had a hard time getting attention from senior management. The research department itself needed to become more responsive to the marketplace, but it still believed that it knew best. Even senior managers who could see the dilemma were caught in the culture, since they could not challenge and overrule some of the powerful research people, and the culture dictated that they stay out of each other's turf. As we saw in the preceding chapter, Multi addressed these problems by scaling down some of its divisions, but it did not change its assumptions about the role of science and research.

In such a situation, the basic choices are between more rapid transformation of parts of the culture to permit the organization to become adaptive once again through some kind of "turnaround," or to destroy the group and its culture through a process of total reorganization via a merger, acquisition, or bankruptcy proceedings. In either case strong new change managers are needed to implement the process, and part of the implementation is to unfreeze the organization before change is even possible. Such unfreezing often results from essentially coercive forces.

Change Mechanism 9: Coercive Persuasion. The concept of coercive persuasion was originally derived from my studies of prisoners of war who had undergone major belief and attitude changes during their three to five years or more of captivity during and after the Korean war (Schein, 1961). The key to understanding some of the dramatic changes that the captives underwent was to realize that if one has no exit option, one is subject to strong unfreezing forces, which, sooner or later, will motivate one to find new information that will permit cognitive redefinition to occur. Thus, prisoners at first vehemently denied their guilt, thought it was ridiculous to be accused of espionage and sabotage, offered to make false confessions, which, however, only produced more severe punishment, and in other ways attempted to cope, but did not question their own assumption base. After months or years of harassment, interrogation, physical punishment, pressure from cellmates, indoctrination, and the threat that they would be in prison forever unless they saw the light and made an honest confession, prisoners would begin to search for an answer. They would find it when they began to realize that such terms as "guilt," "crime," "espionage," and "sabotage" have different meanings in different cultures and political systems. They were able to make sincere confessions of guilt when they understood that their postcards home could conceivably provide economic intelligence information to a recipient who wanted to use the information in this manner, and that crimes in the captor system were measured not by actual harm done but by potential harm. Guilt was established once one was arrested because the government did not make mistakes. Once concepts such as guilt and crime had been cogni-

tively redefined, the prisoner was on the way to solving his
problem.

What does all this have to do with culture change? Situations where elements of the old culture are dysfunctional but
strongly adhered to are comparable to what the captor was up
against with prisoners who asserted their innocence. The key to
producing change in that situation is first to prevent exit and
then to escalate the disconfirming forces while providing psychological safety. This is difficult to execute, but precisely
what effective turnaround managers do. By using the right incentives, they make sure that the people whom they wish to retain in the organization find it difficult to leave. By consistently
challenging the old assumptions, as in the case of the manager
who insisted on painting the trucks white, they make it difficult
for people to sustain the old assumptions. By consistently being
supportive and rewarding any evidence of movement in the direction of new assumptions, they provide some psychological
safety. If psychological safety is sufficient, members of the
group can begin to examine and possibly give up some of their
cognitive defenses.

Change Mechanism 10: Turnaround. Turnaround as a
"mechanism" is really more of a description of a combination
of many mechanisms fashioned into a single program by a talented change manager or team of change agents. In turnaround
situations I have observed or heard about, what strikes me is
that *all* the mechanisms previously described may be used in the
total change process. The first condition for change, as always,
is that the organizational culture must be unfrozen. Either because of external realities that threaten organizational survival
or because of new insights and plans on the part of the board of
directors or the dominant management coalition, the organization must come to recognize that some of its past ways of
thinking, feeling, and doing things are indeed obsolete. If necessary, the change manager uses coercive persuasion to produce
the unfreezing. Once the organization is unfrozen, change is
possible if there is (1) a turnaround manager or team with (2) a
clear sense of where the organization needs to go, (3) a model
of how to change culture to get there, and (4) the power to im-

plement the model. If any of these is lacking, the process will fail.

The key both to unfreezing and to managing change is to create enough psychological safety to permit group members to bear the anxieties that come with reexamining and changing parts of their culture (Schein, 1980). The turnaround management system must have the necessary insight and skill to manage all the above mechanisms without arousing defensive resistance. For example, if major replacement of people in critical positions is involved, that process must be managed in such a way that it is seen as necessary and carried out according to some of the deeper cultural assumptions that may need to be preserved. In the Multi case, it was crucial that those managers who were considered redundant were not to be fired but to be relocated in other divisions or encouraged to retire early, that people really were given a choice because of a variety of financial packages that were offered, and that each person was treated as an individual case. The assumption that people are important was preserved in this process even as people were let go.

Turnarounds usually require the involvement of all organization members, so that the dysfunctional elements of the old culture become clearly visible to everyone. The process of developing new assumptions then is a process of cognitive redefinition through teaching, coaching, changing the structure and processes where necessary, consistently paying attention to and rewarding evidence of learning the new ways, creating new slogans, stories, myths, and rituals, and in other ways coercing people into at least new behavior. All the other mechanisms described earlier may come into play, but it is the willingness to coerce that is the key to turnarounds.

Change Mechanism 11: Reorganization and Rebirth. Little is known or understood about this process, so little will be said about it here. Suffice it to say that if one destroys physically the group that is the carrier of a given culture, by definition that culture is destroyed and whatever new group begins to function begins to build its own new culture. This process is traumatic and therefore not typically used as a deliberate strategy, but it may be relevant if economic survival is at stake.

Conclusion

This chapter has described various mechanisms that change agents and managers use to change culture. As was noted, different functions are served by culture at different organizational stages, and the change issues are therefore different at those stages. In the formative stage of an organization, the culture tends to be a positive growth force, which needs to be elaborated, developed, and articulated. In organizational midlife the culture becomes diverse. Deciding what elements need change or preservation becomes one of the tougher strategic issues that managers face at this time. In the maturity and decline situation, the culture often becomes partly dysfunctional and must change in some areas, creating more drastic problems for managers.

In each case the change process must be understood as involving some unfreezing forces, consisting of disconfirming information and the creation of psychological safety, and some mechanisms to permit cognitive redefinition as a way of developing new assumptions. Though not much was said about it, the change process must also provide the opportunity for refreezing, which occurs when new cultural elements solve problems or reduce anxieties.

13

Analyzing the Change Process

How one goes about analyzing culture change depends on one's frame of reference, one's initial assumptions about the change process, and one's goals. If change processes are to be successful, those who are involved in the design and implementation of culture changes must share the same assumptions about change itself. As I will show later, such consensus may be possible only if we are quite explicit about our assumptions.

Differing Frames of Reference

As Smith (1982) has cogently pointed out, what we define as "change" depends initially on whether we are taking the perspective of (1) a member of the group who is personally affected by a set of events, (2) a change agent who is deliberately attempting to produce new and different responses in members of the group, (3) a group member who is not affected but who observes what may be happening to fellow group members, or

(4) an outside observer or historian reconstructing events. Depending on how a given set of events affects us, and depending on whether we take a short-range or long-run time perspective, we will see either change or continuity.

What we define as "change" depends on immediate effects and what we expect or hope for. The person immediately affected and the person trying to produce the change will be most likely to perceive actual changes, whereas the group member not affected or the outside observer may not even notice that anything has changed and wonder what all the fuss is about. Perception of change also may depend on one's time horizon. If one takes a short-run time perspective, the person directly affected or trying to produce change will be more likely to perceive changes. If one takes a longer-range time perspective, it is the person *not* affected who will be more likely to perceive historical trends and changes that may have been missed by those affected because they were so gradual.

Finally, whether one describes something as having changed or not may depend on one's goals. Politicians who have promised to make changes find all kinds of evidence of change, while entrenched conservatives find all kinds of evidence of stability in those areas for which they want credit. I have observed in my own behavior as a consultant the tendency to notice changes in areas where I am trying to induce them, and to take credit for changes that I consider important, while others may be struck by how little change has occurred and are disappointed that not more has happened.

To give a concrete example of what I mean, in the Redirection Project described in Chapter Eleven, the executives faced with early retirement, their families, and the managers directly involved in the early-retirement procedure saw dramatic and drastic changes in the company, some lamenting the end of an era. Managers in divisions that were profitable saw these same changes as inevitable and said that it was "high time a 'few' things were done to get the company in shape." In their view the early retirements represented a small step toward massive restructuring, which they felt would be needed. Some of the managers in geographically remote areas had been living with severe cost control programs for years and saw hardly any change occurring in headquarters. Those managers and consultants who expected more of a culture change, a real reexamination and redefinition of assumptions, saw no change whatsoever. These differences in perceptions, stemming from different frames of reference, highlight the importance of being clear in one's intentions when one talks of "planned culture change." What precisely is to be changed, and how will one measure resistance and potential impact?

Intentions and Motivations

When we are dealing with social systems (as opposed to biological units), there is no such thing as spontaneous change or mutation. There are no cosmic rays hitting the social genes to produce unpredictable changes. There is always *someone* inside or outside the system who has a motive to make something happen. The actual outcome may be a complex interaction of the forces unleashed by the different intentions of different actors, but the outcome will never be random and unpredictable. The only difficulty may be that events and interactions are so complex that it is not practical to try to unravel them.

Just as perceived change and continuity are two sides of the same coin, the intentions of actors reflect both the desire to change things and to keep them the same. As Lewin (1952) noted long ago, there are always forces in the system toward change and forces in the system toward stability and equilibrium; therefore, human systems exist in "quasi-stationary equilibria."

From the point of view of an outside observer taking a long-range perspective, much of the observed change may *appear* spontaneous or random because the actual causal events cannot be accurately reconstructed. For example, a company that is in economic difficulty hires a new chief executive who "turns out to have just the right kind of personality to save the company," and "Wasn't it fortunate that the board of directors found just the right person?" In fact, one or more board members working with knowledgeable insiders may have been plotting a strategy for years to create a situation where a certain person would be considered for the job, the person may have been secretly groomed for years, intensive political activity may have preceded the appointment, and consent may have been "engineered"; but only a few insiders know all this.

In the sociodynamic space, then, the same kind of assumption can be made that Freud made in the psychodynamic space: that there are no psychic accidents or random events. In fact, if anything, sociodynamic events are overdetermined; that is, so many forces may push an event in a given direction that it may not be historically sound even to settle for a single explanation. For example, in Multi a major structural change was the reshuffling of responsibilities among the members of the executive committee. This reshuffling was quite a dramatic event when it was announced, and one could not decipher why and how it had happened, but one could see at least the following forces all acting in that direction: (1) The poor performance of some of the divisions could have been the responsibility of the executive committee members who were then in charge; hence, shifting those responsibilities would open the door to more effective management of the troubled divisions. (2) If senior managers had to be retired and other severe steps taken, it would be difficult for the managers who had formed relationships with all these people to implement the program. (3) The chairman and board members wanted to find an excuse to put a couple of the "best" executive committee members into the most troubled divisions to ensure problem solution. (4) There had been no rotation of responsibilities in the executive committee for some time; yet such a rotation was considered developmentally desirable. (5) At the planning meetings for the Redirection Project, some executive committee members became very defensive about their divisions, which made it clear to the rest of the group that they would not be able to develop clear, tough change programs. And so on. It would be extremely difficult for a historian to unravel the interactions and formulate a precise set of causes. But the events were hardly fortuitous.

All change, then, is motivated. However, many changes do not go in the direction that the motivated persons wanted them to go. In other words, much of what actually happens as a consequence of initial change efforts may be unplanned and unintended because the change agents may have miscalculated the effects of their action or may have been unaware of other forces that were simultaneously acting. Such miscalculation is especially likely when members of one cultural unit make efforts to change behavior, values, or assumptions in another cultural unit, without fully understanding how their own behavior will be interpreted in the other cultural unit. The result may be new behaviors that neither group intended and that require either cultural redefinition or new cultural assumptions altogether (Sahlins, 1981).

Excellent examples of this process are given by Sahlins in his analysis of the interactions between the British exploration party under Captain Cook and the Hawaiians, which culminated in the killing of Cook by the Hawaiians in 1779. Cook's initial arrival fitted into Hawaiian mythology about the advent of a white god, and his various return visits could similarly be fitted into ritual legends. The myth spells out how a conflict always develops between present chiefs and gods, usually resolved by the ritual killing of the god to reinfuse the power of the chiefs through incorporating the god.

When Captain Cook left the islands in February of 1779, he was not aware that a cycle of such expected behavior had been completed and that he was not expected back for at least a year. Because of trouble with one of his ships, Cook was forced to return within two weeks, an unanticipated and unwelcome event from the Hawaiian point of view. Cook noticed the contrast between the present cool reception and the prior very friendly receptions but obviously did not know how to interpret it. When a conflict developed over a "theft" by the Hawaiians, Cook went ashore and took some chiefs hostage to trade for his equipment. An angry confrontation was precipitated on shore, someone struck an initial blow at Cook, and the event was immediately transformed into the ritual killing ultimately predicted for a later visit (over one hundred Hawaiians stabbed Cook once the first blow was struck). Cook then was glorified because he had fulfilled his mission as a god, and the consequent strong identification of the Hawaiians with the British lasted for several decades and strongly influenced the economic and political course of events in the islands.

Sahlins further documents how the aggressive sexual behavior of the native women was interpreted as a willing prostitution by the sailors but was, in fact, motivated by their desire to consort with "gods" and bear children by the gods because that was culturally desirable. The fact that the sailors viewed it in the context of prostitution, however, led them to give material gifts to the women, which had the secondary effect of creating important economic advantages to the Hawaiian men and led them to encourage the practice of the women's giving themselves. The Hawaiians especially liked iron implements, so the sailors were not above giving away essential items, even pulling up nails from the deck of the ship (and possibly damaging the ship so that it was forced to return to the islands).

The thriving trade of sex for various material objects worked well for the Hawaiian commoners but severely strained the relationships between the commoners and the chiefs, because the chiefs wanted to have a monopoly on trade relations. The chiefs became more aggressive toward the commoners but also found their power waning because of the correlated changes going on in the sex-role structure as the women maintained the sexual relations and thereby increased their own economic strength. Cook was puzzled at the growing aggression from chiefs to commoners and never understood the social causes of such behavior. He viewed it as evidence of the natives' primitive nature.

In fact, what was going on is explained by Sahlins as follows. The women in the Hawaiian social structure were clearly set apart by their observance of strict taboos about what they ate and with whom they ate (not with men). That kept the male role very clear. But when the women were on board ship with their boyfriends, they were encouraged to and did break many of the taboos, by eating forbidden food and consorting with the men. Recognition that the taboos had been broken but that nothing disastrous happened and that there was no point in punishing the women because they were bringing in valued goods forced a reinterpretation of some of the most basic struc-

tural categories of the society, further opening the door to political change that was not intended or anticipated.

Specifically, if the role of women as clearly subordinate
and often tabooed objects was weakened, this, in turn, weakened the absolute strength of the male role, and since power in
the society was tied up with the male role, the power of the
chiefs was gradually undermined. Sahlins makes the cogent
point that these events were outcomes of the interaction of
complex but understandable forces that produced culture
change through creating behavior that initially did not fit
into the cultural paradigm and therefore required new interpretations to rationalize what was going on.

Real history is fantastically complex, difficult to unravel,
and itself culture bound. Therefore, according to Sahlins, cultures simplify and reinterpret the events to fit into themes that
make cultural sense. The Hawaiian version emphasizes the role
of Cook in religious legends, while American history books purchased today in Hawaii emphasize economic and political factors and the "misfortune" that Cook was killed on his unintended repair stopover.

Organizational change is every bit as complex and difficult to unravel as social change of the sort Sahlins tackled.
Various cultural assumptions in various units of the organization interact in unanticipated ways, creating new behavior that
then has to be fitted into existing cultural paradigms or forces
revision of the paradigms. But we rarely analyze organizational
events at the level of historical and ethnographic detail that
would reveal in this fashion what *really* happened and *why*.

Theoretical Assumptions and Implicit Models

Much of the debate concerning whether or not certain
change strategies will work may be the result of misunderstanding of the implicit assumptions about what the process of
change "actually" is. Specifically, when we refer to a "change,"
we might have in mind any of a number of basic process models.

Change as General Evolutionary Process. The implicit assumptions in this model are that forces for change come from

within the group and are natural and inevitable. In addition, it is usually assumed that there are *stages* of evolution from lower to higher stages of development. The "organizational life cycle" (Kimberly and Miles, 1980) implies by its very title that there is a "natural" cycle that organizations go through, often based on the analogy to biological evolution (McKelvey, 1982). For example, according to a number of theorists, organizations move from autocracy to paternalism, to some form of bureaucracy, then to consultative and participative models. Just as some anthropologists see primitive societies evolving into complex civilizations, so the evolutionary model assumes that first-generation autocracies evolve into complex industrial bureaucracies and maybe beyond (Harbison and Myers, 1959; Bennis, 1966; Bennis and Slater, 1968; Likert, 1967).

      Built into this model is often an implicit theory that the stages follow in a set sequence and that the course of evolution is from lower and simpler to higher and more complex forms. Bureaucracy always comes after some stage of autocracy, the nation-state always comes after feudalism, and so on. Some branches of anthropology are built on theories of general evolution, arguing that all societies inevitably go through the same evolutionary sequence, though such theories may disagree on the nature of the actual stages and on the underlying reasons for the evolutionary process (Steward, 1955; Sahlins and Service, 1960; Service, 1971). Organizational evolution models also lack a clear theory of what drives the process from one stage or form to another. The ability to harness energy from the environment through increasingly improved technology (Sahlins and Service, 1960) or the ability to process ever greater amounts of complex information in an increasingly turbulent environment may offer clues to why organizational forms change and become more complex (Galbraith, 1973; Perrow, 1979; Thompson, 1967).

     Change as Adaptation, Learning, or Specific Evolutionary Process. Those change agents who hold as their implicit model some version of general evolution will be predisposed toward minimizing external manipulations, seeking instead change mechanisms that take advantage of the internal dynamics. Many change theorists, especially those influenced by Skinnerian learning theory (Skinner, 1953), assume that what goes on *inside* the learning system is not as critical to understand as what goes on in the environment. The properties of the environment cause certain group responses to be rewarded or punished and thereby cause the group to learn or adapt to the environment. In a sense, the ecological opportunities and constraints select out those group properties that maximize the group's chance of survival. The change agent operating from this theory would emphasize environmental manipulations as the keys to change.

Change as Therapeutic Process. The change agent operating from a therapeutic model would assume that change comes about inside the group but as a result of the interaction of insiders and outsiders and that the aim of the change is to improve the group's adaptive ability or level of integration. Implicit in this model is the assumption that change is related somehow to the action of a change agent whose intent is to improve the situation, as contrasted with the action of more impersonal forces implicit in the evolutionary and adaptive models.

The most direct analogue to therapeutic cultural change is found in the work of family or group therapists, who define their client from the outset as a social system, not an individual. Family therapy deals directly with one kind of culture change, insofar as the parental unit not only develops its own group culture but also represents a socialization unit of the larger culture and is therefore in the business of directly transmitting culture to the next generation (Madanes, 1981, 1984). Models of therapy show many of the variations described here in the discussion of change models, from those that emphasize the surfacing of unconscious assumptions (Bion, 1959) to those that emphasize behavior modification based on Skinnerian learning theory. Of most relevance to culture change, however, are those models that emphasize the cognitive complexity underlying human behavior and the fact that humans are always embedded in groups.

Some family therapists attempt to produce cognitive redefinition directly by various uncommon stratagems or "paradoxical" interventions (Haley, 1973, 1976; Watzlawick, Weakland, and Fisch, 1974; Fisch, Weakland, and Segal, 1982). For example, a depressed patient may reveal that her depression results from frequent unsuccessful social encounters, which lead to casual unsatisfactory relationships, thus paralyzing her and keeping her from making any social contacts. The therapist points out how fortunate it is that she is depressed, since it keeps her at home and safe from casual and unsatisfactory encounters. What was thought to be a destructive unhealthy feeling state gets recast as possibly a functional healthy feeling, which opens up new avenues of thought to the patient. Or, to take another example, the depressed patient is given the task to maximize the depression, to learn how to feel "really" depressed, but to do so at certain times of day, preferably when she would prefer to do something else. The assumption that feelings are not under our control is directly challenged by the task to feel even more of the undesired feeling, thus creating the idea that if one can feel more of something one can also feel less of that something.

More extreme versions, called "ordeal therapy," set the patient onerous tasks to be performed in place of symptomatic behavior (Haley, 1984). Thus, the person with insomnia is ordered to stay up five nights in a row or, if unable to sleep on a given night, to go run two miles, and to repeat this ordeal on every subsequent night if sleep is impossible. These interventions are designed to change the assumptions that the patient is making about himself and the nature of feelings and symptoms.

How does all this apply to culture change? Culture operates as a set of implicit and silent assumptions, which cannot change unless they are brought to the surface and confronted. Many of the cognitively oriented change models provide useful ways not only of bringing such assumptions to the surface but helping the person examine how they enhance or constrain behavior. What is applied by therapists to personal assumptions that we make about ourselves and that produce self-defeating behavior can as well be applied to cultural assumptions that we take for granted and that often also produce behavior out of line with some of our goals. The manager described in Chapter Twelve who ordered the delivery trucks to be painted white, to create a concern for marketing the delivery services, was using the equivalent of such an uncommon or paradoxical intervention. Many of the techniques of seduction or coercive persuasion work because they produce new perceptions and thus facilitate the surfacing and reexamination of assumptions.

To take this approach to the group level, instead of working with the sick person in the family, the systems-oriented family therapist will attempt to identify which member of the family is most capable of making behavioral changes and will work on that person. Thus, the wife of a depressed husband who has become totally inactive and unable to do even simple chores around the house is given the task of carefully monitoring the husband's behavior and systematically rewarding any active coping behavior. The husband is told that his problem is not depression but failure to be responsible and is given some simple tasks to do at home, to be monitored by the wife. Or the children of a couple with marital problems are asked to reward the parents by praising them when they concentrate on having fun together. The aim here is to train the parents to identify those areas where they do get along instead of being obsessed by the areas where they do not get along. The assumption is made that the system is in a quasi-stationary equilibrium and that, if any portion of the system is changed, other parts of the system will have to change as well. The change mechanisms that were labeled "technological seduction" in Chapter Twelve often work because they produce change in one part of an interdependent group, which forces other parts to adapt.

Borwick (1983) has taken this model to the level of executive groups and attempted to intervene at a systems level. Twenty to thirty interdependent managers are asked to attend a workshop, where each manager analyzes his own role in the organization and his relationship to the other managers. Each manager then develops a hypothesis, in role terms, of why certain problems in the system are occurring (for example, "Engineering and Manufacturing are not getting along"). After all the hypotheses are heard, the managers use this new information to reanalyze their roles. Instead of trying to locate individual responsibility, this model emphasizes role behavior and understanding of relationships. The emphasis is on giving each manager insight into his own part in the total network. Therapeutic change then occurs as each person redefines and monitors his own behavior rather than asking others to change their behavior, and the total system changes without anyone's having been specifically asked to change.

These kinds of change tactics applied at the individual or group level clearly assume that dramatic change in assumptions is possible in systems if the right set of interactions occur between motivated parties and appropriate change agents. The culture change theorist who operates with such assumptions will not be daunted by arguments about the monolithic quality of cultural forces or the inevitability of ecological or evolutionary mechanisms. And, again, my point is not to determine at this stage of the evolution of our field who is right and who is wrong, but for theorists to be explicit about the kinds of change assumptions with which they start.

Change as Revolutionary Process. Most organization theorists implicitly assume a revolutionary model when they argue that *power* is a key variable in human organizations, because the working out of power struggles between individuals and groups inevitably will lead to some form of revolutionary process, whether it is labeled as such or not. Management successions, turnarounds, and organizational restructurings usually involve loss of power on the part of one dominant coalition, which can be thought of as revolutions on a minor scale.

Whether we are analyzing class struggles, labor-management conflicts, functional group relationships, politics in the executive suite, or proxy fights, the same underlying model is used: that the change will be the result of new people with new sets of assumptions gaining control of key power positions. Cultural factors tend to be ignored in this model, in the sense that not much attention is given to the *meaning* of power in the different groups. Power is defined in terms of actual control of resources, the ability to reward or punish, and the possession of critical items of information. Whether or not culture changes as a result of such revolutionary changes becomes a secondary issue.

Change as Managed Process. Each of the above models assumes some forces that are and some that are not under the control of managers in the organization or the outside change agent. The theorist who operates from a model of managed change attempts to focus on and build a theory around those forces that can to some degree be controlled (Bennis and others, 1976). This theory is most often an extension of Lewinian change theory and systems-based therapeutic theory, as described above, because of the focus in those theories on what can and cannot be manipulated.

Conclusion

Theorists and change managers often debate about "change models" without specifying which implicit model of the change process they have in mind. The "change through seduction" manager may well have in mind a model based on paradoxical therapy, while the "incrementalist" manager may have in mind a model based on evolution. The "turnaround" manager thinks in terms of revolutionary change ideas, while the "organization development" manager thinks in therapeutic terms. Some managers will have an adaptational view, leading to proposals for action and then "letting the marketplace decide"; others, operating more from evolutionary models, will look for internally integrative solutions before leaping into action. If one person views culture change as evolution, while a second views it as adaptation, while a third views it as managed, they are likely to end up in confusion and disagreement. The same observed change can probably be analyzed from any of these points of view, as long as one is clear about it and has agreement.

Anthropologists who approach cultural change from extremes such as "historical particularism" (one can explain cultures only if one understands their specific antecedents, and every culture is unique), "evolutionism" (every culture goes through a predictable and directional process toward ever higher stages), and "ecological functionalism" (culture can be explained only by the adaptive functions that its various elements fulfill) are increasingly recognizing that these are not competing but complementary points of view, each of which is needed for full understanding of the observed phenomena (Abernathy, 1979;

Diener, Nonini, and Robkin, 1980; Boehm, 1982; Dougherty, 1984). For example, while ecologically one cannot predict what kind of culture will in fact survive in a given environment, especially when that environment is itself changing, one need not assume that cultures enter that environment on a pure trial-and-error basis, passively waiting for the environment to act on them. Genetic experiments may be blind, but experiments on human social systems are not. The members of a group themselves worry about their survival, analyze their environments, make the best prediction they can about what it will take to survive, and then attempt to create a culture that will have survival potential.

The group is always working actively on both the external survival and the internal integration issues. How effectively these issues are addressed is ultimately a function of leadership, in that it is leaders who must, in the end, make the complex calculations of how best to ensure that both sets of issues are addressed.

14

Leadership as Managed Culture Change

The dynamic perspective that has guided the analysis of organizational culture throughout this book has a number of implications. For the *scholar/researcher,* the message is that we simply cannot understand organizational phenomena without considering culture both as a cause of and as a way of explaining such phenomena. As Chapters One and Two indicate, misunderstandings, failures to reach consensus, and conflicts among individuals, groups, and organizations are caused to some degree by what I have defined as "culture." When such conflicts and misunderstandings are explained in cultural terms, our attention is drawn to quite different mechanisms for resolving them. Instead of attributing problems to the personalities and motives of the individuals in the situation, we can search for causes in the shared learning that those individuals have experienced in the groups and organizations to which they have belonged.

As I have argued in Chapters Three and Four, culture develops around the external and internal problems that groups face and gradually becomes abstracted into general and basic assumptions about the nature of reality; the world and the place of the group within it; and the nature of time, space, human nature, human activity, and human relationships. Culture can be thought of as the stable solutions to these problems, and the pattern of particular assumptions that represents these solutions can be thought of as the underlying "essence" that gives any given group its particular character. Though culture is ultimately *manifested* in overt behavior patterns, it should not be confused with overt behavior patterns. Culture is not visible; only its manifestations are.

The deciphering of a cultural paradigm requires the joint work of an outside researcher/consultant and willing insiders. This process of deciphering is difficult and hazardous, as Chapters Five and Six indicate; but it is not as difficult as the ethnographic research that anthropologists conduct in foreign cultures. Organizational cultures form within societal, ethnic, and occupational cultures. As long as the researcher/consultant comes from the same host culture, he should be able to understand much of what goes on in emerging and mature organizations. But, because culture is unconscious and taken for granted by the insiders, it cannot be studied through obtrusive methods such as questionnaires. To get at underlying assumptions, one must observe and interview and then work out the assumptions jointly with insiders who are willing to attempt to bring their assumptions to the surface.

Culture solves problems for the group or organization, and, even more important, it contains and reduces anxiety. The taken-for-granted assumptions that influence the ways in which group members perceive, think, and feel about the world stabilize that world, give meaning to it, and thereby reduce the anxiety that would result if we did not know how to categorize and respond to the environment. In this sense culture gives a group its character, and that character serves for the group the function that character and defense mechanisms serve for the individual. Learning theory, psychoanalytical theory, and sociodynamic theory are, therefore, elements that need to be brought together with leadership theory into a dynamic model of cul-

ture. The relevant theories for this integrative attempt are outlined in Chapter Seven, and they are applied in Chapter Eight
to show how culture actually forms in the small-group setting.

The emotional issues that individual members bring with
them when they enter new groups lead to coping behavior that
ultimately results in predictable stages of group evolution.
These stages are the result of a complex interplay between individuals attempting to exercise leadership and group members attempting to solve problems of authority, intimacy, and identity
for themselves. In resolving these issues, the group members
also learn how to work and how to solve the problems of survival
in the external environment. As solutions are worked out, they
become shared assumptions that are passed on to new members
and eventually become taken for granted and unconscious. All
cultural definitions emphasize that culture is the product of
shared meanings among group members, but the process by
which something comes to be shared in a group is still not well
understood. Chapters Eight, Nine, and Ten attempt to explain
the process in the small group and in the emerging larger organization.

The importance of shared assumptions in the emotional
life of the group will vary according to the stage at which the
group finds itself, which, in turn, will determine whether the
culture can be changed or only enhanced at any given stage. The
role of leadership is therefore very different at different stages
of group development, as we will see later.

Once an organization has evolved a mature culture because it has had a long and rich history, that culture creates the
patterns of perception, thought, and feeling of every new generation in the organization and, therefore, also "causes" the organization to be predisposed to certain kinds of leadership. In
that sense the mature group, through its culture, also creates its
own leaders. As scholars we must understand this paradox:
Leaders create cultures, but cultures, in turn, create their next
generation of leaders.

What makes culture an exciting concept is that its analysis forces one to take an integrative perspective toward organizational phenomena, a perspective that brings together key ideas

from psychology, sociology, anthropology, social psychology, systems theory, and psychotherapy. Our basic knowledge of how culture works is still very fragmentary, but there is no more important research agenda for organizational theory than culture dynamics.

Implications for the Manager

For the *manager* the message is "Give culture its due."

1. Do not oversimplify and do not confuse culture with other useful concepts, such as "climate," "values," or "corporate philosophy." Culture operates at one level below these others and largely *determines* them. Climate, values, and philosophies *can* be managed in the traditional sense of management; but, as I have argued throughout, it is not at all clear whether the underlying culture can be. But culture needs to be understood in order to determine what kinds of climate, values, and philosophies are possible and desirable for a given organization.

2. Do not assume that culture applies only to the human side of an organization's functioning. Culture determines not only the ways in which the internal system of authority, communication, and work is organized and managed but also the organization's most basic sense of mission and goals. Focusing on how people relate to each other in the organization and labeling that aspect "the culture" can be a dangerous trap because it draws attention away from shared basic assumptions about the nature of the product, the market, the organization's mission, and other factors that may have far more influence on how effective the organization is ultimately.

3. Do not assume that culture can be manipulated like other matters under the control of managers. Culture controls the manager more than the manager controls culture, through the automatic filters that bias the manager's perceptions, thoughts, and feelings. As culture arises and gains strength, it becomes pervasive and influences *everything* the manager does, even his own thinking and feeling. This point is especially important because most of the elements that the manager views as aspects of "effective" management—setting objectives, measuring, following up, controlling, giving performance feedback, and

so on—are themselves culturally biased to an unknown degree in any given organization. There is no such thing as a culture-free concept of management.

4. Do not assume that there is a "correct" or "better" culture, and do not assume that "strong" cultures are better than weak cultures. What is correct or whether strength is good or bad depends on the match between cultural assumptions and environmental realities. A strong culture can be effective at one point and ineffective at another point because external realities have changed.

5. Do not assume that all aspects of the culture are relevant to the effectiveness of the organization. Any group with any history will have a culture, but many elements of that culture may be essentially irrelevant to that group's functioning. Much of the time, therefore, the manager need not concern himself with cultural issues; or, if problems of effectiveness arise, the manager must learn how to focus on only those cultural issues that are relevant rather than getting bogged down in total cultural analyses. Those involved in the major change program described in Chapter Eleven thought that "a lot of culture change" had occurred; in retrospect, however, it seems clear that only superficial aspects of the actual culture changed, even though there was a major organizational restructuring and a change in personnel policy. In fact, it was the strength of the underlying culture that made the policy changes, the cutbacks, and the organization's redesign possible.

The operating manager in most organizations needs to be aware of his own culture only in the same sense that any individual needs to be aware of his own character and personality. Most of the time, we do not need this awareness; but when we get into trouble, when things do not work out as they are supposed to, then we need to know how our own silent assumptions contribute to the problem. Like self-awareness, insight into an organization's culture is therefore highly desirable but not something that we work on or dwell on constantly.

Insight into the culture of one's own organization contributes another layer of explanation for why things do or do not work out. When managers observe communication or problem-solving failures, when they cannot get people to work to-

gether effectively, they need to go beyond individual explanations. The problem may not be their own lack of managerial
skill or limitations in the personalities of the people involved.
Often the problem is that those people started with different assumptions, different languages, different world views—in short,
different cultures. Recognizing such cultural differences is
essential, so that the manager can explain how things can go
wrong even if everyone has the same good intentions to make
them work.

If interpersonal, intergroup, interdepartmental, and inter-
organizational problems are often best understood from the cultural perspective, then the solution to such problems is often
achieved only by the creation of intercultural interventions,
such as those described in Chapter Thirteen. These interventions
have to be geared to an understanding of what particular functions the culture is serving for the group, the stage of group evolution, the sources of cultural stability, and the dynamics of culture change.

If the manager is outside the cultures that are in conflict,
he may be able to perceive accurately what is needed, perhaps
bringing representatives of the two groups together around a
new task that is involving enough to create a new group experience and thus a "bridging culture." But if the manager is trying
to understand the issue from the perspective of an insider, a
much greater level of self-insight is needed. Such insight is theoretically possible but not easily achieved. And even if the manager achieves insight, it often tells him that what needs to be
done cannot really be done without major interventions that
may be beyond the manager's power or skill. When such implementation becomes essential because organizational survival or
well-being is at stake, we are going beyond the realm of what is
typically meant by "managing" and into the realm I would like
to identify as "leadership."

Implications for Leaders and the Concept of Leadership

A dynamic analysis of organizational culture makes it
clear that leadership is intertwined with culture formation, evolution, transformation, and destruction. Culture is created in

the first instance by the actions of leaders; culture also is embedded and strengthened by leaders. When culture becomes dysfunctional, leadership is needed to help the group unlearn some of its cultural assumptions and learn new assumptions. Such transformations require what amounts to conscious and deliberate destruction of cultural elements, and it is this aspect of cultural dynamics that makes leadership important and difficult to define. In fact, the endless discussion of what leadership is and is not could, perhaps, be simplified if we recognized that *the unique and essential function of leadership is the manipulation of culture.*

It is this function that provides the most difficult challenge for leadership. It sometimes involves nothing less than surmounting one's own taken-for-granted assumptions, seeing what is needed to ensure the health and survival of the group, and making things happen that enable the group to evolve toward new cultural assumptions. Without leadership, groups would not be able to adapt to changing environmental conditions. Let us examine leadership more closely from this perspective by seeing what is really needed at each major stage of group evolution.

Leadership in Culture Creation

In a growing organization, as described in Chapters Nine and Ten, the leadership externalizes its own assumptions and embeds them gradually and consistently in the mission, goals, structures, and working procedures of the group. Whether we call these basic assumptions the guiding beliefs, the theories-in-use, the basic principles, or the guiding visions on which a founder operates, there is little question that they become major elements of the emerging culture of the organization (Argyris, 1976; Pettigrew, 1979; Bennis, 1983; Donaldson and Lorsch, 1983; Dyer, 1983; Schein, 1983; Davis, 1984).

At this stage the leader needs both *vision* and the *ability to articulate* it and *enforce* it. Inasmuch as the new members of the organization arrive with prior organizational and cultural experiences, a common set of assumptions is only forged by clear and consistent messages as the group encounters and survives its own crises. The culture creation leader therefore needs *persistence* and *patience* as well.

As groups and organizations develop, certain key emotional issues arise, those having to do with dependence on the leader, with peer relationships, and with how to work effectively. At each of these stages of group development, leadership is needed to help the group identify the issues and deal with them. During these stages leaders often *absorb and contain the anxiety* that is unleashed when things do not work as they should (Schein, 1983). The leader may not have the answer, but he must *provide temporary stability and emotional reassurance* while the answer is being worked out.

This anxiety-containing function seems especially relevant in entrepreneurs and founders of companies. The traumas of growth appear to be so constant and so powerful that, unless a strong leader plays the role of anxiety and risk absorber, the group cannot get through its early stages of growth and fails. Being in an ownership position helps, since everyone then realizes that the founder is in fact taking a greater personal financial risk, but ownership does not automatically create the ability to absorb anxiety. Rather, it seems to be the other way around: that people with certain kinds of creative needs, building skills, and emotional strengths are able to create, own, and develop new organizations.

If the shape of the culture that the group will develop is heavily determined by initial leadership behavior, then we as historians and students of organizations must attempt to understand how the early leaders of the group set about to create and manage it and how the culture of the group reflects these early activities. When leaders launch new enterprises, they must be mindful of the power they have to impose on those enterprises their own assumptions about what is right and proper, how the world works, and how things should be done. Leaders should not apologize for or be cautious about their assumptions. Rather, it is intrinsic to the leadership role to create order out of chaos, and leaders are expected to provide their own assumptions as an initial road map into the uncertain future. And the more aware they are of this process, the more consistent and effective they can be in implementing it.

This process of culture creation, embedding, and reinforcement brings with it problems as well as solutions. Many organizations survive and grow but, at the same time, operate inconsistently or do things that seem mutually contradictory. One explanation of this phenomenon is that leaders not only embed in their organizations what they intend consciously to get across, but they also convey their own inner conflicts and the inconsistencies in their own personal makeup (Schein, 1983; Kets de Vries and Miller, 1984). The most powerful signal that subordinates respond to is what catches a leader's attention consistently, particularly what arouses him emotionally. But many of the things that they respond to emotionally reflect not so much their conscious intentions as their unconscious conflicts. The organization then develops a culture around these inconsistencies and conflicts, or the leader gradually loses his position of influence if his behavior begins to be seen as too disruptive or actually destructive. In extreme cases the organization isolates or ejects the founder; in doing so, however, it is not rejecting all of the founder's assumptions but only those that are inconsistent with the core assumptions on which the organization was built.

The period of culture creation, therefore, puts an additional burden on the founder/creator—to obtain enough self-insight to avoid unwittingly undermining his own creation. It is often difficult for founding leaders to recognize that the very qualities that made them successful initially, their strong convictions, can become sources of difficulty later on, and that they also must grow as their organizations grow. Such insight becomes especially important as issues of leadership succession have to be faced, because succession discussions force into the open aspects of the culture that previously may not have surfaced.

Let me summarize this first major point. Organizational culture does not start from scratch or come into being accidentally. Organizations are created by people, and the creators of organizations also create culture through the articulation of their own assumptions. Although the final form of an organization's culture reflects the complex interaction between the thrust provided by the founder, the reactions of the group members, and their shared historical experiences, there is little doubt that the initial shaping force is the personality and belief system of that founder.

Leadership at Organizational Midlife

Once the organization develops a substantial history of its own, its culture becomes more of a cause than an effect. The culture now influences the strategy, the structure, the procedures, and the ways in which the group members will relate to each other. Culture becomes a powerful influence on members' perceiving, thinking, and feeling; and these predispositions, along with situational factors, will influence the members' behavior. Because it serves an important anxiety-reducing function, culture will be clung to even if it becomes dysfunctional in relationship to environmental opportunities and constraints.

Midlife organizations show two basically different patterns, however. Some, under the influence of one or more generations of leaders, have developed a highly integrated culture even though they have become large and diversified; others have allowed growth and diversification in cultural assumptions as well and, therefore, can be described as culturally diverse with respect to their business, functional, and geographical units. How leaders manage culture at this stage of organizational evolution depends on which pattern they perceive and which pattern they decide is best for the future.

As Chapter Twelve attempts to show, leaders at this stage need above all the insight to know how to help the organization evolve to whatever will make it most effective in the future. In some instances this may mean increasing cultural diversity, allowing some of the uniformity that may have been built up in the growth stage to erode; in other instances it may mean pulling together a culturally diverse set of organizational units and attempting to impose new common assumptions on them. In either case what the leader most needs is *insight into the ways in which culture can aid or hinder the fulfillment of the organization's mission* and the *intervention skills to make desired changes happen.*

Most of the prescriptive analyses of how to bring organizations through this period emphasize that the leader must have certain insights and skills, but they say nothing about how a given organization can find and install such a leader. In United States organizations in particular, the outside board members probably play a critical role in this process, but if the organization has had a strong founding culture, its board may be composed exclusively of people who share the founder's vision. Consequently, real changes in direction may not become possible until the organization gets into serious survival difficulties. Until that happens, the organization is, by definition, managed but not led.

Breaking the Tyranny of Culture:
Leadership in Mature Organizations

In the mature organization—if it has developed a strong unifying culture—culture now defines what is to be thought of as "leadership," what is heroic or sinful behavior, and how authority and power are to be allocated and managed. Thus, what leadership has created now either blindly perpetuates itself or creates new definitions of leadership, which may not even include the kinds of entrepreneurial assumptions that started the organization in the first place.

What leaders must do at this point in the organization's history depends on the degree to which the culture of the organization has, in fact, enabled the group to adapt to its environmental realities. If the culture has not facilitated adaptation, the organization either will not survive or will find a way to change its culture. If it is to change its culture, it must be led by someone who can, in effect, break the tyranny of the old culture.

A leader capable of such managed culture change can come from inside the organization if he has acquired objectivity and insight into elements of the culture. However, the formally designated senior managers of a given organization may not be willing or able to provide culture change leadership. Leadership in this form then may have to come from other boundary spanners in the organization or from outsiders. It may even come from a number of people in the organization, so that it makes sense to talk of turnaround teams or multiple leadership. If the formally designated senior managers do not have the insight, skill, or vision to change the culture in whatever ways might be needed, then the culture will change under the impact of other forms of leadership, or it will atrophy and the group will disappear as a social entity. In any event, no change will occur without leadership from somewhere.

If a leader is imposed from the outside, he must have the skill to diagnose accurately what the culture of the organization is, what elements are well adapted and what elements are problematic for future adaptation, and how to change that which needs changing. The leader must therefore be a skilled change manager who first learns what the present state of the culture is, unfreezes it, redefines and changes it, and then refreezes the new assumptions. Talented turnaround managers seem to be able to manage all phases of such changes, but sometimes different leaders will be involved in the different steps over a considerable period of time. They will use all the mechanisms listed in Chapter Twelve in the appropriate combinations to get the job done, provided they have the authority and power to use extreme measures, such as replacing the people who perpetuate the old cultural assumptions.

The more interesting case is how leadership can operate from within. Is it possible for the insider to surmount his own culture and change those aspects that need to be changed? Such a process would seem to be the ultimate in leadership. For that to happen, let us look at what would be required.

Perception and Insight. First, the leader must perceive the problem, must have the insight into the culture and its dysfunctional elements. Such boundary-spanning perception can be difficult because it requires one to see one's own weaknesses, to perceive that one's own defenses not only help in managing anxiety but can also hinder one's efforts to be effective. In the change processes reviewed in Chapters Eleven and Twelve, the most successful architects of change were those who had a high degree of objectivity about themselves and their own organizations. In many instances they had acquired such objectivity because they had spent portions of their careers in diverse settings that permitted them to compare and contrast different cultures. Often they had actually worked in another culture, which can produce greater insight than mere cross-functional or cross-divisional movement.

Individuals often are aided in becoming objective about themselves through counseling and psychotherapy. One might conjecture that leaders can benefit from comparable processes and that one of the functions of outside consultants or board members is to provide the kind of counseling that produces cultural insight. From this perspective it is far more important for the consultant to help the leader figure himself out than to provide recommendations on what the company should do. The consultant also might serve as a "cultural therapist," helping the leader figure out what the culture is and what parts of it are more or less adaptive.

Motivation and Skill. Internal leadership requires not only insight into the dynamics of the culture but the motivation and skill to intervene in one's own cultural process. To change any elements of the culture, leaders must be willing to unfreeze their own organization. Unfreezing requires disconfirmation, a process that is inevitably painful for many. The leader must find a way to say to his own organization that things are not all right and, if necessary, must enlist the aid of outsiders in getting this message across. Such willingness requires a great ability to be concerned for the organization above and beyond the self, to communicate *dedication* or *commitment* to the *group* above and beyond self-interest.

Emotional Strength. Unfreezing also requires the creation of psychological safety, which means that the leader must have the emotional strength to absorb much of the anxiety that change brings with it, and he must have the ability to remain supportive to the organization through the transition phase even if group members become angry and obstructive. The leader is likely to be the target of anger and criticism because, by definition, he must challenge some of what the group has taken for granted. He may have to close down the division in the company that was the original source of the company's growth and the basis of many employees' source of pride and identity. He may have to lay off or retire loyal, dedicated employees and old friends. Worst of all, he may have to get the message across that some of the founder's most cherished assumptions are wrong in the contemporary context.

It is here that dedication and commitment are especially needed, to demonstrate to the organization that the leader genuinely cares about the welfare of the total organization even as parts of it come under challenge. The leader must remember that giving up a cultural element requires one to take some risk, the risk that one will be very anxious and in the end worse off, yet must have the strength to push into this unknown territory.

Ability to Change the Cultural Assumptions. If an assumption is to be given up, it must be replaced or redefined in another form, and it is the burden of leadership to make that happen. Leaders, in other words, must have the ability to induce "cognitive redefinition" by articulating and selling new visions and concepts. They must be able to bring to the surface, review, and change some of the group's basic assumptions.

At Multi this process had only begun in the change program described in Chapter Eleven. Many managers were beginning to doubt that the organization's commitment to science-based technical products could sustain the company in the long run. But so far no strong leader had emerged to convince the organization that consumer goods marketed through strong customer-oriented organizations could be a source of pride for the company. Many other companies that started with a scientific or technical emphasis must undergo a similar kind of redefinition; that is, they must be made to feel that a consumer orientation is not incompatible with the making of useful and valuable products.

Creation of Involvement and Participation. A paradox of culture change leadership is that the leader must be able not only to lead but also to listen, to involve the group in achieving its own insights into its cultural dilemmas, and to be genuinely participative in his approach to change. The leader of social, religious, or political movements can rely on his personal charisma and let the followers do what they will. But in an organization, the leader is bound to work with the group that exists at the moment, because he is dependent on the people to carry out the organization's mission. The leader must recognize that, in the end, cognitive redefinition must occur inside the heads of many members of the organization and that will happen only if they are actively involved in the process. The whole organization must achieve insight and develop motivation to change before any real change will occur, and the leader must create this involvement even as he sells his vision.

Depth of Vision. In order to work at the level of the group's deepest assumptions about the nature of reality and its own identity in relationship to its environment, a leader must have a great depth of vision and extraordinary insight into thoughts and feelings that are normally taken for granted and therefore not articulated. Leadership in this sense means the ability to step outside one's culture even as one continues to live within it. It is not enough just to set goals and sell symbols. The goals and symbols and the assumptions on which they are based must be "correct" in the sense that they will indeed solve key problems for the group and will fit with other deep cultural assumptions. The effective leader needs to use his deeper vision before trying to sell anything.

To illustrate the kinds of mistakes that are possible, we need remember only the period in Atari's history when Warner Communications, the parent company, decided to improve Atari's marketing by bringing in as president an experienced marketing executive from the food industry. This executive brought with him the assumption that the key to success is high motivation and high rewards based on individual performance. He created and sold an incentive system designed to pick out the engineers who were doing the best job in inventing and designing new computer games and gave them large monetary rewards. Soon some of the best engineers were leaving, and the company was getting into technical difficulty.

What was wrong? The new executive had created and articulated clear symbols, and everyone had rallied around them. Apparently what was wrong was the assumption that the incentives and rewards should be based on *individual* effort. What the president failed to understand, coming from the product-management–oriented food industry, was that the computer games were designed by groups and teams and that the assignment of individual responsibility was considered neither possible nor necessary by the engineers. They were happy being group members and would have responded to group incentives, but unfortunately the symbol chosen was the wrong symbol from this point of view. They also noted that the president, with his nontechnical background, was not adept at picking out the best engineers, since their key assumption was that "best" was the product of group effort, not individual brilliance. It is no surprise, given these incompatibilities in assumptions, that the president did not last long. Unfortunately, the damage—the loss of employees and esprit—had been done.

So when I speak of depth of vision, I mean the ability to sense both the external and the internal cultural factors, so that the leadership effort in the end is allocated to the right things, based on an accurate perception of what is going on.

Final Implications

1. If leadership is critical both to the formation of culture and to culture change, we should examine more carefully the development of this form of leader, the *culture manager.*

2. If leadership is culture management, do we develop in our leaders the emotional strength, depth of vision, and capacity for self-insight and objectivity that are necessary for culture to be managed?

3. Do our management development processes nurture "creative individualists," emotionally strong boundary spanners with high objectivity and tolerance of deviant points of view (Van Maanen and Schein, 1979)?

4. If the environment in which organizations have to function is changing ever more rapidly, can we specify what kind of organizational culture will be most adaptive, or is the real implication that the more rapidly things change, the more dependent we are on leaders to manage the changes? If so, are

we developing enough leaders so that they will be available when they are needed?

5. Have we in the United States put so much emphasis on self-actualization that leadership in the culture management sense is itself culturally unpopular because it requires actively challenging the assumptions of some group members? It is an interesting historical fact that the small-group training developed in the 1940s at the National Training Laboratories—which later became the "encounter group movement" oriented toward "personal growth and human potential"—started under its founders as "leadership training." But in the rush for everyone to self-actualize, we may have lost the leadership emphasis. Is the assumption that everyone can and should achieve self-actualization one of these cultural assumptions that has in itself become tyrannical, so that the true challenge for leadership will be a greater vision to see how the United States and the organizations within it can become truly adaptive in the increasingly turbulent environments that world conditions are creating?

If there is to be a single final conclusion drawn from this intellectual journey through parts of organization theory, social psychology, and anthropology, it is that leadership and culture management are so central to understanding organizations and making them effective that we cannot afford to be complacent about either one.

References

Abernathy, V. *Population Pressure and Cultural Adjustment.* New York: Human Sciences Press, 1979.

Adorno, T., and others. *The Authoritarian Personality.* New York: Harper & Row, 1950.

Alderfer, C. P. "Group and Intergroup Relations." In J. R. Hackman and J. L. Suttle (Eds.), *Improving Life at Work.* Santa Monica, Calif.: Goodyear, 1977.

Alderfer, C. P., and Cooper, C. L. (Eds.). *Advances in Experiential Social Processes.* Vol. 2. New York: Wiley, 1980.

Allen, R. F., and Kraft, C. *The Organizational Unconscious.* Englewood Cliffs, N.J.: Prentice-Hall, 1982.

Allen, T. J. *Managing the Flow of Technology.* Cambridge, Mass.: MIT Press, 1977.

Argyris, C. *Integrating the Individual and the Organization.* New York: Wiley, 1964.

Argyris, C. *Increasing Leadership Effectiveness.* New York: Wiley-Interscience, 1976.

Argyris, C., and Schön, D. A. *Theory in Practice: Increasing Professional Effectiveness.* San Francisco: Jossey-Bass, 1974.

329

Argyris, C., and Schön, D. A. *Organizational Learning.* Reading, Mass.: Addison-Wesley, 1978.

Bailyn, L. "Accommodation of Work to Family." In R. Rapoport and R. N. Rapoport (Eds.), *Working Couples.* London: Routledge & Kegan Paul, 1978.

Bailyn, L. "The Apprenticeship Model of Organizational Careers: A Response to Changes in the Relationship Between Work and Family." In P. A. Wallace (Ed.), *Women in the Workplace.* Boston: Auburn House, 1982.

Baker, E. L. "Managing Organizational Culture." *Management Review,* July 1980, pp. 8–13.

Bales, R. F. *Interaction Process Analysis.* Chicago: University of Chicago Press, 1950.

Bales, R. F., and Cohen, S. P. *SYMLOG: A System for the Multiple Level Observation of Groups.* New York: Free Press, 1979.

Barley, S. R. "Semiotics and the Study of Occupational and Organizational Cultures." *Administrative Science Quarterly,* 1983, *28,* 393–413.

Barley, S. R. "The Professional, the Semi-Professional, and the Machine: The Social Implications of Computer Based Imaging in Radiology." Unpublished doctoral dissertation, Sloan School of Management, MIT, 1984a.

Barley, S. R. *Technology as an Occasion for Structuration: Observations on CT Scanners and the Social Order of Radiology Departments.* Cambridge, Mass.: Sloan School of Management, MIT, 1984b.

Bass, B. M. *Stogdill's Handbook of Leadership.* (Rev. ed.) New York: Free Press, 1981.

Bass, B. M., and Ryterband, E. C. *Organizational Psychology.* (2nd ed.) Boston: Allyn & Bacon, 1979.

Beck, A. P. "Developmental Characteristics of the System Forming Process." In J. E. Durkin (Ed.), *Living Groups: Group Psychotherapy and General Systems Theory.* New York: Brunner/Mazel, 1981.

Becker, H. S., and others. *Boys in White: Student Culture in Medical School.* Chicago: University of Chicago Press, 1961.

Beckhard, R. *Organization Development: Strategies and Models.* Reading, Mass.: Addison-Wesley, 1969.

Beckhard, R., and Dyer, W. G. "Managing Change in the Family Firm: Issues and Strategies." *Sloan Management Review,* 1983, *24* (3), 59–65.

Beckhard, R., and Harris, R. T. *Organizational Transitions: Managing Complex Change.* Reading, Mass.: Addison-Wesley, 1977.

Beer, M. *Organization Change and Development: A System View.* Santa Monica, Calif.: Goodyear, 1980.

Benne, K., and Sheats, P. "Functional Roles of Group Members." *Journal of Social Issues,* 1948, *2,* 42–47.

Bennis, W. G. *Changing Organizations.* New York: McGraw-Hill, 1966.

Bennis, W. G. *Organization Development: Its Nature, Origins, and Prospects.* Reading, Mass.: Addison-Wesley, 1969.

Bennis, W. G. "The Artform of Leadership." In S. Srivastva and Associates, *The Executive Mind: New Insights on Managerial Thought and Action.* San Francisco: Jossey-Bass, 1983.

Bennis, W. G., and Shepard, H. A. "A Theory of Group Development." *Human Relations,* 1956, *9* (4), 415–437.

Bennis, W. G., and Slater, P. E. *The Temporary Society.* New York: Harper & Row, 1968.

Bennis, W. G., and others. *The Planning of Change.* (3rd ed.) New York: Holt, Rinehart and Winston, 1976.

Bion, W. R. *Experiences in Groups.* London: Tavistock, 1959.

Blake, R. R., and Mouton, J. S. "Reactions to Intergroup Competition Under Win-Lose Conditions." *Management Science,* 1961, *7,* 420–435.

Blake, R. R., and Mouton, J. S. *The Managerial Grid.* Houston: Gulf, 1964.

Boehm, C. "A Fresh Outlook on Cultural Selection." *American Anthropologist,* 1982, *84,* 105–125.

Bolman, L. G., and Deal, T. E. *Modern Approaches to Understanding and Managing Organizations.* San Francisco: Jossey-Bass, 1984.

Borwick, I. "Footnotes to Change." Unpublished paper, 1983.

Bradford, L. P., Gibb, J. R., and Benne, K. D. (Eds.). *T-Group Theory and Laboratory Method.* New York: Wiley, 1964.

Brandt, S. C. *Strategic Planning in Emerging Companies.* Reading, Mass.: Addison-Wesley, 1981.

Brislin, R. W. "Cross-Cultural Research in Psychology." *Annual Review of Psychology,* 1983, *34,* 363-400.

Bronsema, G. S., and Keen, P. G. W. "Education Intervention and Implementation in MIS." *Sloan Management Review,* 1983, *24,* 35-43.

Brooks, F. P., Jr. *The Mythical Man-Month.* Reading, Mass.: Addison-Wesley, 1975.

Burke, W. W. (Ed.). *The Cutting Edge: Current Theory and Practice in Organization Development.* La Jolla, Calif.: University Associates, 1978.

Butterfield, F. *China, Alive in the Bitter Sea.* New York: Times Books, 1982.

Castaneda, C. *The Teachings of Don Juan.* New York: Pocket Books, 1968.

Castaneda, C. *Journey to Ixtlan.* New York: Simon & Schuster, 1972.

Chibnik, M. "The Evolution of Cultural Rules." *Journal of Anthropological Research,* 1981, *37,* 256-268.

Cohen, A. M., and Smith, R. D. *Critical Incidents in Growth Groups: Theory and Techniques.* La Jolla, Calif.: University Associates, 1976.

Colman, A. D., and Bexton, W. H. (Eds.). *Group Relations Reader.* Sausalito, Calif.: GREX, 1975.

Cooper, C. L., and Alderfer, C. P. (Eds.). *Advances in Experiential Social Processes.* Vol. 1. New York: Wiley, 1978.

Cooper, J., and Croyle, R. T. "Attitudes and Attitude Change." *Annual Review of Psychology,* 1984, *35,* 395-426.

Cyert, R. M., and March, J. G. *A Behavioral Theory of the Firm.* Englewood Cliffs, N.J.: Prentice-Hall, 1963.

Dandridge, T. C., Mitroff, I. I., and Joyce, W. "Organizational Symbolism: A Topic to Expand Organizational Analysis." *Academy of Management Review,* 1980, *5* (1), 77-82.

Davis, S. M. "Transforming Organizations: The Key to Strategy Is Context." *Organizational Dynamics,* Winter 1982, pp. 64-80.

Davis, S. M. *Managing Corporate Culture.* Cambridge, Mass.: Ballinger, 1984.

Deal, T. E., and Kennedy, A. A. *Corporate Cultures.* Reading, Mass.: Addison-Wesley, 1982.

DeBoard, R. *The Psychoanalysis of Organizations.* London: Tavistock, 1978.

Dickinson, A., and Mackintosh, N. J. "Classical Conditioning in Animals." *Annual Review of Psychology,* 1978, *29,* 587–612.

Diener, P., Nonini, D., and Robkin, E. E. "Ecology and Evolution in Cultural Anthropology." *Man,* 1980, *15,* 1–31.

Donaldson, G., and Lorsch, J. W. *Decision Making at the Top.* New York: Basic Books, 1983.

Dougherty, D. *From Genes to Generations, from Minds to Majesties: Theories of Culture, Change, and Processes in Anthropology.* Cambridge, Mass.: Sloan School of Management, MIT, 1984.

Duncan, R. B. "The Characteristics of Organizational Environments and Perceived Environmental Uncertainty." *Administrative Science Quarterly,* 1972, *17,* 313–327.

Durkin, J. E. (Ed.). *Living Groups: Group Psychotherapy and General Systems Theory.* New York: Brunner/Mazel, 1981.

Dyer, W. G. *Team Building.* Reading, Mass.: Addison-Wesley, 1977.

Dyer, W. G., Jr. "Culture in Organizations: A Case Study and Analysis." Unpublished paper, Sloan School of Management, MIT, 1982.

Dyer, W. G., Jr. "Organizational Evolution." Unpublished paper, Sloan School of Management, MIT, 1983.

Dyer, W. G., Jr. "The Cycle of Cultural Evolution in Organizations." Unpublished paper, Sloan School of Management, MIT, 1984.

England, G. *The Manager and His Values.* Cambridge, Mass.: Ballinger, 1975.

Etzioni, A. *A Comparative Analysis of Complex Organizations.* (Rev. ed.) New York: Free Press, 1975.

Evans, J. M. *America: The View from Europe.* Stanford, Calif.: Stanford Alumni Assoc., 1976.

Evered, R., and Louis, M. R. "Alternative Perspectives in the Organizational Sciences: 'Inquiry from the Inside' and 'Inquiry from the Outside.' " *Academy of Management Review,* 1981, *6,* 385–395.

Faucheux, C., Amado, G., and Laurent, A. "Organization Development and Change." *Annual Review of Psychology,* 1982, *33,* 343–370.

Festinger, L. *A Theory of Cognitive Dissonance.* New York: Harper & Row, 1957.

Fiedler, F. E. *A Theory of Leadership Effectiveness.* New York: McGraw-Hill, 1967.

Fisch, R., Weakland, J. H., and Segal, L. *The Tactics of Change: Doing Therapy Briefly.* San Francisco: Jossey-Bass, 1982.

Flax, S. "The Toughest Bosses in America." *Fortune,* Aug. 6, 1984, pp. 18–23.

Fleishman, E. A. "Twenty Years of Consideration and Structure." In E. A. Fleishman and J. G. Hunt (Eds.), *Current Developments in the Study of Leadership.* Carbondale: Southern Illinois University Press, 1973.

Fox, R. "The Evolution of Mind: An Anthropological Approach." *Journal of Anthropological Research,* 1979, *35,* 138–156.

Frake, C. O. "Notes on Queries in Ethnography." *American Anthropologist,* 1964, *66,* 132–145.

French, W. L., and Bell, C. H., Jr. *Organization Development.* Englewood Cliffs, N.J.: Prentice-Hall, 1978.

Galbraith, J. *Designing Complex Organizations.* Reading, Mass.: Addison-Wesley, 1973.

Gibbard, G. S., Hartman, J. J., and Mann, R. D. (Eds.). *Analysis of Groups: Contributions to Theory, Research, and Practice.* San Francisco: Jossey-Bass, 1973.

Goffman, E. *The Presentation of Self in Everyday Life.* New York: Doubleday, 1959.

Goffman, E. *Interaction Ritual.* Hawthorne, N.Y.: Aldine, 1967.

Golding, W. *The Lord of the Flies.* London: Faber & Faber, 1958.

Greiner, L. E. "Evolution and Revolution as Organizations Grow." *Harvard Business Review,* 1972, *50,* 37–46.

Gustafson, J. P., and Cooper, L. "Unconscious Planning in Small Groups." *Human Relations,* 1979, *32,* 1039–1064.

Haley, J. *Uncommon Therapy.* New York: Norton, 1973.

Haley, J. *Problem-Solving Therapy: New Strategies for Effective Family Therapy.* San Francisco: Jossey-Bass, 1976.

Haley, J. *Ordeal Therapy: Unusual Ways to Change Behavior.* San Francisco: Jossey-Bass, 1984.

Hall, E. T. *The Silent Language.* New York: Doubleday, 1959.

Hall, E. T. *The Hidden Dimension.* New York: Doubleday, 1966.

Hall, E. T. *Beyond Culture.* New York: Doubleday, 1977.

Handy, C. *The Gods of Management.* New York: Penguin Books, 1978.

Harbison, F., and Myers, C. A. *Management in the Industrial World.* New York: McGraw-Hill, 1959.

Hare, A. *Handbook of Small Group Research.* (2nd ed.) New York: Free Press, 1976.

Harris, M. *America Now.* New York: Simon & Schuster, 1981.

Harrison, R. "Understanding Your Organization's Character." *Harvard Business Review,* 1972, *3,* 119-128.

Havrylyshyn, B. *Road Maps to the Future.* Oxford, England: Pergamon Press, 1980.

Hax, A. C., and Majluf, N. S. *Strategic Management: An Integrative Perspective.* Englewood Cliffs, N.J.: Prentice-Hall, 1984.

Hebb, D. "The Social Significance of Animal Studies." In G. Lindzey (Ed.), *Handbook of Social Psychology.* Vol. 2. Reading, Mass.: Addison-Wesley, 1954.

Hedberg, B. "Career Dynamics in a Steelworks of the Future." *Journal of Occupational Behaviour,* 1984, *5,* 53-69.

Heider, F. *The Psychology of Interpersonal Relations.* New York: Wiley, 1958.

Hemphill, J. K. *Leader Behavior Description.* Columbus: Bureau of Business Research, Ohio State University, 1950.

Hirsch, P. M., and Andrews, J. A. Y. "Ambushes, Shootouts, and Knights of the Round Table: The Language of Corporate Take-Overs." In L. R. Pondy and others (Eds.), *Organizational Symbolism.* Greenwich, Conn.: JAI Press, 1983.

Hofstede, G. *Culture's Consequences.* Beverly Hills, Calif.: Sage, 1980.

Homans, G. *The Human Group.* New York: Harcourt Brace Jovanovich, 1950.

Horney, K. *Our Inner Conflicts.* New York: Norton, 1945.

Hughes, E. C. *Men and Their Work.* New York: Free Press, 1958.

Hunt, J. McV. "Psychological Development: Early Experience." *Annual Review of Psychology,* 1979, *30,* 103-143.

Inaba, M. "Organization Development—A Critical and Comparative View." *Yokohama Business Review,* 1981, *2,* 119-128.

Janis, I. L. *Victims of Group Think.* Boston: Houghton Mifflin, 1972.

Jaques, E. *The Changing Culture of a Factory.* London: Tavistock, 1951.

Jaques, E. "Social Systems as a Defense Against Persecutory and Depressive Anxiety." In M. Klein, P. Heimann, and R. Money-Kyrle (Eds.), *New Directions in Psychoanalysis.* London: Tavistock, 1955.

Jaques, E. *The Forms of Time.* London: Heinemann, 1982.

Jelinek, M., Smircich, L., and Hirsch, P. "Introduction: A Code of Many Colors." *Administrative Science Quarterly,* 1983, *28,* 331-338.

Johnstad, T. (Ed.). *Group Dynamics and Society: A Multinational Approach.* Cambridge, Mass.: Oelgeschlager, Gunn & Hain, 1980.

Jones, E. E., and Nisbett, R. E. *The Actor and the Observer: Divergent Perceptions of the Causes of Behavior.* Morristown, N.J.: General Learning Press, 1971.

Jones, G. R. "Transaction Costs, Property Rights, and Organizational Culture: An Exchange Perspective." *Administrative Science Quarterly,* 1983, *28,* 454-467.

Jung, C. G. *Psychological Types.* London: Routledge & Kegan Paul, 1923.

Katz, R. "The Effects of Group Longevity on Project Communication and Performance." *Administrative Science Quarterly,* 1982, *27,* 81-104.

Keen, P. G. W. "Cognitive Style and Career Specialization." In J. Van Maanen (Ed.), *Organizational Careers: Some New Perspectives.* New York: Wiley, 1977.

Keen, P. G. W., Bronsema, G. S., and Zuboff, S. "Implementing Common Systems: One Organization's Experience." *Systems, Objectives, Solutions,* August 1982, pp. 125-142.

Kets de Vries, M. F. R., and Miller, D. *The Neurotic Organiza-*

tion: Diagnosing and Changing Counterproductive Styles of Management. San Francisco: Jossey-Bass, 1984.

Kilmann, R. H. *Beyond the Quick Fix: Managing Five Tracks to Organizational Success.* San Francisco: Jossey-Bass, 1984.

Kimberly, J. R., Miles, R. H., and Associates. *The Organizational Life Cycle: Issues in the Creation, Transformation, and Decline of Organizations.* San Francisco: Jossey-Bass, 1980.

Klein, E. B. "An Overview of Recent Tavistock Work in the United States." In C. L. Cooper and C. P. Alderfer (Eds.), *Advances in Experiential Social Processes.* Vol. 1. New York: Wiley, 1978.

Klein, M. "Our Adult World and Its Roots in Infancy." *Human Relations,* 1959, *12,* 291-303.

Kluckhohn, F. R., and Strodtbeck, F. L. *Variations in Value Orientations.* New York: Harper & Row, 1961.

Koprowski, E. J. "Cultural Myths: Clues to Effective Management." *Organizational Dynamics,* Autumn 1983, pp. 39-51.

Kotter, J. *Organizational Dynamics: Diagnosis and Intervention.* Reading, Mass.: Addison-Wesley, 1978.

Lawrence, B. S. "Age Grading: The Implicit Organizational Timetable." *Journal of Occupational Behaviour,* 1984, *5,* 23-35.

Lawrence, P. R., and Lorsch, J. W. *Organization and Environment.* Boston: Harvard Graduate School of Business Administration, 1967.

Leavitt, H. J. "Suppose We Took Groups Seriously." In E. L. Cass and F. G. Zimmer (Eds.), *Man and Work in Society.* New York: Van Nostrand Reinhold, 1975.

Lesieur, F. *The Scanlon Plan.* New York: Wiley, 1958.

Levinson, H. *The Exceptional Executive.* Cambridge, Mass.: Harvard University Press, 1968.

Lewin, K. "Group Decision and Social Change." In G. E. Swanson, T. N. Newcomb, and E. L. Hartley (Eds.), *Readings in Social Psychology.* (Rev. ed.) New York: Holt, Rinehart and Winston, 1952.

Lewis, G. "The Management of Strategic Change." Unpublished doctoral dissertation, London Graduate Business School, 1983.

Likert, R. *New Patterns of Management.* New York: McGraw-Hill, 1961.

Likert, R. *The Human Organization.* New York: McGraw-Hill, 1967.

Lilly, J. In *Factors Used to Increase the Susceptibility of Individuals to Forceful Indoctrination: Observations and Experiments.* New York: Group for the Advancement of Psychiatry, 1956.

Lilly, J. In *Methods of Forceful Indoctrination: Observations and Interviews.* New York: Group for the Advancement of Psychiatry, 1957.

Louis, M. R. "Surprise and Sense Making." *Administrative Science Quarterly,* 1980, *25,* 226–251.

Louis, M. R. "A Cultural Perspective on Organizations." *Human Systems Management,* 1981, *2,* 246–258.

Louis, M. R. "Organizations as Culture Bearing Milieux." In L. R. Pondy and others (Eds.), *Organizational Symbolism.* Greenwich, Conn.: JAI Press, 1983.

Maccoby, M. *The Gamesman.* New York: Simon & Schuster, 1976.

McGrath, J. E. *Groups: Interaction and Performance.* Englewood Cliffs, N.J.: Prentice-Hall, 1984.

McGregor, D. M. *The Human Side of Enterprise.* New York: McGraw-Hill, 1960.

McKelvey, W. *Organizational Systematics: Taxonomy, Evolution, Classification.* Berkeley: University of California Press, 1982.

McKenney, J. L., and Keen, P. G. W. "How Managers' Minds Work." *Harvard Business Review,* 1974, *52* (3), 79–90.

Madanes, C. *Strategic Family Therapy.* San Francisco: Jossey-Bass, 1981.

Madanes, C. *Behind the One-Way Mirror: Advances in the Practice of Strategic Therapy.* San Francisco: Jossey-Bass, 1984.

Manning, P. "Metaphors of the Field: Varieties of Organizational Discourse." *Administrative Science Quarterly,* 1979, *24,* 660–671.

March, J. G., and Simon, H. A. *Organizations.* New York: Wiley, 1958.

Martin, J. "Stories and Scripts in Organizational Settings." In
A. Hastorf and A. Isen (Eds.), *Cognitive Social Psychology*.
New York: Elsevier, 1982.

Martin, J., and Powers, M. E. "Truth or Corporate Propaganda:
The Value of a Good War Story." In L. R. Pondy and others
(Eds.), *Organizational Symbolism*. Greenwich, Conn.: JAI
Press, 1983.

Martin, J., and Siehl, C. "Organizational Culture and Counter
Culture: An Uneasy Symbiosis." *Organizational Dynamics*,
Autumn 1983, pp. 52–64.

Martin, J., and others. "The Uniqueness Paradox in Organizational Stories." *Administrative Science Quarterly*, 1983, *28*,
438–453.

Maruyama, M. "Paradigmatology and Its Application to Cross-
Disciplinary, Cross-Professional, and Cross-Cultural Communication." *Dialectica*, 1974, *28*, 135–196.

Maslow, A. *Motivation and Personality*. New York: Harper &
Row, 1954.

Mednick, S. A. *Learning*. Englewood Cliffs, N.J.: Prentice-Hall,
1964.

Menzies, I. E. P. "A Case Study in the Functioning of Social
Systems as a Defense Against Anxiety." *Human Relations*,
1960, *13*, 95–121.

Merton, R. K. *Social Theory and Social Structure*. (Rev. ed.)
New York: Free Press, 1957.

Miller, E. J., and Rice, A. K. *Systems of Organization*. London:
Tavistock, 1967.

Mintzberg, H. *The Structuring of Organizations*. Englewood
Cliffs, N.J.: Prentice-Hall, 1979.

Mintzberg, H. *Power in and Around Organizations*. Englewood
Cliffs, N.J.: Prentice-Hall, 1983.

Mitroff, I. I. *Stakeholders of the Organizational Mind: Toward a
New View of Organizational Policy Making*. San Francisco:
Jossey-Bass, 1983.

Mitroff, I. I., and Kilmann, R. H. "Stories Managers Tell: A
New Tool for Organizational Problem Solving." *Management
Review*, 1975, *64* (7), 18–28.

Mitroff, I. I., and Kilmann, R. H. "On Organizational Stories:

An Approach to the Design and Analysis of Organizations Through Myths and Stories." In R. H. Kilmann, L. R. Pondy, and L. Sleven (Eds.), *The Management of Organization Design.* New York: Elsevier, 1976.

Morris, C. *Varieties of Human Value.* Chicago: University of Chicago Press, 1956.

Myers, I. B. *Manual: The Myers-Briggs Type Indicator.* Palo Alto, Calif.: Consulting Psychologists Press, 1975. (Originally published 1962.)

National Commission on Productivity and Work Quality. *A Plant-Wide Productivity Plan in Action: Three Years of Experience with the Scanlon Plan.* Washington, D.C.: National Commission on Productivity and Work Quality, 1975.

Newman, W. "Cultural Assumptions Underlying U.S. Management Concepts." In J. L. Massie and J. Luytjes (Eds.), *Management in an International Context.* New York: Harper & Row, 1972.

Nur, M. M. "A Case Study of Corporate Culture: Hastings Manufacturing Co., Inc." Unpublished master's thesis, Pepperdine University, 1983.

O'Toole, J. J. "Corporate and Managerial Cultures." In C. L. Cooper (Ed.), *Behavioral Problems in Organizations.* Englewood Cliffs, N.J.: Prentice-Hall, 1979.

Ouchi, W. G. *Theory Z.* Reading, Mass.: Addison-Wesley, 1981.

Pages, M. *The Emotional Life of Groups.* Paris: Dunod, 1968.

Pages, M. "The Collective Unconscious and Social Change." In T. Johnstad (Ed.), *Group Dynamics and Society: A Multinational Approach.* Cambridge, Mass.: Oelgeschlager, Gunn & Hain, 1980.

Parsons, T. *The Social System.* New York: Free Press, 1951.

Pascale, R. T., and Athos, A. G. *The Art of Japanese Management.* New York: Simon & Schuster, 1981.

Perrow, C. B. *Organizational Analysis.* Monterey, Calif.: Brooks/Cole, 1970.

Perrow, C. B. *Complex Organizations: A Critical Essay.* (2nd ed.) Glenview, Ill.: Scott, Foresman, 1979.

Peters, T. J. "Management Systems: The Language of Organizational Character and Competence." *Organizational Dynamics,* Summer 1980, pp. 2–26.

Peters, T. J., and Waterman, R. H., Jr. *In Search of Excellence.* New York: Harper & Row, 1982.

Pettigrew, A. M. "On Studying Organizational Cultures." *Administrative Science Quarterly,* 1979, *24,* 570-581.

Pfeffer, J. "Management as Symbolic Action." In L. L. Cummings and B. M. Staw (Eds.), *Research in Organizational Behavior.* Vol. 3. Greenwich, Conn.: JAI Press, 1981.

Piaget, J. *The Psychology of Intelligence.* Paterson, N.J.: Littlefield, Adams, 1947.

Pondy, L. R., and others (Eds.). *Organizational Symbolism.* Greenwich, Conn.: JAI Press, 1983.

Pugh, D. S. "The Measurement of Organization Structure." *Organizational Dynamics,* 1973, *1,* 19-34.

Pulliam, H. R., and Dunford, C. *Programmed to Learn: An Essay on the Evolution of Culture.* New York: Columbia University Press, 1980.

Quinn, J. B. "Strategic Change: 'Logical Incrementalism.' " *Sloan Management Review,* 1978, *20,* 7-21.

Redding, S. G., and Martyn-Johns, T. A. "Paradigm Differences and Their Relation to Management, with Reference to Southeast Asia." In G. W. England, A. R. Neghandi, and B. Wilpert (Eds.), *Organizational Functioning in a Cross-Cultural Perspective.* Kent, Ohio: Comparative Administration Research Unit, Kent State University, 1979.

Rice, A. K. *The Enterprise and Its Environment.* London: Tavistock, 1963.

Rioch, M. J. "The Work of Wilfred Bion on Groups." In A. D. Colman and W. H. Bexton (Eds.), *Group Relations Reader.* Sausalito, Calif.: GREX, 1975.

Ritti, R. R., and Funkhouser, G. R. *The Ropes to Skip and the Ropes to Know.* Columbus, Ohio: Grid, 1982.

Roethlisberger, F. J., and Dickson, W. J. *Management and the Worker.* Cambridge, Mass.: Harvard University Press, 1939.

Rotter, J. B. "Generalized Expectancies for Internal Versus External Control of Reinforcement." *Psychological Monographs,* 1966, *80* (Whole No. 609).

Roy, D. "Banana Time: Job Satisfaction and Informal Interaction." *Human Organization,* 1960, *18,* 158-169.

Sahlins, M. *Historical Metaphors and Mythical Realities.* Ann Arbor: University of Michigan Press, 1981.

Sahlins, M., and Service, E. R. (Eds.). *Evolution and Culture.* Ann Arbor: University of Michigan Press, 1960.

Sathe, V. *Managerial Action and Corporate Culture.* Homewood, Ill.: Irwin, 1985.

Schein, E. H. *Coercive Persuasion.* New York: Norton, 1961.

Schein, E. H. "How to Break in the College Graduate." *Harvard Business Review,* 1964, *42,* 68-76.

Schein, E. H. "The Problem of Moral Education for the Business Manager." *Industrial Management Review,* 1966, *8,* 3-14.

Schein, E. H. "Organizational Socialization and the Profession of Management." *Industrial Management Review,* 1968, *9,* 1-15.

Schein, E. H. *Process Consultation.* Reading, Mass.: Addison-Wesley, 1969.

Schein, E. H. "The Individual, the Organization, and the Career: A Conceptual Scheme." *Journal of Applied Behavioral Science,* 1971, *7,* 401-426.

Schein, E. H. *Professional Education: Some New Directions.* New York: McGraw-Hill, 1972.

Schein, E. H. *Career Dynamics: Matching Individual and Organizational Needs.* Reading, Mass.: Addison-Wesley, 1978.

Schein, E. H. *Organizational Psychology.* (3rd ed.) Englewood Cliffs, N.J.: Prentice-Hall, 1980. (First published 1965, 2nd ed. 1970.)

Schein, E. H. "Does Japanese Management Style Have a Message for American Managers?" *Sloan Management Review,* 1981a, *23,* 55-68.

Schein, E. H. "Improving Face-to-Face Relationships." *Sloan Management Review,* 1981b, *22,* 42-52.

Schein, E. H. "The Role of the Founder in Creating Organizational Culture." *Organizational Dynamics,* Summer 1983, pp. 13-28.

Schein, E. H. "Coming to a New Awareness of Organizational Culture." *Sloan Management Review,* 1984, *25,* 3-16.

Schein, E. H., and Bennis, W. G. *Personal and Organizational Change Through Group Methods.* New York: Wiley, 1965.

Schein, E. H., and Lippitt, G. L. "Supervisory Attitudes Toward the Legitimacy of Influencing Subordinates." *Journal of Applied Behavioral Science,* 1966, *2,* 199-209.

Schein, E. H., and Ott, J. S. "The Legitimacy of Organizational Influence." *American Journal of Sociology,* 1962, *67,* 682-689.

Schrank, R. *Ten Thousand Working Days.* Cambridge, Mass.: MIT Press, 1978.

Schutz, W. *FIRO: A Three Dimensional Theory of Interpersonal Behavior.* New York: Holt, Rinehart and Winston, 1958.

Schwartz, H., and Davis, S. M. "Matching Corporate Culture and Business Strategy." *Organizational Dynamics,* Summer 1981, pp. 30-48.

Service, E. R. *Cultural Evolutionism: Theory in Practice.* New York: Holt, Rinehart and Winston, 1971.

Sherif, M., and others. *Intergroup Conflict and Cooperation.* Norman, Okla.: University Book Exchange, 1961.

Shrivastava, P. "A Typology of Organizational Learning Systems." *Journal of Management Studies,* 1983, *20,* 7-28.

Silverzweig, S., and Allen, R. F. "Changing the Corporate Culture." *Sloan Management Review,* 1976, *17,* 33-49.

Simon, H. A. *The New Science of Management Decisions.* New York: Harper & Row, 1960.

Sithi-Amnuai, P. "The Asian Mind." *Asia,* Spring 1968, pp. 78-91.

Skinner, B. F. *Science and Behavior.* New York: Macmillan. 1953.

Slater, P. *The Pursuit of Loneliness.* Boston: Beacon Press, 1970.

Smircich, L. "Concepts of Culture and Organizational Analysis." *Administrative Science Quarterly,* 1983, *28,* 339-358.

Smith, K. K., and Simmons, V. M. "A Rumpelstiltskin Organization: Metaphors on Metaphors in Field Research." *Administrative Science Quarterly,* 1983, *28,* 377-392.

Smith, M. E. "The Process of Sociocultural Continuity." *Current Anthropology,* 1982, *23* (2), 127-142.

Sofer, C. *The Organization from Within.* New York: Quadrangle Books, 1961.

Solomon, R. L., Kamin, L. J., and Wynne, L. C. "Traumatic Avoidance Learning: The Outcomes of Several Extinction

Procedures with Dogs." *Journal of Abnormal and Social Psychology,* 1953, *48,* 291–302.

Solomon, R. L., and Wynne, L. C. "Avoidance Conditioning." *Psychological Monographs,* 1953, *67* (Whole No. 354).

Spradley, J. P. *The Ethnographic Interview.* New York: Holt, Rinehart and Winston, 1979.

Srivastva, S., and Associates. *The Executive Mind: New Insights on Managerial Thought and Action.* San Francisco: Jossey-Bass, 1983.

Steele, F. I. *Physical Settings and Organization Development.* Reading, Mass.: Addison-Wesley, 1973.

Steele, F. I. *The Sense of Place.* Boston: CBI Publishing, 1981.

Steward, J. H. *Theory of Culture Change.* Urbana: University of Illinois Press, 1955.

Steward, J. H. *Evolution and Ecology.* Urbana: University of Illinois Press, 1977.

Stogdill, R. M., and Coons, A. E. (Eds.). *Leader Behavior: Its Description and Measurement.* Columbus: Bureau of Business Research, Ohio State University, 1957.

Stonich, P. J. (Ed.). *Implementing Strategy.* Cambridge, Mass.: Ballinger, 1982.

Tagiuri, R., and Litwin, G. H. (Eds.). *Organizational Climate: Exploration of a Concept.* Boston: Division of Research, Harvard Graduate School of Business, 1968.

Tannenbaum, R., and Schmidt, H. W. "How to Choose a Leadership Pattern." *Harvard Business Review,* 1958, *36* (2), 95–101.

Thompson, J. D. *Organizations in Action.* New York: McGraw-Hill, 1967.

Thompson, J. D., and McEwen, W. K. "Organizational Goals and Environment." *American Sociological Review,* 1958, *23,* 23–30.

Tichy, N. M. *Managing Strategic Change.* New York: Wiley, 1983.

Trist, E. L., and Bamforth, K. W. "Some Social and Psychological Consequences of the Long-Wall Method of Coal Getting." *Human Relations,* 1951, *4,* 1–38.

Trist, E. L., and others. *Organizational Choice.* London: Tavistock, 1963.

Tuckman, B. W. "Developmental Sequence in Small Groups." *Psychological Bulletin,* 1965, *63,* 384–399.

Tuckman, B. W., and Jensen, M. A. C. "Stages of Small-Group Development Revisited." *Group and Organizational Studies,* 1977, *2,* 419–427.

Turquet, P. M. "Leadership: The Individual and the Group." In G. S. Gibbard, J. J. Hartman, and R. D. Mann (Eds.), *Analysis of Groups: Contributions to Theory, Research, and Practice.* San Francisco: Jossey-Bass, 1973.

Uttal, B. "The Corporate Culture Vultures." *Fortune,* Oct. 17, 1983, pp. 66–72.

Van Maanen, J. "Police Socialization." *Administrative Science Quarterly,* 1975, *20,* 207–228.

Van Maanen, J. "Breaking In: Socialization to Work." In R. Dubin (Ed.), *Handbook of Work, Organization and Society.* Chicago: Rand McNally, 1976.

Van Maanen, J. "Experiencing Organizations." In J. Van Maanen (Ed.), *Organizational Careers: Some New Perspectives.* New York: Wiley, 1977.

Van Maanen, J. "The Fact of Fiction in Organizational Ethnography." *Administrative Science Quarterly,* 1979a, *24,* 539–550.

Van Maanen, J. "The Self, the Situation, and the Rules of Interpersonal Relations." In W. Bennis and others, *Essays in Interpersonal Dynamics.* Homewood, Ill.: Dorsey Press, 1979b.

Van Maanen, J., and Barley, S. R. "Occupational Communities: Culture and Control in Organizations." In B. M. Staw and L. L. Cummings (Eds.), *Research in Organizational Behavior.* Vol. 6. Greenwich, Conn.: JAI Press, 1984.

Van Maanen, J., and Schein, E. H. "Toward a Theory of Organizational Socialization." In B. M. Staw and L. L. Cummings (Eds.), *Research in Organizational Behavior.* Vol. 1. Greenwich, Conn.: JAI Press, 1979.

Vroom, V. H. "Can Leaders Learn to Lead?" *Organizational Dynamics,* Winter 1976, pp. 17–28.

Vroom, V. H., and Yetton, P. W. *Leadership and Decision Making.* Pittsburgh, Penn.: University of Pittsburgh Press, 1973.

Wallen, R. W. "The 3 Types of Executive Personality." *Dun's Review,* Feb. 1963, pp. 54–56, 106.

Watzlawick, P., Beavin, J. H., and Jackson, D. D. *Pragmatics of Human Communication.* New York: Norton, 1967.

Watzlawick, P., Weakland, J., and Fisch, R. *Change: Principles of Problem Formulation and Problem Resolution.* New York: Norton, 1974.

Weber, M. *The Theory of Social and Economic Organization.* (T. Parsons, Ed.) New York: Free Press, 1947.

Weick, K. E. "Cognitive Processes in Organizations." In B. M. Staw and L. L. Cummings (Eds.), *Research in Organizational Behavior.* Vol. 1. Greenwich, Conn.: JAI Press, 1979.

Wells, L., Jr. "The Group-as-a-Whole: A Systemic Socio-Analytic Perspective on Interpersonal and Group Relations." In C. P. Alderfer and C. L. Cooper (Eds.), *Advances in Experiential Social Processes.* Vol. 2. New York: Wiley, 1980.

Whyte, W. F. *Money and Motivation.* New York: Harper & Row, 1955.

Wilkins, A. L. "Organizational Stories as Symbols Which Control the Organization." In L. R. Pondy and others (Eds.), *Organizational Symbolism.* Greenwich, Conn.: JAI Press, 1983.

Wilkins, A. L., and Ouchi, W. G. "Efficient Cultures: Exploring the Relationship Between Culture and Organizational Performance." *Administrative Science Quarterly,* 1983, *28,* 468–481.

Woodward, J. *Industrial Organization.* London: Oxford University Press, 1965.

Wright, J. P. *On a Clear Day You Can See General Motors.* New York: Wright Enterprises, 1979.

Zaleznik, A. *Human Dilemmas of Leadership.* New York: Harper & Row, 1966.

Zaleznik, A. "Charismatic and Consensus Leaders: A Psychological Comparison." *Bulletin of the Menninger Clinic,* 1974, *39,* 67–78.

Zaleznik, A., and Kets de Vries, M. F. R. *Power and the Corporate Mind.* Boston: Houghton Mifflin, 1975.

Index

A

Abernathy, V., 309, 329

Action Company: assumptions in, 19; birth and early growth stage of, 273, 275-276, 279-280; critical incident in, 166, 167-168; cultural paradigm of, 110; and culture change, 245, 246-247, 268-269; culture shaped by founder of, 216-221; embedding culture in, 229-230, 231, 233, 236-237, 238, 240-241; environmental relationship of, 88; as example, 2, 9-11, 12; goals of, 55-56; group boundaries of, 70-71; as high-context, 91; human activity to, 102; human nature to, 101; human relationships in, 105-106, 108; ideology in, 80, 81-82; means of, 58-59; measurement in, 62; overprojection in, 29; parts and whole of, 46; patterning in, 28; peer relationships in, 75-77; potency of culture in, 25; power in, 73-74; pragmatism of, 93; reality to, 89; remediation in, 63; rewards and punishments in, 78; space to, 97, 98; strategy at, 32; time to, 95; uncovering assumptions in, 114-119

Adaptation. *See* External adaptation

Adorno, T., 92, 329

Aggression, cultural norms for, 73

Alderfer, C. P., 39, 50, 148-149, 329, 332

Allen, R. F., 33, 113, 329, 343

Allen, T. J., 39, 41-42, 329

Allport, G., xi, xv

Amado, G., 333-334

American Express, merger of, 35

Andrews, J. A. Y., 180, 335

Anxiety: cognitive, 179-180; cultural reduction of, 82-83; primary existential, 179-182; reduction, and learning theory,

347

cerns, 150-151; satisfaction of, and culture, 30-44

Information and control system, data from, 122-125

Insubordination, as critical incident, 231-232

Intergroup conflicts, in organizations, 39-40

Internal integration: analysis of issues in, 65-82; critical incidents in, 231-232; and group boundaries, 66, 70-72; and ideology, 66, 79-82; language and concepts for, 65-69; and peer relationships, 66, 74-77; and power, 66, 72-74; and rewards and punishments, 66, 77-79

Interviews: group, 127-135; iterative, 113-119; methodology for, 119-120

Intrapsychic conflict, emotional issues in, 155-158

Israel, power distance in, 105

J

Jackson, D. D., 346

Janis, I. L., 157, 336

Japan: consensus in, 258; crowding in, 59; dynamics of culture in, 44-45, 146; human relationships in, 105; reality and truth in, 91; sex roles in, 103

Jaques, E., 95, 96, 149, 156, 172, 178, 182, 336

Jelinek, M., xi, 336

Jensen, M. A. C., 163, 345

Johnson, B., xvi

Johnstad, T., 336

Jones, E. E., 27, 336

Jones, G. R., 107, 336

Jones Company: culture shaped by founder of, 210-215; embedding culture in, 223-224, 226, 228-229, 232-233; and succession phase, 275

Joyce, W., 81, 332

Jung, C. G., 103, 158, 159, 336

K

Kamin, L. J., 174, 343-344

Katz, R., 336

Keen, P. G. W., 37, 158, 332, 336, 338

Kennedy, A. A., x, 6, 24, 283, 332

Kets de Vries, M. F. R., 24, 64, 172-173, 319, 336-337, 346

Kilmann, R. H., x, 81, 113, 337, 339-340

Kimberly, J. R., 304, 337

Klein, E. B., 337

Klein, M., 155-156, 337

Kluckhohn, C., xi

Kluckhohn, F. R., xi, xv, 18, 86, 96, 98, 101, 102, 103, 104, 109, 337

Kolb, D., xv-xvi

Koprowski, E. J., 81, 337

Kotter, J., 337

Kraft, C., 33, 329

Kunda, G., xv

L

Language and concepts, common: and emotional coping styles, 154; for internal integration, 65-69

Laurent, A., 333-334

Lawn care business: birth and early growth stage of, 274; strategy of, 32-33

Lawrence, B. S., xv, 337

Lawrence, P. R., 39, 95, 278, 284, 337

Leaders: analysis of role of, 311-327; for anxiety containment, 318; attention of, and embedding, 225-230; background on, 311-314; in birth and early growth stage, 317-320; and critical incidents, 230-232; cultural assumptions changed by, 324; cultural implications for, 316-326; culture embedded and transmitted by, 223-243; and culture formation, 2, 50-51, 313, 317-320; as culture managers, 326-

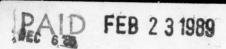